Perspectives on Mormon Theology

Perspectives on Mormon Theology

Perspectives on Mormon Theology is designed to facilitate and advance the academic study of Latter-day Saint thought. As Mormon Studies continues to develop as an academic field, there is increasing demand for scholarship that engages theological studies and the philosophy of religion. This series is a response to this need and is designed to provide interested readers additional resources in understanding this rich and intriguing religious tradition. Each volume engages a specific theological topic and exhibits a variety of perspectives in the topic area. The series is not intended to defend any particular position, but rather to provide a forum within which a range of approaches and methodologies are given voice.

Other titles in the series:

Scriptural Theology, edited by James E. Faulconer and Joseph M. Spencer
Apologetics, edited by Blair Van Dyke and Loyd Isao Ericson
Grace, edited by Jacob T. Baker and Robert L. Millet
Atonement, edited by Deidre Green and Erid D. Huntsman
Revelation, edited by Brian D. Birch and Richard Livingston

Perspectives on Mormon Theology

Scriptural Theology

Edited by
James E. Faulconer
and Joseph M. Spencer

Series edited by
Brian D. Birch
and Loyd Isao Ericson

GREG KOFFORD BOOKS
SALT LAKE CITY, 2015

Cover design by Loyd Ericson

Published in the USA.

Greg Kofford Books
P.O. Box 1362
Draper, UT 84020
www.gregkofford.com
facebook.com/gkbooks

Also available in ebook.

2019 18 17 16 15 5 4 3 2 1

Library of Congress Cataloging-in-Publication Data

Contents

SERIES INTRODUCTION

Perspectives on Mormon Theology

Brian D. Birch and Loyd Isao Ericson,
Series Editors

From its beginnings, Mormonism has challenged the boundaries of Christian theology. On the one hand, it affirms the core features of the Christian faith—including a belief in the Bible as God's word and the divinity, atonement for the sins of humanity, resurrection, ascension, and second coming of Jesus Christ—and yet it does so within a remarkably unorthodox framework.

The primary source of these ideas is Joseph Smith who, between 1829 and 1844, produced a remarkable 750 pages of additional scripture. These works—the Book of Mormon, Doctrine and Covenants, and Pearl of Great Price—do not replace the Bible; rather they are understood by Latter-day Saints to affirm, clarify, and ultimately complement the Biblical text.

The ability to produce new scripture is borne from Smith's self-understanding as a prophet for the latter days. His revelations are understood to constitute not only a restoration of the ancient Christian church, but to be the "restoration of all things" in which the God's activities across the ages are brought to a fulfillment in anticipation of the second coming of Jesus Christ. This sweeping narrative includes the belief that the fullness of God's truths and plan for humanity were given to Adam and Eve and other biblical Patriarchs but had been lost and recovered through multiple restorations.

This robust concept of restoration led historian Jan Shipps to argue that Mormonism is a "new religious tradition" that emerged out of Christianity in a similar fashion to that of Christianity out of Judaism.[1]

1. Jan Shipps, *Mormonism: The Story of a New Religious Tradition* (Urbana: University of Illinois Press, 1987).

This designation has also proven useful as well for Christian leaders anxious to distance Mormonism from mainstream Christianity. Richard Land, a longtime point person for the Southern Baptist Convention, said in a *Time* magazine article that "the fairest and most charitable way to define Mormonism would be to call it the fourth Abrahamic religion."[2]

The production of new revelation created a fluid and dynamic environment in the early years of Mormonism. Theology, ritual, and church governance were being shaped and reshaped in accordance with Smith's expanding canon. This developmental dynamic has had interesting implications for Mormon theological studies. Mormonism's earliest new scripture, the Book of Mormon, fit more comfortably within early nineteenth-century Protestant theology. Critics of Mormonism rarely raised concerns over the theological content of the Book of Mormon but rather drew contempt over Smith's claim of producing additional scripture on par with the Bible. They were also discomfited by stories of the miraculous events surrounding its coming forth, which included angelic visitation, buried golden plates, and the miraculous use of seer stones to aid in the translation process.

However, the theological comfort present in the earliest years of Mormonism soon disappeared. In the decade and a half following the publication of the Book of Mormon and a formal establishment of a church in 1830, Smith's revelations proclaimed new doctrines that further separated Mormon theology from its Christian environs. Among these new teachings, Smith reconceptualized heaven and hell, separated the Trinity into physically distinct beings, embodied God with flesh and bone, and taught that marriage was an essential ordinance for human deification.

Among the more intriguing features of Mormonism is that, despite its centralized authority, there has been no theological tradition to synthesize their unique doctrines. Historically, the Church of Jesus Christ of Latter-day Saints has discouraged attempts within its ranks to apply rigorous philosophical and theological analysis to its doctrinal teachings. This has been largely informed by the Church's emphasis on continuing revelation and, with it, the understanding that theology is largely unnecessary because living prophets and apostles provide whatever guidance is necessary in interpreting and applying Latter-day Saint scripture and doctrine. This sensibility is readily observed in the absence of theological

2. David Van Biema, "What is Mormonism? A Baptist Answer," *Time,* October 24, 2007, available at http://content.time.com/time/nation/article/0,8599,1675308,00.html (accessed February 2, 2015).

training for its lay leadership who are overwhelmingly selected based upon pastoral and organizational skills. While some early Mormon authorities attempted to provide rigorous philosophical and exegetical analyses of Mormon thought, their works never gained authoritative status and have little direct influence on church teachings today.

In the twentieth century, the first significant theoretical treatment of Mormon theology was Sterling M. McMurrin's *The Theological Foundations of the Mormon Religion.*[3] A self-described agnostic Mormon, McMurrin began his career in the LDS Church's Church Educational System (CES) and migrated to academia where he taught philosophy at the University of Utah and served in a variety of administrative positions. Published in 1965, McMurrin's book stood alone for a generation as the only attempt at a sustained theological engagement with the Christian tradition.

The landscape has changed in recent years, however, as a number of Latter-day Saint scholars have pursued formal academic training in theology and the philosophy of religion, and they have applied this training within the context of an emerging interdisciplinary field of Mormon Studies. The work of Truman Madsen, David Paulsen, Robert Millet, and James Faulconer at Brigham Young University paved the way through their efforts to create dialogue between Mormon thinkers and the broader Christian theological community. In 2007, Paulsen co-edited a volume with Baptist theologian Donald Musser entitled *Mormonism in Dialogue with Contemporary Christian Theologies.*[4] Four years prior, the Society for Mormon Philosophy was formed at the Yale Divinity School during a major academic conference on Mormon history, thought, and culture.

Blake Ostler, an independent scholar and theologian, has offered the most thorough examination of a Latter-day Saint theology in his *Exploring Mormon Thought* series.[5] These and other publications on Mormon thought in the late twentieth and current century have largely been limited to either monographic works portraying a single perspective on Mormon theology, such as the works by McMurrin and Ostler, or scat-

3. Sterling M. McMurrin, *The Theological Foundations of the Mormon Religion* (Salt Lake City: University of Utah Press, 1965).

4. David L. Paulsen and Donald W. Musser, *Mormonism in Dialogue with Contemporary Christian Theologies* (Macon, Ga.: Mercer University Press, 2007).

5. Blake T. Ostler, *Exploring Mormon Thought: The Attributes of God* (Salt Lake City: Greg Kofford Books, 2001), *Exploring Mormon Thought: The Problems of Theism and the Love of God* (Salt Lake City: Greg Kofford Books, 2006), *Exploring Mormon Thought: Of God and Gods* (Salt Lake City: Greg Kofford Books, 2008).

tered across various scholarly journals and anthologies.[6] The most recent full-length treatment of Mormon thought is Terryl Givens's *Wrestling the Angel: The Foundations of Mormon Thought.*[7]

As Mormon Studies continues to develop as an academic field, there is increasing demand for scholarship that engages theological studies and the philosophy of religion. *Perspectives on Mormon Theology* is a response to this need and is designed to provide interested readers additional resources in understanding this rich and intriguing religious tradition. This series is designed to both facilitate and advance the academic study of the Latter-day Saint thought. Each volume engages a specific theological topic and exhibits a variety of perspectives in the topic area. The series is not intended to defend any particular position, but rather to provide a forum within which a range of approaches and methodologies are given voice.

We begin the series with scriptural theology, the most primary form of theological reflection. James Faulconer and Joseph Spencer have gathered scholars from diverse disciplines to examine the role of scripture and to demonstrate the connection between theological reflection and scriptural exegesis. Subsequent volumes will explore the atonement, grace, revelation, and apologetics to name a few. We are grateful to all who have contributed to this series and look forward to quality dialogue on the issues contained therein.

Brian D. Birch
Loyd Isao Ericson

---

6. These journals include *Dialogue: A Journal of Mormon Thought, Faith and Philosophy, Element: The Journal of the Society for Mormon Philosophy and Theology, BYU Studies,* and *Sunstone.* Anthologies include Jacob T. Baker, *Mormonism at the Crossroads of Philosophy and Theology* (Salt Lake City: Greg Kofford Books, 2012), James McLachlan and Loyd Ericson, *Discourses in Mormon Theology: Philosophical and Theological Possibilities* (Salt Lake City: Greg Kofford Books, 2007). Charles Harrell offers a historical analysis of Mormon thought in his *This is My Doctrine: The Development of Mormon Theology* (Salt Lake City, Greg Kofford Books, 2011).

7. Terryl L. Givens, *Wrestling the Angel: The Foundations of Mormon Thought: God, Cosmos, Humanity* (New York: Oxford University Press, 2014).

Perspectives on Mormon Theology

Scriptural Theology

INTRODUCTION

Scriptural Theology

James E. Faulconer and Joseph M. Spencer

The phrase "theology of scripture" can be understood in two distinct ways. First, theology of scripture would be reflection on the nature of scripture, asking questions about what it means for a person or a people to be oriented by a written text (rather than or in addition to an oral tradition or a ritual tradition). In this first sense, theology of scripture would form a relatively minor part of the broader theological project, since the nature of scripture is just *one* of many things on which theologians reflect. Second, theology of scripture would be theological reflection guided by scripture, asking questions of scriptural texts and allowing those texts to shape the direction the theologian's thoughts pursue. In this second sense, theology of scripture would be less a part of the larger theological project than a way of doing theology, since whatever the theologian takes up reflectively, she investigates through the lens of scripture.

The essays making up this collection reflect attentiveness to both ways of understanding the phrase "theology of scripture." Each essay takes up the relatively un-self-conscious work of reading a scriptural text but then—at some point or another—asks the self-conscious question of exactly what she or he is doing in the work of reading scripture. We have thus attempted in this book (1) to create a dialogue concerning what scripture is for Latter-day Saints, and (2) to focus that dialogue on concrete examples of Latter-day Saints reading actual scripture texts.

In fact, this volume has grown out of an actual dialogue. It began in the summer of 2010 with an online seminar (available in its entirety at http://scripturaltheology.wordpress.com/), during which the several contributors were able to present to each other readings of particular scriptural texts and reflections on what it means to read scripture as a Latter-day Saint. When the online discussions came to an end, some conclusions were presented and further discussed in a one-day symposium, "Mormon

Scriptural Theology," held at Brigham Young University on October 4, 2010, and graciously hosted jointly by the Richard L. Evans Chair of Religious Understanding and Greg Kofford Books. The present book crystallizes that ongoing conversation at a moment in its development—a development that we hope continues into the future.

This collection is a dialogue in a still profounder sense as well. From the outset, we aimed to bring together diverse voices. All participants were selected in part because of their interest in scripture, but we also tried to bring together people with varied backgrounds and distinct kinds of training. Participants hail from philosophy (Faulconer, Miller, and Spencer), humanities (Webb and Handley), English (Hafen and Jorgensen), religious studies (Huntsman), history (Bushman), and even finance (Couch). Moreover, as the essays demonstrate, even those trained in the same discipline have rather different scriptural and theological interests. While Webb offers a close reading of Doctrine and Covenants 128 largely guided by her interest in scripture's reflection on textuality, Handley is guided to the Book of Moses by his ecological concerns; while Hafen's interest in Doctrine and Covenants 46 is driven by her personal and academic interest in questions of community, Jorgensen's reading of Alma 37 is heavily inflected by his formalist training; Faulconer's attention to Moses 5 is driven by his interest in ritual and presence, Miller turns to Matthew 6 as part of his larger project of investigating consciousness, and Spencer addresses Job 19 because of his interest in the uniqueness of the Book of Mormon. The dialogue that has resulted from the variety of perspectives and interests has been most fruitful and edifying for us; we hope it will be similarly fruitful and edifying for those who are listening in on the conversation.

What has guided our approach from the beginning is the (in our eyes unfortunate) fact that relatively little—indeed, almost nothing—has been published about serious theology of scripture in the Mormon tradition. Our intention in carrying on this dialogue, and then in capturing it in this volume, is to lay some of the groundwork for a conversation that largely remains to be held. If we will have drawn attention to the basic questions, we will have succeeded. If not, we can take comfort in the fact that we have immensely enjoyed talking together about scripture.

A few words of introduction to the several essays might be in order.

The first two essays address texts from the Old Testament. Both focus profoundly on how uniquely Mormon scripture should inflect the interpretation of the Hebrew scriptures, though each does so in a rather different way. In "A Mormon Reading of Job 19:23–25a," Joseph Spencer draws on the Book of Mormon and the Doctrine and Covenants in order to construct a framework for the interpretation of the Old Testament—thus bringing non-biblical scriptural texts to bear directly on a biblical text. The result is a speculative interpretation of the Book of Job in which Spencer takes it to have been oriented to the eschatological event to which Joseph Smith gave the name "Adam-ondi-Ahman." In "'Without Money,'" however, Robert Couch traces quotations of and allusions to a particular Old Testament text in the Book of Mormon—thus asking how biblical texts worm their way into non-biblical scriptural texts. Further, Couch uses the passage from Isaiah 55 that is his focus to assess the limits of certain modern academic approaches to scriptural themes, arguing that the social and economic ideals set forth in scripture outstrip especially contemporary political and economic discourse.

The New Testament is the focus of the next two essays. Here, the focus is a bit different. In "'Take No Thought,'" Adam Miller uses a passage from Jesus's Sermon on the Mount to model what in an addendum he calls a hermeneutics of "semiotic materialism," a style of interpretation that takes the words of scripture to be as material as the concrete objects of everyday experience. In the actual work of his reading, moreover, he displays a still deeper concern with conscious dwelling in a world of material realities, finding in Jesus's words so much counsel to avoid fantastic flights from the work of paying attention to the here and now. For his part, Eric Huntsman, in "Jesus on Jesus," roots exposition in strict, traditional exegesis while nonetheless asking at every point how the carefully interpreted biblical text relates to Restoration texts and teachings. Looking closely at a few of Jesus's teachings in the Gospel of John, Huntsman pays particularly close attention to the role of the symbolic in scripture.

Turning to uniquely Mormon scripture, the next two essays address themselves to the Book of Mormon. Where there has been a consistent emphasis in the first four essays to determine what it means to read scriptural texts that Latter-day Saints share with other faith traditions, these essays begin to ask what it means to read scripture unique to the Mormon tradition. In "I, Nephi," Claudia Bushman demonstrates the power of taking the Book of Mormon's claim to historicity seriously by reading the text of First Nephi as she would any other historical text—asking about what the author veils over as much as about what the author puts on display. Bushman thus outlines a kind of hermeneutics of suspicion that is ultimately inseparable from the commitments of her faith. In a somewhat similar vein, Bruce Jorgensen, in "Alma's Wisdom-Poem to Helaman," openly doubts whether there is anything unique about a specifically "Mormon" interpretation of texts—scriptural or otherwise. But rather than bringing the tools of the historian's trade to the task of reading the Book of Mormon, Jorgensen uses his training as a formalist to mine several poetic lines from Alma 37 for meaning.

The Doctrine and Covenants, naturally, is the focus of the next two essays. As the only book of Mormon scripture exclusively containing modern revelation, the Doctrine and Covenants raises some unique questions. This can be sensed in these two essays. Jane Hafen's profoundly personal essay, "Seek Ye Earnestly the Best Gifts," models the immediate relevance of modern revelation to the contemporary Church by taking the words of section 46 to describe exactly how the community that is today's Church should work. As she shows over the course of her essay, a heightened sense of normativity can lead, in a community that is seldom fully attentive to scripture, to tension and fractures that can be painful. Because Jenny Webb, in "Records, Reading, and Writing in Doctrine and Covenants 128," looks at a canonized letter from the Doctrine and Covenants rather than a revelation, she understands the immediate relevance of the scriptural text somewhat differently—finding in Joseph Smith's creativity with the biblical texts on which he draws a kind of model for engaging with scripture. Along with providing a most provocative reading of section 128 of the Doctrine and Covenants, Webb asks what it means for Latter-day Saints to engage with the scriptures on a daily basis, and argues that there is something essential about the experience of reading scripture consistently, whether or not there is a particular goal or project guiding such reading.

Finally, the last two essays in this collection are dedicated to the Pearl of Great Price. Given the complexity of the relationship between most of this last of the Standard Works to the Old Testament—a complexity that has raised more serious doubts about the historicity of uniquely Mormon scripture than any other single source—it might seem that the principal focus of these last essays should be historical and exegetical. As it turns out, however, neither contributor privileges such questions; each, instead, reads the Pearl of Great Price simply as scripture. Thus, in "Faith and the Ethics of Climate Change," George Handley takes the Book of Moses as a canonical and therefore binding text to be interpreted faithfully by the believing Latter-day Saint, always from within the context of the reader's historical and social milieu. More important to his approach than tortuous questions of historicity, then, are the ethical demands of contemporary life—demands that he carefully (and impressively) uproots from political ideology in order to plant them securely in faith—and Handley shows how dutiful attention to both the text and such demands allows scripture to speak profoundly to contemporary concerns. For his part, James Faulconer, in "The Way toward the Garden: Moses 5:1–12," pays somewhat more attention to the relationship between the Book of Moses and the Book of Genesis, but he does so to better understand the meaning and implications of the canonical text. With nuanced attention to the details of Moses 5, Faulconer shows how scripture reveals what it means to live in the world in the way God ordains.

The telling variety of these essays, we believe, demonstrates how much this discussion needs to continue to take place. We therefore express our gratitude to everyone who has helped to make this project possible. We owe thanks to Brian Birch and Loyd Ericson, general editors of the *Perspectives on Mormon Theology* series, for inviting us to produce this volume. Obviously, we owe thanks to all the contributors, as well as to other potential contributors we approached who, for one reason or another, could not participate with us. The conference in which these papers were first presented would not have been possible without generous financial assistance from the Richard L. Evans Chair of Religious Understanding at Brigham Young University, nor without the support, more generally, of both Brigham Young University and Greg Kofford Books. Particularly helpful in organizing the conference was Karen Lambert. We are grateful also to Nate Noorlander, who provided some formatting and editorial assistance. Two essays in this volume appeared in *Dialogue: A Journal of Mormon Thought* after they were presented at the conference; we express our thanks to Kristine Haglund for her interest in our project and for being happy to see those essays appear in this volume as well as the journal she has more than ably edited. Finally, and most especially, we express gratitude to our families, who are far more supportive of our efforts than we deserve.

ONE

A Mormon Reading of Job 19:23–25a

Joseph M. Spencer

I take as my task here to read, with the eyes of a Mormon theologian, a text from the Old Testament.[1] The eyes of a Mormon theologian—that implies two things. First, the reading I will offer here is that of a theologian. It will be, therefore, speculative. Second, the reading I will offer here is that of a Mormon. It will be, therefore, oriented by the events, the texts, and the truths that motivate Mormonism. Speculative in methodology and Mormon in orientation, what I set forth in this paper will be an attempt to embody the interpretive implications of what Joseph Smith said in his eighth article of faith. That is, if Mormons "believe the Bible to be the word of God as far as it is translated correctly," then it seems they have the task, whenever they read the Bible, to transform the received text into the word of God through what I can only understand to be a theological endeavor. It is that task that I assume here.

What follows comes in two parts. In the first part, I want to say a little bit more about what I have just outlined, that is, what did Joseph Smith mean—or what *might* he have meant—when he spoke of translating the Bible correctly? In the second part of the paper, I will turn to the task of actually reading a passage from the Old Testament in a distinctly Mormon and explicitly theological way. The text I will consider is Job 19:23–25a, and I will have a good deal more to say by way of introduction to that passage when I come to the second part of the paper.

---

1. For a broad-stroke analysis of the history of biblical interpretation in the LDS tradition, see Philip L. Barlow, *Mormons and the Bible: The Place of the Latter-day Saints in Religion* (New York: Oxford University Press, 1991).

I

I suspect that the eighth article of faith was in part inspired by Nephi.[2] In the Book of Mormon, Nephi offers both a forthright affirmation of biblical inspiration and an equally forthright denial of biblical sufficiency. Importantly, according to Nephi—or rather, according to the angel to whom Nephi attributes the words—both the inspired nature of the Bible and its essential insufficiency are revealed specifically by the Book of Mormon. In the words to be found in Nephi's writings, at once the Book of Mormon "shall establish the truth" of the Bible and "shall make known the plain and precious things which have been taken away" from it (1 Ne. 13:40). This double gesture—or at least its spirit—clearly lies behind the claim that we Mormons "believe the Bible to be the word of God as far as it is translated correctly," while we "believe the Book of Mormon to be the word of God" pure and simple. Thus, to approach the Bible from an irremediably Mormon point of view is to regard the received biblical text both with a vow of faithful obedience and with a vow of suspicious rigor.[3]

From the angel's words to Nephi an initial picture might be drawn up of what Joseph Smith meant when he spoke of the Bible being translated correctly.[4] It is, at the very least, a matter of reading the Bible through the lens of the Book of Mormon, and doing so in a way that both establishes the Bible's truth and makes known the plain and precious things taken from it. Of course, each of the two crucial elements of this formulation deserves to be clarified in some detail. What does it mean to "establish the

---

2. The eighth article of faith, along with the other articles of faith, was largely drawn from Orson Pratt's pamphlet, "Remarkable Visions." It thus draws on but subtly reworks Orson Pratt's statement there: "The gospel in the 'Book of Mormon,' is the same as that in the New Testament, and is revealed in great plainness, so that no one that reads it can misunderstand its principles." See Orson P. Pratt, *Remarkable Visions* (Liverpool: R. James, 1848).

3. I use here the language of Paul Ricoeur. See Paul Ricoeur, *Freud and Philosophy: An Essay on Interpretation*, trans. Denis Savage (New Haven: Yale University Press, 1970), 27. It is worth noting, however, that Ricoeur's and the Latter-day Saint's motivations for doubling fidelity with suspicion in the work of interpretation are distinct. Ricoeur's commitment to suspicion is drawn from the philosophical insights of Marx, Nietzsche, and Freud; the Latter-day Saint's commitment to suspicion is drawn directly from scripture. That difference seems to me crucial.

4. Regarding just the word "to translate" in Joseph Smith's thinking, it is worth reviewing Hugh Nibley's important remarks in Hugh Nibley, *The Message of the Joseph Smith Papyri: An Egyptian Endowment* (Salt Lake City: Deseret Book, 1976), 47–54.

truth" of something? And what does it mean to speak of "the plain and precious things" supposedly taken from the Bible?

Regarding the first of these two questions, the essential ambiguity of the phrase "to establish the truth of something" should be noted. This phrase can have reference either to establishing that the "something" in question is true (to establish, for example, that the proposition "the Bible is true" is in fact the case) or to discovering and elaborating a truth indiscernibly proper to the "something" in question (to discover and elaborate, for example, the truth that is proper to the Bible). I suspect that most of Nephi's readers assume he means the first of these two options—the Book of Mormon establishes the fact that the Bible is true—but I want to make a case for the possibility that he means the second, that he means in fact to suggest that the Book of Mormon allows one to discover and even to elaborate the truth around which the whole Bible circulates without ever quite stating it overtly.

In order to defend such a reading, however, it is necessary to address the second question above. What does it mean to speak of "the plain and precious things" supposedly taken from the Bible? On this point Nephi's angel could not be clearer. When Nephi first sees the emergence of the Bible in his vision, the angel explains to him: "The book that thou beholdest is a record of the Jews, which contains the covenants of the Lord, which he hath made unto the house of Israel; and it also containeth many of the prophecies of the holy prophets" (1 Ne. 13:23). The Bible as Nephi sees it gathers together a historical record and a collection of prophecies, but what binds it together is, it seems, "the *covenants* . . . made unto the house of Israel." The angel again emphasizes this covenantal theme only moments later in his words to Nephi. Though the book seen in vision is not so large as the brass plates Nephi brought from Jerusalem, "nevertheless, they contain the *covenants* of the Lord, which he hath made unto the house of Israel; *wherefore*, they are of great worth unto the Gentiles" (v. 23; emphases mine). What made the first Gentile readers so deeply interested in the Bible they received as it "proceede[d] out of the mouth of a Jew" (v. 23) was, specifically, its *covenantal* content.

What has this covenantal focus to do with the plain and precious things? Nephi goes on in his vision to see "the formation of that great and abominable church, which is most abominable above all other churches," concerning which event the angel explains: "they have taken away from the gospel of the Lamb many parts which are plain and most precious; and also *many covenants of the Lord have they taken away*" (1 Ne. 13:26; emphasis mine). This is, it seems to me, absolutely crucial. What is lost from the Bible in the course of its Gentile appropriation is first and foremost an emphasis on the covenant. Whether any actual passages were removed or altered we do not know—and we in fact have reason to doubt. But that the meaning and centrality of the Abrahamic covenant were downplayed seems clear. And that is Nephi's focus.

Is it too much, then, to suggest that what it means to translate the Bible correctly—what it means to read the Bible through the truth-establishing lens of the Book of Mormon—is to restore to the Bible its covenantal center? It is something like this that, I suspect, Nephi has in mind when he says that the Book of Mormon and the Bible "shall be established in one" (1 Ne. 13:41). To translate the Bible correctly is to read the letter of the biblical text with a spiritual eye trained on the covenantal focus of the Book of Mormon—on the covenantal focus that is established at length in Nephi's writings and brought back to the Lehites' attention during Christ's climactic visit to the New World. The task of the translator, it would seem, is less a question of sorting out the Hebrew or the Greek originals, or of sifting through mounds of manuscript finds to establish an earliest biblical text, than of establishing the covenantal focus of the Bible. Obviously, such a covenantal focus is particularly important in reading the Old Testament.

A confirmation of the approach I am laying out here can perhaps be found in Joseph Smith's own efforts at translating the Bible. Those efforts took two rather distinct shapes over the course of Joseph's prophetic career. Between 1830 and 1833, Joseph was at work on what he called the "New Translation" (but what Latter-day Saints commonly call the "Joseph Smith Translation") of the Bible. Subsequently, beginning especially in 1835 in Kirtland's "school of the prophets," Joseph launched a second, ongoing but intermittent, attempt to translate the Bible, though never with the aim of producing a complete or systematic translation. These two efforts at translation, investigated carefully, make clear that what Joseph understood by "translation" was nothing like the mechanical work of shifting intellectual content from one language to another. While working on the New Translation between 1830 and 1833, Joseph never even pretended to consult the "original" Hebrew of the Old Testament or Greek of the New Testament. Instead, he seems simply to have worked from the English of the King James Version, making alterations wherever he felt inspired to do so, regardless—and often against the grain—of the actual Hebrew or Greek "originals."[5] Again, when in 1835 Joseph began seriously to study the strictly biblical languages (especially Hebrew) and so turned his attention anew to translation, it is clear that his intent was not to provide a straightforwardly accurate rendering of the "original." Instead, up through the last sermons he gave before his martyrdom, his efforts aimed at using the nuances of the biblical languages to launch radically innovative and theologically expansive interpretations of otherwise relatively banal biblical passages.[6]

If it is clear that Joseph Smith did not understand the translation of the Bible simply to be the slavish reproduction of the plain meaning of the "original" text, what, *positively*, did he mean by "translation"? What was common to Joseph's two distinct attempts to translate the Bible was his intention to rework the received biblical text—whether the received English of the KJV or the *textus receptus* of the Hebrew and Greek "originals"—in terms of the scriptures and revelations he had himself prophetically provided to the Saints. On one occasion in 1844, Joseph intimated as much while commending Luther's German translation of the Bible: "I have been reading the German: I find it to be the most correct that I have found and it corresponds the nearest to the revelations that I have given the last 16 years."[7] What seems to have guided Joseph's efforts to translate the Bible correctly first and foremost was the need to reorient the received text to the events, the texts, and the truths that he had himself produced.[8]

---

5. Though it represents only a first—and not entirely rigorous—approach, the standard work on the New Translation remains Robert J. Matthews, *"A Plainer Translation": Joseph Smith's Translation of the Bible, A History and Commentary* (Provo, Utah: Brigham Young University Press, 1985). See also, of course, Scott H. Faulring, Kent P. Jackson, and Robert J. Matthews, eds., *Joseph Smith's New Translation of the Bible: Original Manuscripts* (Provo, Utah: BYU Religious Studies Center, 2004).

6. The most famous such interpretation—a wildly speculative but theologically fascinating reading of Genesis 1:1 offered in the course of the famous "King Follett Discourse"—perfectly illustrates the kind of "translation" project that interested Joseph. See Joseph Smith Jr., *The Words of Joseph Smith: The Contemporary Accounts of the Nauvoo Discourses of the Prophet Joseph*, ed. Andrew F. Ehat and Lyndon W. Cook (Provo, Utah: BYU Religious Studies Center, 1980), 340–62.

7. Ibid., 351. I have expanded the occasional abbreviations found in Thomas Bullock's notes.

8. It may be that the Book of Abraham fits more into Joseph's efforts at translating the Bible than it does into his efforts at translating original, ancient documents. The close relationship between the Book of Abraham and the Book of Genesis is unmistakable. In some ways, the Book of Abraham is to Joseph's

All of this is to say, I think, that Joseph Smith's efforts at translation were an experiment in Mormon theology. What Joseph produced in his ongoing engagement with biblical texts was speculative, and he launched his theological speculations from a deliberately Mormon platform. But what does it mean to say that Joseph's translations were theological or speculative? I have in mind here what Adam Miller has described very well in the following words:

> Theology is an attempt to explore the range of meanings that scripture is capable of producing beyond the bounds of its historical, doctrinal, and devotional responses. Theology runs experiments for the sake of mapping a text's own latent patterns. Its power to illuminate these unseen, latent patterns derives from its freedom to pose hypothetical questions: *if* such and such were the case, *then* what meaningful pattern would the text produce in response?[9]

Theological speculation, contrary to what is often said about it among Latter-day Saints, is anything but so much spinning in the void, anything but asking pointless or unanswerable questions, anything but sensational attention to so-called mysteries. Theological speculation is, rather, an attempt, undertaken in the name of charity, to see what scriptural texts have to teach us and to see what scripture can do in addition to providing grist for the historical mill and confirming doctrine we all already know to be true. To speculate is to hold a mirror up to the scriptures, to allow them to reflect on themselves, to give them something to say to us about their meaning and significance.

Joseph Smith was a speculator. And the mirror he held up to the Bible in his efforts at translation was a distinctly Mormon one, constructed of the events that had started him on his prophetic career, the texts that had been given to the world through him, and the truths that had been forced on him by his experiences. If the Bible is to be translated correctly, it seems to me that it has to be approached in the way that Joseph approached it. That is, Latter-day Saints must approach it speculatively, and must do so in a distinctly Mormon fashion. The task of the translator is to put to each biblical text a set of questions that arise in connection with the unique founding events of Mormonism, questions that emerge from close study of uniquely Mormon scripture, and questions that issue from unswerving commitment to the truths uniquely set forth in the Restoration. Mormon

---

efforts at translating the Bible after 1835 as the Book of Moses is to his efforts at translating the Bible before 1835.

9. Adam Miller, ed., *An Experiment on the Word: Reading Alma 32* (Provo: Maxwell Institute Press, 2014), 4; emphases in original.

theological speculation yields profit only (1) when it is undertaken with the hope of profiting from its distinctly Mormon investment, (2) when it invests specifically in the Bible and does so with full faith, and (3) when it aims to give away what profits it yields in real charity.

Of course, to quote Adam Miller again, "it is essential to remember that, because it is fundamentally hypothetical, theology is always tentative and nonbinding. Theology, though sensitive to what is normatively binding, never decides doctrine."[10] This seems, curiously, to have been largely true even of Joseph Smith's work at translating the Bible. Although a few chapters of the 1830–1833 project have been canonized (in the Pearl of Great Price), almost all of Joseph's extensive efforts at translating the Bible—from 1830 to 1844—remain nonbinding for the Latter-day Saint. Joseph's translations, despite the fact that they occupied more of his prophetic attention than any other project during the course of his life, have not—have *never*—decided doctrine.[11]

Perhaps for this last reason above all, I think it is prudent to suggest that every Latter-day Saint has the freedom—if not the responsibility—to translate the Bible in something like the way that Joseph Smith did. But what shape—what *specific* shape—might such a translation take? Does Joseph's example provide some guidance about how one is to move forward? I think it does, and spelling out that guidance will pave the way at last to the attempt I would like to wager here of reading Job 19:23–25a.

As I have already made clear, Joseph Smith's own work on the Bible unfolded in two distinct sequences: a first between 1830 and 1833, the product of which was the New Translation, and a second beginning in 1835 and lasting until the prophet's death, the product of which was a smattering of writings and sermons that dealt with biblical texts. Each of

---

10. Ibid., 6.

11. One might point out that the close relationship between the New Translation and the revelations making up the bulk of the Doctrine and Covenants suggests that the New Translation was indeed doctrinally binding. But this proves precisely the opposite. The fact that the doctrines that would become binding had to appear in the revelations that would be canonized in the Doctrine and Covenants makes all the clearer that what appeared only in the New Translation was not binding. On the relationship between the New Translation and Joseph Smith's revelations, see Kerry Muhlestein, "One Continuous Flow: Revelations Surrounding the 'New Translation,'" in *The Doctrine and Covenants: Revelations in Context*, ed. J. Spencer Fluhman and Alonzo Gaskill (Salt Lake City and Provo, Utah: Deseret Book and BYU Religious Studies Center, 2008), 40–65.

these projects allows one to put a finer point on what Joseph Smith taught us by his example about translating the Bible correctly.

What, then, can be learned from Joseph's efforts with the Bible between 1830 and 1833? The motivation for this project seems to have been the Book of Mormon—or, more specifically, two crucial but subtle theological innovations introduced by the Book of Mormon. First, the Book of Mormon launches a remarkably complex and startlingly sophisticated theology of writing, rooted in nuanced interpretations of Isaiah and exposited in great detail in the writings of Nephi especially (though clearly relied on in the subsequent editorial work of Mormon and Moroni).[12] This Nephite theology of writing seems to have informed every stage of Mormonism's early development, culminating in the remarkable and too-often ignored section 128 of the Doctrine and Covenants.[13]

Second, the Book of Mormon organizes from its very beginning and with consistent clarity through to its end a markedly unique messianic theology, a theology that even within the Nephite volume itself called for systematic reinterpretation of major biblical themes, from the Abrahamic covenant through the Law of Moses, to the resurrection and salvation by grace. In my view, these two Book of Mormon themes—the Nephite theology of writing and Nephite messianism—were in large part what called for the revisionary program of the New Translation.

Significantly for Mormon interpretation of the Old Testament, neither Nephite messianism nor the Nephite theology of writing is presented in the Book of Mormon as being a uniquely New World phenomenon. Rather, the Nephite understanding of the Messiah is often attributed in the Book of Mormon to the prophets of the Old World, and Nephi so closely connects his theology of writing to the Isaianic tradition that it is impossible to describe it solely as a New World development. As if following out the implications of such Nephite confidence in their continuity with the Old World, Joseph Smith's early work on the New Translation finds him emending the biblical text in precisely these two directions. The Book of Moses in particular, which represents Joseph's first months at work on the Bible, reads like an investigation of the possibility of finding in the biblical text—in particular in the narratives dealing with Adam and Eve and their immediate descendants—traces of both Nephite messian-

12. I work through some details of the Nephite theology of writing in Joseph M. Spencer, *An Other Testament: On Typology* (Salem, Ore.: Salt Press, 2012).

13. For an excellent study of the theme of writing in Doctrine and Covenants 128, see Jenny Webb's contribution to the present volume.

ism and Nephite understandings of writing.[14] And from this one might draw a somewhat clearer picture of what, concretely, "correct" translation of the Bible meant in Joseph Smith's own thinking. It seems to have been, at least at first, an attempt to trace distinctly Nephite theological themes to biblical sources, and even to revise the biblical text—whether slightly or drastically—in fidelity to Nephite claims that such theological themes had come to them from the Old Testament.

What, in turn, might be drawn from Joseph Smith's later work with the Bible? In many ways, the second sequence of Joseph's work on the Bible is a development or even an expansion of the first. Once Joseph began to study ancient languages, his interest in returning to and revising his revisions of the Bible became insatiable. With these new tools ready at hand, Joseph seems to have felt more prepared than before to do serious work on making sense of biblical texts. Not only might he work with the received English rendering in order to trace ideas and theological conceptions introduced in uniquely LDS scripture, but now he might return to the original languages—as well as come for the first time to other important translations. (Joseph was deeply interested in the German translation of the Bible especially.) Thus finding himself occupying the space between different renderings of the biblical text—the space between the lines of interlinear translations, as it were—Joseph was caught between what is traditionally taken to be the two "conflicting tendencies" of translation: "fidelity and freedom."[15]

Joseph Smith's later work on the Bible is thus characterized by a double tendency, a double tendency that pulled him in opposite directions. On the one hand, by adding to his familiarity with the King James Version some facility with Hebrew, Greek, Latin, and German renderings of the Bible, Joseph added what might loosely be called an academic edge to his interpretation. At any rate, Joseph began to make reference in his sermons to the "learned men," and not only to bolster the authority of his inter-

---

14. To see this as clearly as possible, it is best to look at both versions of the Book of Moses, as can be found in Faulring, Jackson, and Matthews, *Joseph Smith's New Translation*, 83–113, 591–625. See also the interesting theological discussion of this point in Terryl L. Givens, "Joseph Smith: Prophecy, Process, and Plenitude," *BYU Studies* 44, no. 4 (2005): 55–68.

15. See Walter Benjamin, "The Task of the Translator: An Introduction to the Translation of Baudelaire's *Tableaux Parisiens*," trans. Harry Zohn, in *Illuminations: Essays and Reflections*, ed., Hannah Arendt (New York: Schocken Books, 2007), 69–82.

pretations ("if you do not believe it you do not believe the learned man of God"), but also to challenge the scholarly world to contradict his interpretations of the Hebrew ("come here ye learned men & read if you can")![16]

On the other hand, by placing himself at the complex intersection of radically distinct languages, Joseph gave himself to much more imaginative interpretations, playing off the nuances of several drastically different renderings of a single text. His willingness to make reference to three or four different languages in justifying a single interpretation makes clear that he was attuned to the freedom of interpretation that comes with looking at alternative translations.[17] Joseph's later work on the Bible thus at once forced him to be more careful and rigorous and allowed him the most unrestrained interpretive freedom imaginable.[18]

Importantly, it was in the thick of this relatively late work on the Bible that Joseph wrote the eighth article of faith with its affirmation of the Bible's divinity "as far as it is translated correctly." Not only was he at that time continuing in essence what he had begun in his work on the New Translation—continuing, in other words, to rework the biblical text from the specific perspective of Book of Mormon theological innovations—but he was doing so with the increased rigor and multiplied imagination of looking at original sources, the slipperiness of language, and the play of inventive translations. All of this, it seems to me, puts a finer point on what a distinctly Mormon interpretation of the Bible—or, for my purposes here, specifically of the Old Testament—might look like. Fidelity to the text as it stands is crucial and should even been attended by academic rigor, underpinned by serious study of languages, history, and texts. It is not good, at the same time, for this fidelity to be alone; rather, it should be accompanied by a strong commitment to imagination or theological speculation (in the sense discussed above). And from both the early and the late attempts on Joseph's part to take up the speculative task, it is clear that what orients every imaginative gesture is the deepest commitment to the most consistent theological innovations of the Book of Mormon.

---

16. Smith, *The Words of Joseph Smith*, 351.

17. See ibid. Also, see Samuel Brown, "The Translator and the Ghostwriter: Joseph Smith and W. W. Phelps," *Journal of Mormon History* 34, no. 1 (Winter 2008): 26–62.

18. I think it is crucially significant that whereas Joseph Smith's early work at translating the Bible amounted to an alteration of the received text, his late work replaced alteration with imaginative recasting rooted in the original.

Such, I think, is what Joseph Smith had in mind when he spoke of translating the Bible correctly. And it is this sort of program I will follow next, turning my attention directly to an Old Testament text: Job 19:23–25a. I should note briefly that Joseph Smith had nothing, really, to say about this passage. The Book of Job received only marginal treatment in the New Translation. Indeed, only four slight changes to the entire book are to be found in the manuscripts, none of them enormously significant theologically. Chapter 19, like most of the chapters of the Book of Job, is simply labeled, "Correct."[19] Nevertheless, I wonder whether, had Joseph given more time and attention to Job during his most sustained efforts at translation, we might not have a rather different reading provided to us. In what remains I will in part be exploring how Joseph Smith *might* have reworked or at least have reinterpreted one passage from Job—though, obviously, I do not at all pretend to have the same prophetic ability or authority that Joseph Smith himself had.

II

I understand grace to be the central theme of the Book of Job. The textual cue is Job 2:3, in which God brags to Satan about Job's steadfastness after the first round of disasters: "still he [Job] holdeth fast his integrity, although thou [Satan] movedst me against him, to destroy him *without cause*" (emphasis mine). "Without cause" in this passage translates the adverbial form of the Hebrew word *hen*, grace. It thus means "without cause," but also could be translated "freely," "gracefully," even "as a gift."[20]

19. See Faulring, Jackson, and Matthews, *Joseph Smith's New Translation*, 738–43. The changes actually made are as a follows: (1) in Job 1:6, "sons of God" is changed to "children of God"; (2) in Job 2:1, "sons of God" is again changed to "children of God"; (3) in Job 2:3, the word "me" is crossed out of "thou movedst me against him"; and (4) in Job 6:29, "my righteousness is in it" is changed to "my righteousness in me."

20. Wyclif translated it "in veyn," but all other English translations have more or less followed the "without cause" translation: the Bishop's Bible and the Geneva Bible at the time of the KJV; the RSV more modernly—the NIV and ESV translate it similarly: "without any reason." Luther translated it similarly to the KJV tradition (*ohne Ursache*), as did the translators of the Louis Segond version (*sans motif*) and the Reina Valera (*sin causa*). As for ancient versions, the Septuagint translates it *diakeneis*, "emptily" or "in vain," and the Vulgate renders it with the somewhat ambiguous *frustra*, which does indeed mean "without cause," but which can also mean "wrongly."

However bizarre it might sound, I want to wager that the point of the narrative of the Book of Job is to track the process through which its main character comes to see the absurd horror of his life as a manifestation of grace, as a gift. On this reading, what is so adversarial about the speeches of Job's friends is not simply that they adhere to the God of retribution or wrongfully accuse Job of wickedness. Rather, the difficulty is that such adherence or accusation—not to mention their constant interruptions of Job's attempts to ask God about his situation—impedes Job's full recognition that his situation is one of grace. Job must come to see his sufferings as unearned if he is to begin to get a sense for the nature of grace, but his friends are constantly telling him that all he is going through is something he has himself brought about.

The passage I will be considering in detail comes in the second round of debate between Job and his friends—at a point, specifically, when Job seems to have left off calling on God so as to fight off the accusations of his adversaries. At the heart of this second round, Job offers what is generally regarded among Latter-day Saints as the book's high point, his declaration that he has a living advocate who will—even if only after his own death—vindicate him (Job 19:25–27). The celebrated actual announcement of the advocate's existence ("I know that my redeemer liveth," etc.) is, it turns out, among the most difficult passages in scripture.[21] Christians traditionally read the passage typologically, taking the mentioned advocate or redeemer to be Jesus Christ. This is, of course, not an entirely unjustified interpretation, but it should be ventured only with full recognition that the Hebrew of the passage is so difficult, if not actually corrupt, that one cannot be responsibly confident about any interpretation of the text.[22] I will be considering only the first line of Job's famous confession (Job

21. After translating the first line of verse 25 ("As for me, I know my avenger lives"), Edwin M. Good confesses: Job "goes on for six more lines, in which I can read each word, but they do not combine into sentences that make sense to me." See Edwin M. Good, "The Problem of Evil in the Book of Job," in *The Voice from the Whirlwind*, ed. Leo G. Perdue and W. Clark Gilpin (Nashville: Abingdon, 1992), 60. See also Janzen's helpful discussion of the history of the passage's interpretation in J. Gerald Janzen, *Job* (Atlanta: John Know, 1985), 134–50.

22. In what amounts to the only serious full-length Mormon book on Job, published only since I had finished my work on this essay, Michael Austin has provided a lengthy critique of the traditional Mormon (and traditional Christian) interpretation of Job 19. His criticisms echo those of modern biblical interpreters rather generally. Obviously, the criteria guiding my own interpretive approach are different from Austin's, despite the fact that I too part ways with the traditional

19:25a), coupling and contextualizing it with the two verses that precede and introduce it (Job 19:23–24). In offering a distinctly Mormon interpretation of this passage, I will ultimately suggest what might seem an entirely unconventional reading, even for a Latter-day Saint, but one that I can easily see Joseph Smith himself having produced.

I am not entirely unsatisfied with the King James rendering of Job 19:23–25a ("Oh that my words were now written! oh that they were printed in a book! That they were graven with an iron pen and lead in the rock for ever! For I know that my redeemer liveth . . ."), since it matters little to me how one translates the various technical terms associated with ancient writing practices.[23] I want, nonetheless, to raise a question about the Hebrew phrase *my yitten* (unvoiced: *my ytn*), which is translated as "Oh that . . . !" in the KJV despite the fact that it literally means "Who will give/grant . . . ?" Following a more literalist translational tradition, I will render the passage as follows: "Who will give now, and my words are written? Who will give, and they are printed in a book—graven with an iron pen and lead in the rock for ever? For I know that my redeemer liveth . . ."[24] The emphasis on "giving" that comes along with this translation of the text seems to me to square

interpretation. See Michael Austin, *Re-reading Job: Understanding the Ancient World's Greatest Poem* (Salt Lake City: Greg Kofford Books, 2014), 103–17.

23. Commentaries focus, *ad nauseum*, on the theologically immaterial details: Is "written" quite right, or should it be rendered "carved"? Certainly "printed" should be replaced by something less anachronistic! Is it quite appropriate to speak of "books" at the time? How should the word behind "iron pen" be translated? What curious technique lies behind the mention of "lead"? Is "rock" meant to point to a stela, a simple stone inscription, a cliff wall, or what? And so on.

24. In English, see Wyclif's translation, as well as the Douay Rheims Bible, among the earlier translations. Note also that both the Septuagint (Greek) and the Vulgate (Latin) translated the Hebrew literally in their renderings, among the ancient sources. One might justifiably object, however, that experts in Hebrew grammar universally note that the use of *my ytn* in Job 19:23 is in a late, attenuated form and so should not be taken literally. See Wilheml Gesenius, *Gesenius' Hebrew Grammar*, ed. E. Kautzsch, trans. A. E. Cowley (Mineola, New York: Dover, 2006), 476–77; B. Jongeling, "L'expression *my ytn* dans l'ancien testament," *Vetus Testamentum* 24 (1974): 32–40; and Edwin M. Good, *In Turns of Tempest: A Reading of Job with a Translation* (Stanford, Calif.: Stanford University Press, 1990), 257. In response, however, one might suggest, with Dermot Cox, that the author of Job "prescinds from [standard] Hebrew usage," and that, at any rate, "no creative writer—much less a poet—holds himself bound to strict grammatical usage." Dermot Cox, *The Triumph of Impotence* (Rome: Universitá Gregoriana), 34.

nicely with the larger theme of grace that, on my reading, characterizes the whole Book of Job.

Now, what words does Job want written? Traditionally, readers have assumed that the testimony of verses 25–27 ("I know that my redeemer liveth," etc.) is what Job wishes to have inscribed in a book. More modern interpreters, however, generally agree that the words to be written are actually all of Job's words, everything he says in the course of the whole Book of Job—his consistent case for his own innocence.[25] This more modern approach calls for a reworking of the relationship between verses 23–24 on the one hand, and verses 25–27 on the other. Various models have been proposed,[26] but the most intriguing, in my opinion, takes the connection to be causal: Job's awareness of the advent of an advocate (verses 25–27) makes him desirous to begin assembling a dossier of his innocence, a written record of his defense that then could be used by that advocate in court with God (verses 23–24).[27] That approach makes Job's "Who will give . . . ?" sound a bit more hopeful than it appears at first.[28] Perhaps the implicit answer to Job's "Who will give . . . ?" is not, in the end, "No one!"

And indeed, is it not clear that the answer to Job's question or cry cannot actually be "No one!" for the simple fact that his words *have* been written? We only know of Job's desire to have his words written because that desire, along with Job's words more generally, has indeed been printed in a book. Commentators, of course, generally recognize this irony, though

25. See, for example, David J. A. Clines, *Job 1–20* (Waco: Word Books, 1989), 456.

26. See Franz Delitzsch, *Biblical Commentary on the Book of Job* (Edinburgh: Clark, 1866), 354; H. Torczyner, *The Book of Job* (Jerusalem: Hebrew University Press, 1941), 302–4; and Robert Gordis, *The Book of Job: Commentary, New Translation, and Special Studies* (New York: Jewish Theological Seminary Press, 1978), 204.

27. For this interpretation, see Norman C. Habel, *The Book of Job: A Commentary* (Philadelphia: Westminster Press, 1985), 303: "Job wants more than 'words' recorded; he wants the details of the case which justifies his innocence publicly recorded. Job's final cry in 31:35 is a challenge to God, his adversary at law, to follow suit and also write down the particulars of his legal case against Job. Job's written testimony would be available for his defender to utilize when he rose to support Job's case (v. 25)." Note that other texts in Job make clear that God in heaven, against whom Job's advocate will be arguing, has already written out an indictment against Job.

28. Commentators generally see Job's cry as indicative of complete despair. See, in particular, Cox, *The Triumph of Impotence*, 34–35.

they do not, I believe, probe its significance enough.[29] Job's written wish to have his words written deserves far more attention, particularly if, as commentators universally claim, the speeches in the Book of Job are inventions by the book's author, not the actual words spoken in the course of whatever historical events lie behind the text.[30] If the writer (or writers) of Job's discourses produced them whole cloth, then there was never a real gap between the "expression" of Job's desire to have his words written and the actual putting of his words into writing.[31] Job's wish, in a word, was fulfilled in its very expression. And this is, I believe, essential—rather than incidental—to the purposes of the text. It is not, I suspect, something unintended by the author (or authors) that only "we moderns" recognize.

One way—an unmistakably theological way—of sorting out the difficulty posed by this irony would be to suggest that Job had reference,

---

29. See Good, *In Turns of Tempest*, 257: "The irony is, of course, that Job's words *are* written, are nothing but written"; Robert D. Sacks, *The Book of Job with Commentary: A Translation for Our Time* (Atlanta: Scholars Press, 1999), 191: "When one reads this verse, it is hard not to be aware of the fact that there was a[t] least one man who did in fact provide that place. The Book of Job lies open before us"; Habel, *The Book of Job*, 303: "Ironically, it was not a stone witness but the book that bears Job's name which survived to clear his name"; and Strahan, quoted in Clines, *Job 1–20*, 456: "Yet how splendidly his idea has been realized! His singular fancy of a testimony 'in the rocks' could not be gratified, but he has his *apologia* . . . 'in a book' which is the masterpiece of Hebrew poetic genius."

30. Because some Latter-day Saints argue, on the basis of D&C 121:10, that the Book of Job is entirely historical, it is necessary to say a word about the historicity of the Book of Job. First, it should be noted that a mere mention of Job in a divine communication to Joseph Smith does not amount to a confirmation of historicity in any sense. Still more, the First Presidency, when asked about the historicity of Job in 1922, officially stated that the historicity of the Book of Job "is of little significance" next to "what is set forth therein." See Thomas G. Alexander, *Mormonism in Transition: A History of the Latter-day Saints, 1890–1930* (Urbana and Chicago: University of Illinois Press, 1986), 283. Though a good case can be made that there is a historical kernel behind the literary Book of Job, the reader is certainly not meant to believe a scribe sat near Job and his friends, copying down every poetic word. Whatever historical reality lies behind the Book of Job, the canonical text is largely the work of poetic invention. For a good, moderate Mormon take on Job's historicity, see John S. Tanner, "Why Latter-day Saints Should Read Job: An Exegesis on Suffering, Endurance, and Revelation," *Sunstone* 78 (August 1990): 38–47.

31. Only if Job actually said the words in Job 19:23–25 would there be any real gap between wish and fulfillment.

when he spoke of writing, to something other than mechanical transcription of what he otherwise communicated orally. That is, if we give real force both to Job's expressed desire and to the too-obvious fulfillment of the too-obvious interpretation of the meaning of that expressed desire, we might conclude that when Job says he desires his words to be written, he cannot mean that he desires to have his words written in the shape they appear in the Book of Job. There is, it is worth suggesting, *some other kind of writing* to which Job has reference, or at least *something more about the act of writing than mere transcription* that Job has in mind. Job might be said, given the emphatic "now" of his plea ("Who will give *now* . . . ?"), to be gesturing not only toward a *redeemer* still-to-come, but just as much to a *writing* still-to-come. Job and the author (or authors) of the Book of Job are together in search of another writing, if not—to be a bit playful—in search of a writing of the other.[32]

It might sound here as if I am transitioning to the language of "postmodern" thought—perhaps in particular that of Jacques Derrida—and thus preparing to mingle my reading of scripture with what is regarded as the most dangerous (or at least the silliest) of the philosophies of men. Actually, a Derridean reading of the text would be interesting and, I think, fruitful, but it is not one that I care to pursue here.[33] My aim, as I have been saying from the beginning, is to read Job's words in a distinctly Mormon way. Consequently, it seems to me necessary to read Job's "Who will give . . . ?" against the commentators' grain, taking it as an indication not of Job's ineluctable despair, but of his unmistakable hope—hope in the possibility of a sort of writing still-to-come that will give his coming redeemer to redeem him.

In the first half of this paper I mentioned, but said nothing substantial about, the unique theology of writing that is not only to be found in the

---

32. Note that the redeemer is actually described in verse 25, in the Hebrew, as the *aharon*, quite literally "the other." (The word, quite problematically, is translated in the KJV as "latter day," a phrase that usually translates two words in Hebrew, one of them related to *aharon*, but neither reducible to it: *aharit hayammim*.)

33. Regarding Derrida, it is necessary to mention: James G. Williams, "On Job and Writing: Derrida, Girard, and the Remedy-Poison," *Scandinavian Journal of the Old Testament* 7, no. 1 (1993): 32–50. In my opinion, Williams's piece is not very productive. Despite the fact that it does take the passage I am considering here as central to the Book of Job, it does so from the perspective of a certain interpretation of the work of René Girard, an interpretation that I think Girard himself finds problematic. I find the essay's conclusions less than persuasive.

Book of Mormon (and subsequently in the Doctrine and Covenants), but also seems to have guided Joseph Smith's work in translating the Bible. At this point all that becomes quite relevant. Making reference to one of the earliest texts Joseph Smith produced in his work on the Bible, Hugh Nibley connects a certain Mormon concept of writing with the theme of the gift toward which Job points with his "Who will give . . . ?": "If Joseph Smith was right, books and writing are a gift to man from heaven, 'for it was given unto as many as called upon God to write by the spirit of inspiration' (Moses 6:5). The art of writing was a special dispensation, an inestimable boon."[34] To echo Job, the Restoration as Joseph Smith understood it was founded on the granting of just such a divinely bestowed gift of another writing. Everything began, in the words of (the original version of) an early revelation, with "a gift to translate the book," and Joseph was "commanded" to "pretend to no other gift," since God would "grant him no other gift."[35] Joseph began his work this way, and he never left off doing so. Indeed, by 1842 Joseph was speaking more radically of "a very bold doctrine," namely, the idea that there is in the priesthood "a power which records or binds on earth and binds in heaven," thus a coupling of "authority" with keeping "a proper and faithful record" such that the priesthood had the power to produce what would become "a law on earth and in heaven, and could not be annulled, according to the decrees of the great Jehovah" (D&C 128:9). These themes are more than relevant to Job 19:23–25a, but how exactly might they guide interpretation of that passage?

First, I think it is necessary to pay attention to the connections between Job 19:23–25a and two other passages in the Book of Job, connections often noted by commentators. The first of these passages, Job 16:18–22, finds Job pleading in a vein similar to that of Job 19:23–25a: "O earth, cover not thou my blood, and let my cry have no place. Also now, behold, *my witness is in heaven, and my record is on high*. My friends scorn me: but mine eye poureth out tears unto God. O that one might plead for a man with God, as a man pleadeth for his neighbour! When a few years are come, then I shall go the way whence I shall not return" (emphasis mine). Here, as in chapter 19, Job speaks of his words being written, but the phrasing makes clear that the record referred to in chapter 16 is *already* written ("my record *is* on high") and is to be found *in heaven* ("my record is *on high*"). The record referred to in chapter 16 is, then, ap-

34. Hugh Nibley, *Temple and Cosmos: Beyond this Ignorant Present* (Salt Lake City and Provo, Utah: Deseret Book and FARMS, 1992), 462.

35. See Book of Commandments 4:2; cf. D&C 5:2–4. See also Moses 6:7.

parently *already* in the hands of the redeemer or advocate later mentioned in chapter 19. Is it too much to suggest that when these two texts are read together, the implication is that in chapter 19 Job is actually asking for an *earthly* copy of the already existent *heavenly* text mentioned in chapter 16? Perhaps what Job desires in chapter 19 is less an earthly—and therefore necessarily fragmented—transcription of what has been said in the course of the dialogues than a kind of *translation* into earthly terms of a heavenly—and therefore necessarily complete—record of what has taken place. If this interpretation is not entirely amiss (and I confess that it is largely guided by what I am calling the Mormon theology of writing), then it seems that the anticipated advent of Job's advocate, described in chapter 19, would mark as much the arrival of the heavenly record as of the person carrying it, upon which arrival Job could compare his earthly copy of the heavenly book with its original, thus being fully vindicated.

The second connection is with Job 31:35–36: "Oh that one would hear me! behold, my desire is, that the Almighty would answer me, and that *mine adversary had written a book.* Surely I would take it upon my shoulder, and bind it as a crown to me" (emphasis mine). At first, Job's desire here appears to be the reversal of that expressed in 19:23–27. He says now that he wants not his *advocate* but his *adversary* to produce a full record of what has happened. But reflection clarifies the point. In the end, Job wants his advocate-to-come to have access *both* to his own earthly copy of what has already been written in heaven—a copy whose accuracy, Job avers, would be fully vindicated through comparison with the heavenly copy carried in hand by the arriving advocate—*and* to the corrupt accusation written up by his adversary, the corruption of which could be detected in an instant when it too is compared with the heavenly record brought in its purity. In a word, Job seems to desire that his advocate have full access to every earthly account of his sufferings, both that produced by the defense and that produced by the prosecution, in order to present them, side by side with the heavenly "original," before the judge—before the judge who will sit at the last days when the earthly books will be opened to be compared with the singular, incorruptible book of life brought from heaven.[36]

By bringing these two parallel texts from Job to the table, I am continuing the work of linking Job 19:23–25a with distinctly Mormon ideas. It is not difficult to see how Job's desire might echo certain ideas in the Doctrine and Covenants (particularly sections 85 and 128), ideas con-

36. See Revelation 20:12–15 and commentary in D&C 128:2–7.

cerning the matching up of an infinite proliferation of conflicting records on earth with the single and complete book of life kept in heaven. *And* it is not difficult to see how Job's desire might echo certain ideas in the Book of Mormon (particularly in 2 Nephi 25–30), ideas concerning the sudden appearance of an untainted record that changes the stakes of the religious situation drastically at a time when all the relevant records are brought together to formulate a single massive world history.[37] At any rate, I would like to suggest that Job 19:23–25a be read in light of the conviction, presented and developed at length in uniquely Mormon scripture, that an eschatological event yet lies on the horizon during which a kind of reconciliation of earthly and heavenly records is to be worked out, a kind of final "adjustment" that will ensure that everything actually *is* on earth as it is in heaven.

All of this, then, clarifies what I take to be the anticipated *gift* in Job's plea. What, though, can be said about the giver in question? Job does not simply ask for a gift. He does not ask, "Will it be given, and my words are written?" Rather, he asks also and more directly about the *identity* of the giver: "Who will give now, and my words are written?" In whom is Job's hope here? It seems clear, of course, that the giver of verses 23–24 is the redeemer or advocate of verses 25–27. But is it so clear who that redeemer or advocate is meant to be? I have already mentioned the traditional Christian interpretation that takes the redeemer in question to be Jesus Christ, as if Job were looking out from his sufferings to the enactor of every manifestation of grace. As I said before, that is not an entirely unjustified interpretation. I want, however, to suggest another way—a distinctly Mormon way—of making sense of Job's words. In order to address the identity of the giver in question, though, it will be necessary to turn from the Nephite theology of writing to what I called above the unique messianic theology outlined by the same Nephites in the Book of Mormon. As before I had to say a bit more about the theology of writing, it is now necessary to say a bit more about Nephite messianism.

It has long been recognized that there is something strange about the Book of Mormon's presentation of a fully Christian but nonetheless supposedly pre-Christian history. The specificity with which the Nephites anticipated the events of the Christian revelation is startling enough to lead rather straightforwardly to derision on the part of critics of the Book

37. See Richard Lyman Bushman, "The Book of Mormon in Early Mormon History," in *Believing History: Latter-day Saint Essays*, ed. Reid L. Neilson and Jed Woodworth (New York: Columbia University Press, 2004), 65–78.

of Mormon, and even to lead faithful readers of the Book of Mormon on occasion to produce theories of translation that leave substantially more of the final form of the Book of Mormon to Joseph Smith than the strictly orthodox position has traditionally held to be the case.[38] On the other hand, most orthodox Latter-day Saints have taken the fully developed Christianity of the pre-Christian Nephites to be perfectly natural, just another manifestation of the straightforward plainness of the Book of Mormon vis-à-vis the relative obscurity of the Old Testament anticipations of Christ.

Both the critical (or semi-heterodox) and traditional reactions to the Book of Mormon, however, seem to me to miss the theological richness of what the Book of Mormon sets forth.[39] Working from a Pauline Christian theology several centuries before Paul was even born, let alone began his fateful journey on the road to Damascus, the Nephites—even before Christ came—arguably looked forward *from*, rather than looked forward *to*, the Messiah. Or, in more strictly Nephite language, the Nephites were taught "to *look forward unto the Messiah . . . as though he already was*" (Jarom 1:11; emphasis mine). King Benjamin puts it this way: "the Lord God hath sent his holy prophets . . . that thereby whosoever should believe that *Christ should come*, the same might receive remission of their sins, and rejoice with exceedingly great joy, *even as though he had already come among them*" (Mosiah 3:13; emphases mine). And Abinadi was happy simply to speak of "things *to come* as though *they had already come*" (16:6, emphases mine).

Nephite messianism was thus, even before the coming of the Messiah, the messianism of a completed eschatology—of an *always already* completed eschatology. The Lamb was, for the Nephites, indeed slain from the foundation of the world. Nephite messianism—*Mormon* messianism—works forward from a projected-but-already-(in-some-sense)-ful-

38. The most frequently cited example of this position is, of course, Blake T. Ostler, "The Book of Mormon as a Modern Expansion of an Ancient Source," *Dialogue: A Journal of Mormon Thought* 20, no. 1 (Spring 1987): 66–123. More recent and more developed, however, is Brant A. Gardner, *The Gift and Power: Translating the Book of Mormon* (Salt Lake City: Greg Kofford Books, 2011).

39. A very productive approach to this difficulty, though quite distinct from the one I set forth here, can be found in Adam Miller, "Messianic History: Walter Benjamin and the Book of Mormon," in *Discourses in Mormon Theology: Philosophical and Theological Possibilities*, ed. James M. McLaughlan and Loyd Ericson (Salt Lake City: Greg Kofford Books, 2007), 227–45.

filled-messianic-event, rather than, as in traditional messianism, toward a projected-but-always-mysteriously-deferred-messianic-event.

Now, coming back to Job, the question I would like to ask is whether it might be worth claiming that Job's plea-and-testimony issue from the conviction of a Nephite messianism, rather than from the conviction of a traditional messianism. And I want to suggest that what Job anticipates in the form of a redeemer or advocate is not, on a strictly Mormon reading, the Messiah. If what Job anticipates—as I have argued in this emphatically theological, speculative reading—is an event in which there is a kind of final adjustment of records, then it seems clear to me that he anticipates, not the arrival of the Messiah, but the arrival of *another* eschatological figure, the one the Doctrine and Covenants describes as "one mighty and strong": the Ancient of Days, the oldest man, Adam or Michael.

Section 85 of the Doctrine and Covenants—in which the reference to the "one mighty and strong" appears—has a rather turbulent history of interpretation.[40] But despite all of the wildly speculative identifications of the "one mighty and strong," it does not seem difficult to me to figure out who Joseph Smith understood him to be. The mighty and strong one who is going to show up eschatologically to fix the records concerning Zion is none other than Adam, and the event thus predicted is what Joseph Smith consistently referred to as Adam-ondi-Ahman.[41] It is Adam or Michael who will, according to Joseph, come to set in order the inheritances in Zion, whose appearance is described as being the occasion for a balancing of the earthly records with the heavenly record. It thus seems to me quite possible to suggest—from an irremediably Mormon perspective—that Job not only looked out from his sufferings to an event not unlike Adam-ondi-Ahman as Joseph Smith understood it, but more specifically that he placed his hopes for *vindication* in such an appearance of Father Adam, whose task it would be to assume the responsibility for all the translated "books of the dead" as he brought with him the "book of life." This reading is unmistakably speculative, but it is so, I hope, in the way that Joseph Smith's readings of biblical texts were unmistakably speculative.

40. See Brian C. Hales, "John T. Clark: The 'One Mighty and Strong,'" *Dialogue: A Journal of Mormon Thought* 39, no. 3 (Fall 2006): 46–63.

41. The best single source on what Joseph took to be at stake in Adam-ondi-Ahman is the discourse to be found in Smith, *The Words of Joseph Smith*, 8–12. In addition, however, it is necessary to take up close readings of D&C 27, D&C 85, and D&C 128.

What, though, of the Messiah? Has Christ not simply been displaced from the center of the gospel in this interpretation, as the ready accusation of certain of Mormonism's critics might well point out? Actually, I believe that Christ has not been simply excised from Job 19:23–25a in this interpretation, though he does assume a rather different position in the world set forth by the text. Christ is, on the reading I am offering here, no longer the Always-Anticipated, the Ever-Still-To-Come. But perhaps precisely for that reason he is all the more present in Job's sufferings, no longer indefinitely delayed but already present in the flesh, always already making possible the experience of life as such. Though the event in which every wrong will be righted, in which the books will finally be corrected and every deserved vindication will be granted, remains on the horizon, the sufferer experiences the grace of a present made possible precisely by the always already accomplished event of the Atonement. Whether one lives before or after the actual advent of the Messiah in the flesh, life trumps death at every moment because of the universal effects of the resurrection, and it is, according to the longest-standing Mormon interpretation of Job's words, precisely the resurrection that ultimately gives Job whatever confidence he has in his vindication to come.

Perhaps still more radically, Christ is anything but excised in this interpretation from the text of the Book of Job because the point of the book is to bring Job to recognize that he was there when Christ—along with Adam—laid the foundations of the earth. According to yet another longstanding Mormon interpretation of the Book of Job, the purpose of the divine speeches issuing from the whirlwind, with which the book concludes, is to help Job to see that he was among "all the sons of God" who "shouted for joy" (Job 38:7). "Where were you, Job, when the world was created? Don't you know," goes the Mormon reading, "that you were there? Don't you know that you were there with Adam and Eve and all their children not only to assist in the work of creation, but also to witness the slaying of the Lamb, the event that marked the laying of the very cornerstone on which the foundations of the earth were laid?" Though the event to which Job looks forward becomes, on a profoundly Mormon reading, not the event of the Messiah's coming, Christ is all the more central to the text of the Book of Job than he is in any other reading of which I am aware.

Such, at any rate, is my overdetermined and clearly speculative theological reading. But if it is overdetermined, I can only hope that it is overdetermined in more or less the same way that Joseph Smith's interpretations of scripture were generally overdetermined. I might also hope, while I am at it, that Latter-day Saint interpreters of scripture today can attempt to translate the Bible with more dedicated rigor and less apologetic creativity than they have done in recent years. Sterling McMurrin could unfortunately have been speaking about the past couple of decades when he lamented almost fifty years ago that "yesterday [Mormon theology] was vigorous, prophetic, and creative" while "today it is timid and academic and prefers scholastic rationalization to the adventure of ideas."[42] I see no reason, however, why a rebirth of Mormon theology in the most robust sense could not take place. If it is to do so, I believe it will have to begin—as Joseph Smith began—with an attempt to make real, theological sense of scripture.

---

42. Sterling M. McMurrin, *The Theological Foundations of the Mormon Religion* (Salt Lake City: University of Utah Press, 1965), 112.

TWO

"Without Money": Equality and the Transformative Power of God's Word

Robert Couch

In Isaiah 55:1, an invitation to the Lord's salvific feast is made: "Ho, every one that thirsteth, come ye to the waters, and he that hath no money; come ye, buy, and eat; yea, come, buy wine and milk without money and without price." In the Book of Mormon, the phrase "without money and without price" is quoted in three different places: 2 Nephi 9:50, 2 Nephi 26:25, and Alma 1:20. Similar concepts and imagery are employed in a number of other places in the Book of Mormon, as well as in the Doctrine and Covenants.[1] How should the prevalence of Isaiah's phrase in Mormon scripture be understood?

One obvious approach is to begin with a stark contrast in mind between the world and the kingdom of God: the world is rooted in economic relations governed by money; the kingdom of God is not. If this is a reasonable place to begin—and I hope it is, because it is my own starting place in this essay—a question immediately arises for the scriptural theologian: Given that we live in a world largely governed by relations of money, what relevance can Isaiah's apparently utopian phrase have for us? To answer this question, we might try first to translate Isaiah's ancient phrase into modern terms. This undertaking, however, is fraught with danger.

1. Examples include Alma 5:34, 42:27, D&C 10:66. Each of these passages employs some close variation of the phrase "let him take the water of life freely" from Revelation 22:17, a verse that draws heavily from Isaiah 55:1. Also, the account in Alma 6:5 "that the word of God was liberal unto all, that none were deprived" expresses a closely related idea, even if there is less direct word-for-word correspondence with Isaiah 55:1.

First, to attempt to render Isaiah's message in modern terms is implicitly to draw on something like the common Christian idea that, as disciples, we are *in* the world but not *of* the world (John 17:11–16). Although this is a nice and useful way of conceiving the call of Christian discipleship, it nevertheless risks overlooking the sense in which being in the world distorts our conception of the kingdom of God. If our vision of God's kingdom is painted with a worldly brush, it can be very difficult to truly extricate ourselves from the world, despite our best efforts to build the kingdom. Similarly, any attempt to translate Isaiah's phrase into modern terms risks forcing it to conform so much to our modern way of thinking that the very process of translation strips Isaiah's words of their transformative power.

Another challenge arises from a commonly made distinction between devotional and academic discourse. In a collection of essays like this one—billed as scholarly, with a goal to study scripture in a rigorous, intellectual way—there is a temptation to reject devotional discourse in embracing its other, namely academic discourse. The problem with this is that academic discourse is, generally speaking, *of* the world. The tension between these types of discourse is sometimes represented as an either/or conflict, a battle between the mind and the heart with those focusing on the mind maligned as irreligious and those focusing on the heart maligned as irrational.

Cognizant of these difficulties, this essay considers the Isaianic phrase "without money and without price" both in light of contemporary academic discourse and scriptural passages related to the use of this phrase. To keep the scope of this essay manageably narrow, I will focus on the concept of equality as addressed in the relevant scriptural selections. My aim is not to translate the scriptures into the language of academic discourse, but rather to use the scriptures to *interrogate* academic discourse. I say "interrogate" here rather than "criticize" because the latter is likely to conjure an idea of scriptural meaning wholly external to academic discourse—an idea that would further entrench the heart/mind dichotomy mentioned above. Put differently, then, my aim is to use the resources of academic discourse to help *incarnate* an intellectually rigorous interpretation of scripture that is at once true to scripture and cognizant of the intellectual screen on which the meaning of scripture is necessarily projected.[2]

2. See James E. Faulconer, *Faith, Philosophy, Scripture* (Provo, Utah: Neal A. Maxwell Institute for Religious Scholarship, 2010), 151–202.

To avoid producing an interpretation of scripture that is surreptitiously governed by modern academic discourse, I will be guided from the beginning by two commitments. First, I take an interdisciplinary approach. Modern academic discourse has a tendency to work according to disciplinary boundaries—especially in the sciences, where division-of-labor concerns guide an effort to maximize the marginal contribution of each publication. These boundaries, although useful for many purposes, can be an impediment to the faithful incarnation of ancient scripture in our modern world. By drawing on various disciplinary discourses, the background assumptions of each can more easily be brought to light and scrutinized. I begin with sections on the relatively scientific disciplines of economics and politics—largely in order to show the limits of such disciplines in making sense of Isaiah's words. Then, I turn to the humanities and their subjective focus on language in order to show how the transformative and universally available power of language is able to present a way beyond or out of the traps the social sciences set for us.[3]

My second commitment is to stay close to scripture—in particular, to the texts within the Mormon canon that most closely pertain to Isaiah 55:1 (specifically the following chapters, then: Isaiah 55; 2 Nephi 9, 26; and Alma 1). My aim is not to exegetically uncover the original authorial intentions of Isaiah 55:1. Rather, I aim to read scripture in a way that provides an understanding of the world—and of equality, in particular—as refracted through scripture. It will become apparent that, relative to the disciplinary perspectives of economics and politics, scripture will present a vision of equality that is more universally available and transformative.

Economics

In 2 Nephi 26:25, Nephi quotes Isaiah's phrase "without money and without price" as part of an explanation of how God offers salvation to everyone, such that "none are forbidden" (vv. 26–28). Nephi then addresses the nature of priestcraft as follows:

> He commandeth that there shall be no priestcrafts; for, behold, priestcrafts are that men preach and set themselves up for a light unto the world, that

3. The humanities are not, of course, a single discipline, but the disciplines that comprise the humanities, especially those focused on language, do not suffer from the same kind of disciplinary deficiencies endemic to more empirically and scientifically inclined human sciences like economics and politics. For the purposes of this essay, it suffices to treat the humanities as a single discipline.

> they may get gain and praise of the world; but they seek not the welfare of Zion. . . . Wherefore, the Lord God hath given a commandment that all men should have charity. . . . Wherefore, if they should have charity they would not suffer the laborer in Zion to perish. But the laborer in Zion shall labor for Zion; for if they labor for money they shall perish. (vv. 29–31)

Here Nephi establishes a close link between priestcraft and the desire to "get gain," underscored by the warning that those who "labor for money . . . shall perish." A similar idea is expressed later in the Book of Mormon when lawyers and judges are described as using their facility with language to "stir up the people to rioting and all manner of disturbances and wickedness, that they might have more employ, that they might get money" (Alma 11:20). The phrase "get money" not only echoes 2 Nephi 26 but parallels an earlier occurrence in Alma 11:20 of the phrase "get gain."

The idea of laboring for money or gain has resonance with the idea in modern finance theory where corporations have been increasingly conceived as nexuses of economic contracts between managers and various stakeholders made with the overarching objective of maximizing shareholder value. This shareholder maximization paradigm is most often used as a modeling assumption in predicting firm- and market-level behavior; however, it has also been used for normative justification. The argument runs roughly like this: Since shareholders are paid only after all the other stakeholders—employees, suppliers, the government, etc.—maximizing the expected payments to shareholders also maximizes, over time, the ability to pay all other, upstream stakeholders.[4] Although an in-depth discussion of the pros and cons associated with shareholder maximization is not worth pursuing here, a tension nevertheless needs to be addressed between the rather commonsensical idea of individuals and organizations working for the purpose of making money and the scriptural condemnation of working "for money," to "get gain," or to "get money."

The pursuit of money is often taken to be valuable because of the beneficial consequences money can be used to accomplish. Using this consequentialist logic, the pursuit of money can be ethically justified because it can be used to alleviate poverty and produce a prosperous lifestyle

---

4. Milton Friedman, "The Social Responsibility of Business is to Increase its Profits," *The New York Times Magazine*, September 13, 1970, http://doc.cat-v.org/economics/milton_friedman/business_social_responsibility (accessed July 6, 2012). For an account of the historical influence of Friedman's ideas, see Gerald Davis, *Managed by the Markets: How Finance Re-Shaped America* (Oxford: Oxford University Press, 2009).

conducive to happiness for a large number of people. Following this logic, Nephi's admonition to "labor for Zion" might be understood as commensurable with the pursuit of money as an intermediate goal in accomplishing the greater goal of building Zion. This, after all, is a common way to understand Jacob's admonition: "But before ye seek for riches, seek ye for the kingdom of God. And after ye have obtained a hope in Christ ye shall obtain riches, if ye seek them" (Jacob 2:18–19).

A consequentialist idea also appears at work in another of Jacob's sermons where he cites Isaiah 55:1–2, though with an insertion that distances it from the rendering in the King James Version of the Bible. After quoting the Isaianic phrase "without money and without price," and the Isaianic admonition to "hearken diligently" (Isa. 55:2), Jacob inserts the following phrase: "come unto the Holy One of Israel, and feast upon that which perisheth not, neither can be corrupted" (2 Ne. 9:51). The word "corrupt" occurs twenty times in the Book of Mormon, typically in one of three meaning-based contexts: (1) the corruption of a soul, a law, or an institution due to pride, avarice, or lust for power (see 2 Ne. 28:11, 12; Mosiah 29:40; Hel. 4:22, 5:2; Ether 9:6); (2) the corruption of earthly treasures (see 3 Ne. 13:19–20, 27:32); and (3) the corruption of trees that fail to produce good fruit (see Jacob 5:39, 42, 46–48, 75; 3 Ne. 14:17–18). The last of these is especially relevant to consequentialist logic because Jacob's insertion of the term "corrupt" gives voice to a concern about the effects or consequences of corruption: corrupt trees are bad because they fail to produce good fruit.

A certain form of consequentialist logic can also be discerned in Alma 1, but there is an important disrupting twist. The faithful church members are described as becoming "exceedingly rich . . . [and] they did prosper and become far more wealthy than those who did not belong to their church" (vv. 29, 31).[5] It would seem that the prosperous circumstances of the righteous are being held up in this narrative as a consequentialist-based motive to be righteous. However, this meta-narratival logic is subverted by the story itself because the righteous church members are distinguished in the text precisely by their refusal to seek after riches. We read that the

5. Brant Gardner suggests a strong difference between Mormon's use of the terms *wealthy* and *riches*, suggesting that *wealthy* refers to a generous-spirited nature in the community. Be that as it may, Alma 1:29 clearly states that the church members were rich. See volume 4 of Brant A. Gardner, *Second Witness: Analytic and Contextual Commentary on the Book of Mormon* (Salt Lake City: Greg Kofford Books, 2007).

church members "did impart the word of God, one with another, without money and without price" (v. 20), and that they "did not set their heart upon riches" (v. 30). The nonmembers, in contrast, devoted themselves to "the spreading of priestcraft . . . for the sake of riches" (v. 16). The twist at work here follows an inversion pattern which itself can be traced back to Isaiah. Isaiah declares, for example, that the "loftiness . . . and haughtiness of men will be made low" (Isa. 2:17). This is similar to the inverted manner in which nonmembers of the church in Alma 1, who sought after riches, ended up being much poorer than the church members who did not seek riches and ended up "far more wealthy" (v. 31).

Another disruption of consequentialist thinking can be brought to light by examining King Benjamin's condemnation of those who refuse to give to beggars. King Benjamin says, "Perhaps thou shalt say: The man has brought upon himself his misery; therefore I will stay my hand . . . for his punishments are just" (Mosiah 4:17). These rationalizing words echo a version of an argument used by consequentialists to criticize programs and practices that help the poor. The argument asserts that since the poor are often poor as a result of their own laziness, and giving to the poor effectively subsidizes laziness, aid should not be given to the poor.[6] King Benjamin, however, condemns such rationalizing attitudes toward the poor, declaring that those with such attitudes have "great cause to repent" (v. 18).

Returning to Alma 1, a similar link between laziness and the pursuit of riches can be seen at work. The wicked nonmembers of the church are there described as indulging in "idolatry or idleness, and . . . wearing costly apparel" (v. 32). This simultaneous manifestation of both idleness and pride among nonmembers contrasts with the righteous church members, who seem to have had both a diligent work ethic and modest consumer tastes. According to Alma 1:26–27, the church members returned "diligently unto their labors" after hearing God's word, working "every man according to his strength" and "not wear[ing] costly apparel." The phrase "idolatry or idleness" is curious, and brings to mind a desire to avoid work that is manifest in two earlier episodes from the Book of Mosiah: first, the Lamanites are described as "a lazy and an idolatrous people . . . desirous . . . that they might glut themselves with the labor of [the Nephites'] hands" (Mosiah 9:12); second, King Noah and his priests are described as being "supported in their

6. For a book-length treatment that advocates a version of this argument, see Richard Epstein, *Mortal Peril: Our Inalienable Right to Health Care?* (New York: Basic Books, 2000).

laziness, and in their idolatry, and in their whoredoms, by the taxes which king Noah had put upon his people; thus did the people labor exceedingly to support iniquity" (Mosiah 11:6). The linking of pride and idleness in Alma 1 follows naturally from a consequentialist mode of thought, particularly in its utilitarian guise. In the workhorse model of modern economic theory, a rational agent maximizes utility and minimizes costs. Mapping this model to scriptural terms, it seems that maximizing utility corresponds to pride and minimizing of costs corresponds to idleness. The behavior of the wicked nonmembers that we observe in Alma 1 is exactly what modern economic theory predicts: they pursue riches in a way that entails the least amount of effort or work on their part.

The idleness manifested by the nonmembers of the church in Alma can be more deeply understood when considered in light of Nehor's teachings of universal salvation. Nehor teaches "that all mankind should be saved at the last day" (Alma 1:4). This description of universal salvation can be contrasted with a different kind of universality at work later in the chapter where the righteous church members are described as being "liberal unto all" (v. 30). Similarly, Nephi declares that God's invitation to salvation is addressed to "all . . . for he denieth none that come unto him, black and white, bond and free, male and female; and he remembereth the heathen; and all are alike unto God, both Jew and Gentile" (2 Ne. 26:33). A key difference between the universalism at work in Nehor's teaching compared to Nephi's teaching, and the practice of universal giving by the members of the church in Alma 1, is that for Nehor salvation is *guaranteed* to everyone whereas Nephi teaches that salvation is *offered* to everyone. This difference between *guarantee* and *offer* has a certain resonance with the different plans offered in the pre-mortal council by God and Satan. We read, for example, that Satan's plan would "destroy the agency of man" by "redeem[ing] all mankind, that one soul shall not be lost" (Moses 4:1, 3). In its focus on guaranteeing salvation, Satan's plan gives rise to instrumental logic where the ends justify the means: salvation for all is an end worth pursuing, regardless of the means used to obtain that end. In contrast, God's plan, as articulated by Nephi, must be judged as inefficient and risky using the same logic, especially since humanity so frequently ignores the invitation to repent. Because of the seemingly large number of souls being lost to the world, the plan of salvation manifests itself as weak and ineffectual against the consequentialist, means-ends logic we are so accustomed to in modern modes of discourse. To properly understand God's universally offered salvation requires a different mode of reasoning.

Returning to King Benjamin's sermon, we find economic terms being used in a way that further subverts the usual mode of economic reasoning. Although King Benjamin acknowledges that he is "a ruler and a king" over his people (Mosiah 2:11), he emphasizes the fact that he has "not sought gold nor silver nor any manner of riches" from his people (v. 12), and he goes on to explain that he is only a "mortal man," like his people, "subject to all manner of infirmities" (vv. 10–11). Moreover, he maintains that the service he has rendered to his people fails to warrant boasting since he has only been serving God, to whom we are all eternally indebted (vv. 15–26). This theme of indebtedness to God is also referred to in King Benjamin's later discussion of beggars when he explains that we should not judge them unworthy to give to, since we are all ultimately undeserving of the blessings God has given us (Mosiah 4:16–26). Using economic measures as a basis for understanding our relationship to God, King Benjamin reveals how our indebtedness to God is incalculable. Because of this incalculability, we are effectively put on an equal footing with other mortals in a way that undermines rationalizations to withhold from the poor.

This conception of equality that King Benjamin develops represents a very different conception of equality from what dominates modern discourse. The modern idea of economic inequality does not readily map onto the Book of Mormon, although there are a few instances where it does seem that something like a modern conception of economic equality is present. One instance is in Fourth Nephi where we read that the Lehites "had all things common among them; therefore there were not rich and poor, bond and free, but they were all made free, and partakers of the heavenly gift" (4 Ne. 1:3). The scripture here does not, however, make a very explicit claim that economic equality actually existed, as we would conceive it today; rather, we read a different characterization, that there "were not rich and poor," and the people "had all things in common." Similarly, after acknowledging distinctions between rich and poor in Alma 1, the righteous are characterized by their willingness to

> impart of their substance, every man according to that which he had, to the poor, and the needy, . . . [and] they were liberal to all, both old and young, both bond and free, both male and female, whether out of the church or in the church, having no respect of persons as to those who stood in need. (vv. 27, 30)

This passage does not include a description of any economic system or political program aimed at producing equality. Instead, the righteous church members are simply said to be "liberal to all" in a manner that has an immediate, transformative effect on the given economic situation.

Another way to understand the difference between universally offered and universally guaranteed salvation is by the universal workings of money. In Karl Marx's magnum opus *Capital*, he repeatedly refers to money using the adjective "universal" (or the adverb "universally").[7] Money is universal in the sense that any good or service located within the economy can be measured by money, and thus compared to any other good or service within the economy. When market forces of competition are present, a single price for commoditized goods and services gets assigned a single price that uncouples subjective, individual values and the singular objective market value. As this universal, objectifying money-based economy extends its reach—across the globe and into the private, family realm—it becomes more and more possible to buy anything (in this world) with money. Moreover, the incentives to acquire more money increase in a multiplicative feedback loop as the economy increases its scope.[8] Marx observes how the universality of money in the gathering momentum of a capitalist economy leaves "remaining no other nexus between man and man than naked self-interest, than callous 'cash payment,'" dissolving every human bond "in the icy water of egotistical calculation."[9] This reduction to a one-dimensional measure of goods, services, and relations is what gives money its universal, objectifying potency.

Besides the one-dimensional, instrumentalizing tendency described above, there are two other tendencies in modern economic thinking that Book of Mormon appropriations of Isaiah's "without money" phrase call into question: a focus on rationality, and stable preferences. Although there are good and useful scientific reasons for assuming that economic

---

7. Phrases Marx uses in his chapter on "Money, or the Circulation of Commodities" include: "a universal measure of value," "a universal equivalent," "the universal representative of material wealth," "the universal commodity," "the universal subject-matter of all contracts," "universal money," "the universal medium of payment," "the universal means of purchasing," "the universally recognized embodiment of all wealth," and "the universally recognized embodiment of social wealth." See Karl Marx, *Capital, Volume One*, trans. Ben Fowkes (New York: Vintage, 1976), 188–244.

8. The increasing scope of the global economy increases the incentives to acquire more money for two major reasons. First, the range of goods and services money can buy continues to increase. Second, the value of labor relative to capital tends to increase, so that those who depend primarily on labor income (that is, the non-wealthy) must work harder to keep their relative purchasing power the same.

9. Robert C. Tucker, ed., *The Marx-Engels Reader*, 2nd ed. (New York: Norton, 1978), 475.

agents make decisions based on a rational analysis of the possible alternatives, the Book of Mormon tends to use emotional rather than cognitive language when describing attitudes toward money.[10] For example, the church members in Alma 1 "set their hearts upon riches" (v. 30) and are contrasted with Nehor who "began to be lifted up in the pride of his heart" (v. 6), and the nonmembers who are described by the phrase "the hearts of many were hardened" (v. 24). This language invoking the emotional term *heart* echoes many other Book of Mormon passages, but especially noteworthy is Alma's sermon a few chapters later with its focus on a change of heart (Alma 5:12, 14, 26). This focus on a change of heart calls into question the assumption of stable preferences commonly used by economists. Again, there are good and useful reasons for making this simplifying assumption, but in making this assumption modern discourse regarding economic matters tends to underemphasize the sense in which people's hearts and preferences change over time, and the manner in which these changes depend upon the larger societal and communal contexts in which economic transactions take place.

When stable, rational preferences and a reductionist focus on money are combined with the consequentialist logic of economy described above, all the main ingredients are present for the workhorse utilitarian model of modern economics in which individuals and organizations are expected to make rationally calculated decisions that maximize a stable and objectively measured payoff function according to monetarily inscribed cost constraints. Although it is true that limits can be imposed on what kind of maximizing behavior is ethically justified, such ethical constraints do little to disrupt the overarching, money-focused mode of reasoning that pervades public discourse on economic matters. When interrogated by scripture, this approach manifests several weaknesses. First, the Book of Mormon baldly criticizes those who work for the purpose of making money. The prevalence and commonsensical resonance in our modern economy of this idea—working to earn money—suggests that our conscious and unconscious thoughts about economic matters are dominated by worldly conceptions. Developing a robust alternate conception of economic concerns, and training ourselves to think according to such an alternative, will therefore entail great care, attention, and work.

10. The term "heart," for example, occurs in 1,475 distinct verses in the Mormon canon, with 394 of those verses coming from the Book of Mormon, while the term "mind" occurs in only 239 distinct verses in the Mormon canon, with 61 of those verses coming from the Book of Mormon.

Second, whereas the most common mode of modern economic thinking involves a focus on consequences and means-ends logic, a focus on this kind of reasoning is called into question by scripture. Consequentialist logic can at times be found in scripture, including a link between righteousness and economic prosperity; however, there are important subversions of this logic at work in scripture. For example, in Alma 1 the righteous members of the church who do not seek after riches enjoy much greater economic prosperity than the nonmembers who do seek after riches. This inversion casts the controlling tendency of modern scientific thinking about economic problems in sharp relief: whereas a modern economist is apt to think about structuring economic incentives so that the unalterable desires of individual agents are aligned in a way that maximizes an economic measure of societal well-being, the Book of Mormon's appropriation of Isaiah's "without money" phrase suggests that economic prosperity is best obtained, ironically, by a turn away from pursuing economic prosperity.

Finally, this turning away from economic concerns is ultimately bound up with a change in the manner that money is related to, not just cognitively but emotionally as well. This point leads naturally to questions regarding larger political context in which economic agents are embedded.

Politics

As has already been pointed out, it is within the context of Nephi's teachings on universal salvation that the phrase "without money and without price" occurs (2 Ne. 26:25). To get a better sense of the context, note that chapters 25–27 of Second Nephi comprised a single chapter in the original Book of Mormon manuscript,[11] with Nephi offering a midrashic commentary on both Isaiah 55:1 and Isaiah 29:3–24.[12] In the beginning of chapter 26, Nephi discusses his vision recorded in 1 Nephi 11–14 of Christ's then-still-future visit to Lehi's children and the associated four generations of peace that would ensue, only to be followed by a "speedy destruction" of the Nephites (2 Ne. 26:1–11). Nephi then transitions to a discussion of the Gentiles and the Lehites in the last days, explaining the coming forth of the Book of Mormon during a time when pride and secret combinations would thrive among the Gentiles (vv. 14–23). In the

11. Orson Pratt reworked the chapter divisions of the Book of Mormon text late in the nineteenth century.

12. See the various essays in Joseph M. Spencer and Jenny Webb, eds., *Reading Nephi Reading Isaiah: Reading 2 Nephi 26–27* (Salem, Ore.: Salt Press, 2011).

last part of the chapter, Nephi offers theological reflections on God's universal offer of salvation to people of all stripes (vv. 24–33). The role that the coming forth of the Book of Mormon plays in these several discussions will be considered later when I discuss the creative, transformative effects of language. For the moment, I will focus principally on the issues of equality and identity politics in Nephi's discussion.

The text of 2 Nephi 26:33 reads, "and he denieth none that come unto him, black and white, bond and free, male and female; and he remembereth the heathen; and all are alike unto God, both Jew and Gentile." On the one hand, Nephi's explicit mention of race, social standing, gender, and religion affirms politically recognizable identities, with a varying mix of biologically and socially based factors. On the other hand, Nephi undermines this affirmation of political identities in the very next phrase by asserting that "all are alike unto God." The term "alike" has interesting connotations. Although the context strongly suggests that humans who differ across socio-political differences are all alike *before* God, the root term "like" in this phrasing recalls how humans were made in the image and *likeness* of God (see Gen. 1:26–27). This suggests a possible connotation that all human beings are, not just *like each other* in God's eyes, but human beings—all of them—are *like God*. Nevertheless, a tension between Nephi's simultaneous affirmation and denial of socio-political difference remains.

In addition to this tension, another difficulty arises in considering Nephi's words later in this same chapter:

> Hath he commanded any that they should not partake of his salvation? Behold I say unto you, Nay; but he hath given it free for all men; and he hath commanded his people that they should persuade all men to repentance. Behold, hath the Lord commanded any that they should not partake of his goodness? Behold, I say unto you, Nay; but all men are privileged the one like unto the other, and none are forbidden. (2 Ne. 26:27–28)

Similar to the proviso in 1 Nephi 17:35, God's salvation is here offered "free for all men," although all are to be persuaded "to repentance." The difficulty is that Nephi claims in 2 Nephi 26:33 that "bond and free . . . are alike unto God," and the implication is surely that someone in bonds can be as righteous as a free person. But if, as Nephi said earlier, the righteous are favored of God, and we interpret freedom as a favored status over bondage, the implication would be that those who are free are more righteous than those who are in bondage. Surely this is not what Nephi means.

Nephi offers a similar doctrine of equality in his first book when he asserts that "the Lord esteemeth all flesh in one" but then immediately follows this claim with the important proviso, "he that is righteous is favored of God" (1 Ne. 17:35). By taking the contrapositive of this proviso, we seem to get the following: he that is not favored of God is not righteous. A close and unfortunately popular corollary of this claim is a version of the prosperity gospel where material prosperity and righteousness are causally linked. But this is not what Nephi is saying. First, divine favor and material prosperity are not the same thing: being "favored of God" is a concept that can have a wide range of meanings and does not necessarily entail any externally observable manifestation. Second, the common interpretation is to assume an immediate linkage between being righteous and being favored. To force this immediate linkage upon the text is an unwarranted, myopic interpretation, especially given the ongoing concern in scripture with an eternal temporal horizon. Nevertheless, there is still a tension between Nephi's affirmed recognition of various forms of inequality, with an underlying gesture toward theological justification relating inequality and righteousness, and Nephi's simultaneous affirmation of equality. This tension represents a challenge for modern interpreters of Nephi's doctrine of equality.

In addition to these difficulties in Nephi's writing, a similar difficulty can be found in Alma 1, though it takes a bit of work to bring it out. First, a form of inequality regarding labor explicitly manifests itself in Nehor's claim "that every priest and teacher ought to become popular; and they ought not to labor with their hands, but that they ought to be supported by the people" (v. 3). As a result of this teaching, people "began to support [Nehor] and give him money. And [Nehor] began to be lifted up in the pride of his heart, and to wear very costly apparel" (vv. 5–6). The followers of Nehor continued this pattern of "wearing costly apparel" and "being lifted up in the pride of their own eyes" (v. 32), even after Nehor's death. These actions are contrasted in the text with the actions of the members of the church at the time who "did not wear costly apparel" (v. 27) and who maintained relations between the priest and his hearers such that the priest did not esteem "himself above his hearers, for the preacher was no better than the hearer, neither was the teacher any better than the learner; and thus they were all equal, and they did all labor" (v. 26). All of this seems simple enough. But the link between the verb "esteem" used here and Nephi's teaching that the Lord "esteemeth all flesh in one" (1 Ne. 17:35; cf. Philip. 2:6) should not be overlooked, especially since it is here that a difficulty not unlike the one in Nephi's writings regarding equality manifests itself. Although the priest does not esteem himself above his hearers, he nevertheless holds the priesthood and has the privilege of talking. Perhaps it is not difficult for a modern Mormon audience to agree with the text that "they were all equal" in the sense that they had equal access to speak, since in the Church today lay members take turns being instructors and being instructed. However, since the Church does not allow women to become priests, the claim of equality applied to the priest/hearer relationship does not jive with a robust modern understanding of equality. (The difficulty is only heightened for modern Church members by a similar tension at work in "The Family: A Proclamation to the World," where it is asserted that "fathers are to *preside over* their families" even though "fathers and mothers are obligated to help one another as *equal partners*"—a tension that has not escaped the notice of the Mormon blogging community.)[13]

One way to address the problem of equality in these Book of Mormon passages is to confine our understanding of equality to the realm of esteem. That is, although the priest and the hearer were unequal in certain respects, the priest did "not esteem himself above his hearers," just as "the preacher was no better than the hearer."[14] But how should we understand the word *esteem*? Interestingly, in light of our previous discussion of economics, *esteem* has the same etymological roots as the word *estimate*, and the first two definitions in the Oxford English Dictionary for *esteem* read: "(1) To estimate value; to value. (2) To attach value (subjectively) to." The parenthetical reference to a specifically subjective mode of valuation—implicitly opposing it to any objective mode—is important, especially when considered in the light of contemporary political theory where law is thought to work objectively.

In the modern conception of the rule of law, a commonly embraced principle is the granting of universal equal protection under the law so that

13. "The Family: A Proclamation to the World," http://www.lds.org/Static%20Files/PDF/Manuals/TheFamily_AProclamationToTheWorld_35538_eng.pdf (accessed June 6, 2012); emphasis added. For a good example of Mormon bloggers debating the language of the proclamation, see "Reason, Authority, and Ralph Hancock," *By Common Consent*, http://bycommonconsent.com/2012/05/17/reason-authority-and-ralph-hancock/ (accessed June 6, 2012).

14. Besides being equal in these ways, the priest and hearer "did all labor, every man according to his strength" (Alma 1:26) so they could also be considered equal in this additional sense.

the law is blind to political identities. This principle gives law a degree of objectivity that, for example, protects minority groups against arbitrary or oppressive treatment. This objective nature of law is somewhat analogous to the objective nature of money discussed above: just as the law is blind, money too is blind in that money has the same economic (exchange) value regardless of how, or from whom, the money was obtained. This blindness, inherent to both law and money, helps ensure a formal or ideal kind of equality at work: the law treats all subjects equally, just as money treats all market participants equally. This formal, ideal conception of equality has been criticized by suggesting it ignores a more actualized sense of equality that pertains to the actual lived experience of legal subjects and economic participants.[15] The simplest way to understand this difference is in terms of the distribution of economic goods: although money works according to a principle of equality, in the sense that money is blind, the actual distribution of money among market participants can be very unequal. Other forms of political inequality, pertaining to goods and opportunities that are not merely economic, can be understood in a similar manner.

The link between the objective nature of law and the question of equality can be better understood in terms of the switch to the reign of the judges when it was established "that men should be judged according to their crimes . . . therefore, a man was punished only for the crimes which he had done; therefore all men were on equal grounds" (Alma 30:11; cf. Mosiah 29:38–39). In modern ethical theory, the study of rules requiring equal situations to be treated equally is known as *deontology*. This name is significant. The root *deon-* comes from the Greek *deo-(/dei-)*, "to tie or to bind," and connotes the binding obligations or duties we have toward others. A deontological ethical approach is thus rooted in the idea of acting in accordance with one's duty to others.

Because duties and obligations to others are usually conceived juridically, a major danger of the deontological approach is revealed in Jesus's interaction with his legalistic critics. After healing "a woman which had a spirit of infirmity" (Luke 13:11) on the Sabbath day, and being accused of not keeping the principle of the Sabbath which maintains that there are only "six days in which men *ought* to work" (Luke 13:14; emphasis mine), Jesus responds by asking: "And *ought* not this woman . . . whom Satan hath *bound* . . . be loosed from this *bond* on the Sabbath day?" (v. 16; emphases mine). The interplay in this verse between the words

15. See Amartya Sen, *The Idea of Justice* (Cambridge: Belknap Press, 2009).

I have italicized, all of which echo the same Greek root *deo-*, reflects a tension between Greek and Hebrew conceptions of the world: where the Greek worldview is rooted in "the thought of a neutral deity . . . which determines the course of the world," the Hebrew worldview "thinks God in terms of the will which personally summons man and which fashions history according to its plan."[16] For Jesus, the law of the Sabbath cannot be properly understood in neutral, impersonal terms unconnected from a robust conception of the good as revealed by a personal God. The Greek conception of *the good* disconnects it from an ethical conception of *the right*, and it is this disconnect that makes the deontological framework so attractive to modern secular society and its pluralistic conceptions of the good. However, this disconnect also comprises a weakness of the deontological approach because it can lead to the kind of hypocritical legalism against which Jesus preached in his encounters with the Sadducees and Pharisees. This kind of legalism tends to arise in societies where rule-of-law values like universality, neutrality, and equality are privileged over a publicly held conception of the good.

A problem related to this kind of legalism manifests itself in the history of the Nephites after the reign of judges begins. As mentioned above, problems of avarice began to appear in the very first year of the judges' reign when priestcraft thrived and the nonmembers of the church are described as "lov[ing] the vain things of the world" and preaching "for the sake of riches and honor," although "for fear of the law . . . they pretended to preach according to their belief" (Alma 1:16–17). There are two forms of disconnect at work here, both of which undermine the subjective integrity between the law and the person subject to the law. First, desires—because of a desire for riches—are disconnected from the requirements of law. Second, preaching is disconnected from beliefs. These disconnects appear later in the chapter in the form of a tension between the law and the increasingly wicked desires of the nonmembers who

> did indulge themselves; . . . nevertheless, the law was put in force upon all those who did transgress it, inasmuch as it was possible. And it came to pass that by thus exercising the law upon them, every man suffering according to that which he had done, they became more still, and durst not commit any wickedness if it were known; therefore, there was much peace among the people of Nephi until the fifth year of the reign of the judges. (vv. 32–33)

---

16. Gerhard Kittel and Gerhard Friedrich, eds., *Theological Dictionary of the New Testament*, trans. Geoffrey William Bromiley (Grand Rapids, Mich.: Eerdmans, 1964–1976), 1:345.

This problem of heteronomous desire—the tension between the requirements of the law, "force[d] upon all those who did transgress," and diverging desires—eventually works its way into the church, further endangering the tenuous peace described in the passage above.[17] By the eighth year of the reign of the judges, the members of the church also began to be prideful, "set[ting] their hearts upon riches" and "be[ing] scornful, one towards another . . . persecut[ing] those that did not believe according to their own will and pleasure" (Alma 4:8). Interestingly, the reference here to "will and pleasure" is similar to a phrase in Helaman 7:5 where "the wicked go unpunished because of their money . . . and *do according to their own wills*" (emphasis mine). Similar language is also used in a more modern warning given in Doctrine and Covenants 3:4: "if [a man] boasts in his own strength . . . and follows *the dictates of his own will and carnal desires,* he must . . . incur the vengeance of a just God upon him" (emphasis mine). The "own will" and "carnal desires" language in this Doctrine and Covenants passage highlights the tendency in modern conceptions of human agency to conceive of individuals atomistically, and the relation of this idea to the tendency of economic models to posit agency as, effectively, a rational will being exercised in accordance with pre-given, unchanging desires.

In the Book of Mormon, the problem of heteronomous desire arises from a failure to subject desire to law. When this happens, a disconnect arises between individuals' increasingly divergent subjective wills and the law's unchanging, universal objective requirements. Although law helps mediate the conflict of wills in society, the peace achieved in this way is tenuous and temporary. Trust becomes difficult to establish and maintain because of the disconnect of words from beliefs and actions from desires. Within this conflict-of-wills political situation, equality tends to be measured according to external, objective criteria. Based on these political criteria, the kind of subjective equality we find on offer in the Book of Mormon manifests itself as weak, ineffectual, and insufficient. Although salvation is offered equally to all, this salvation seems far off and distant, working according to a remote spiritual horizon rather than a proximate, temporal horizon. In our contemporary world, just as in Nephi's world, we find various power-based manifestations of inequality involving race,

17. For a good treatment of the problem of a version of this problem of heteronomous desire as it relates to law and language, see Giorgio Agamben, *The Sacrament of Language: An Archeology of the Oath*, trans. Adam Kotsko (Stanford, Calif.: Stanford University Press, 2010).

social standing, gender, and religion (2 Ne. 26:33). Against these background inequalities, the equal esteem that God is described as having for all his children appears feeble and inadequate.

God's Word

Most modes of modern economic and political thought share a key weakness: they assume a single ground or measure for evaluation. When economic or political tensions arise, a solution is usually sought by attempting, as it were, to find a point on a horizontal line that optimally balances competing interests of individual wills. The distribution of economic goods and political justice is conceived in such a way that a larger allocation to one party necessitates a smaller allocation to another party. This economizing logic, which saturates modern political discourse as much as economic discourse, does not govern the humanities. If, for example, a writer creates a beautiful phrase, this does not interfere with other writers' ability to come up with their own beautiful phrases—in fact, beautiful writing usually inspires, more than it discourages, other writing. Thus, in contrast to economic and political goods, scarcity is a poor measure of language.

The creative excess characteristic of the humanities is both a weakness and a strength.[18] Scholars in more scientific, quantitative disciplines often become frustrated with the subjective and qualitative nature of the humanities that is a direct consequence of excess and abundance. The subjective, relative nature of art gives those who seek objective truths intellectual vertigo. Progress becomes hard to determine and measure. This is the weakness of the humanities. The flip-side strength is skill in language that has creative and transformative potency lacking in other disciplines. Although technology and the social sciences may have a greater effect on the economy, culture is dominated by those proficient in the subject matter of the humanities. Prophets, in this sense, seem to have more in common with the ability of artists and writers to inspire and motivate than with the ability of engineers to build gadgets and structures with an aim to control and satisfy. This ability to inspire represents a dimension of verticality that is foreign to the social sciences, although it can be very useful for resolving economic and political struggles. Political philosopher Charles Taylor, employing a similar horizontal-vertical metaphor, writes:

18. See Adam S. Miller, *Rube Goldberg Machines: Essays in Mormon Theology* (Salt Lake City: Greg Kofford Books, 2012), 99–105.

"The horizontal space gives you the dimension in which you have to find the point of resolution, the fair 'award,' between two parties. The vertical space opens the possibility that by rising higher, you'll accede to a new horizontal space where the resolution will be less painful/damaging for both parties."[19] In the search for reconciliation and lasting peace, the vital skills of creativity and imagination are required, skills that are most properly valued and cultivated through careful engagement with language. This is the strength of the humanities.

In the Book of Isaiah, the invitation to buy "without money and without price" is followed by an invitation to "incline your ear, and come unto me: hear, and your soul shall live" (Isa. 55:3). This focus on God's word is revisited a few verses later, in what is essentially the beginning of the concluding paragraph of Second Isaiah:

> For as the rain cometh down, and the snow from heaven, and returneth not thither, but watereth the earth, and maketh it bring forth and bud, that it may give seed to the sower, and bread to the eater: So shall my word be that goeth forth out of my mouth: it shall not return unto me void, but it shall accomplish that which I please, and it shall prosper in the thing whereto I sent it. (Isa. 55:10–11)

The theme of God's word going forth, not returning void, and accomplishing God's purposes reinforces themes in earlier parts of the Book of Isaiah—themes that also play a prominent role in the Book of Mormon's appropriations of Isaiah's "without money and without price." For example, in Isaiah 48:3 (and 1 Nephi 20:3), we read: "I have declared the former things from the beginning; and they went forth out of my mouth, and I shewed them; I did them suddenly, and they came to pass" (cf. Isa. 41:22–23; 42:9; 43:9; 44:6–8; 45:21; 46:9–10). The "former things" here are God's prophecies that have not been made in vain, but have proven themselves by actually coming to pass.

Several oblique references to the "former things" of Isaiah 48:3 can be cited in the Book of Mormon. First, the prosperous situation of the righteous members of the church is noted in Alma 1 in a manner that accords with the oft-quoted promise that Lehi's children would prosper if they kept God's commandments. God's promise is thus "brought to pass" as Isaiah claims. Second, since many biblical commentators see Isaiah 40–48 forming a first structural unit of Second Isaiah, and Isaiah 49–55 forming

19. Charles Taylor, *A Secular Age* (Cambridge: Harvard University Press, 2007), 706.

a second structural unit, it is noteworthy that Isaiah 48 is quoted in the Book of Mormon, along with the rest of Isaiah 49–54, and the first part of Isaiah 55.[20] By including Isaiah 48 as, effectively, the opposite bookend to Isaiah 55, the Book of Mormon draws attention to the manner in which the "former things" declared by God's word are eventually fulfilled in the world, "not return[ing] . . . void" (Isa. 55:11). Finally, Nephi's vision of the coming forth of latter-day scripture in 1 Nephi 13 is closely linked with Nephi's citation of Isaiah 48 only a few chapters later.[21] For Nephi, the coming forth of God's word in the latter days is itself a fulfillment of God's promise to fulfill his word, and purposes, in the world.

If the "former things" mentioned in Isaiah 48:3 are taken to correspond with the summary allusion in Isaiah 55:10 that God's word "shall not return . . . void," the contrast with the "new things" mentioned in Isaiah 48:6 can be taken to correspond to the summary allusion in Isaiah 55:10 that God's word "shall accomplish that which [God] please[s]." The claim in Isaiah 48:6 is: "I have shewed thee new things from this time, even hidden things, and thou didst not know them." These "new things" correspond to the vertical dimension where the effect of God's word is innovative and creative, finding transformative solutions that go beyond the one-dimensional disciplinary models and concepts that currently dominate the social sciences. In his commentary on Isaiah, John Oswalt writes about Isaiah 48:6:

> We humans have a desperate need to bring our diverse environment under control, both intellectually, through organization and data, and actually, through manipulation of the environmental elements. What we do not want are surprises. Thus, if God . . . fulfilled prophecy in the past, he must fulfill it in exactly the same way now. But Isaiah has been saying that this kind

20. Joseph Blenkinsopp summarizes: "Most commentators agree that chs. 40–48, which are bracketed with their own inclusive passage (48:20–22 cf. 40:3–5), form a section that is quite different in theme and tone from 49–55." *Isaiah 40–55: A New Translation with Introduction and Commentary* (New York: Doubleday, 2000), 59. The Book of Mormon, interestingly, seems to group Isaiah 48 with Isaiah 49–55. At least one interesting biblical scholar suggests that that is the better way of dividing up the two parts of Second Isaiah. See Edward W. Conrad, *Reading Isaiah* (Minneapolis: Fortress Press, 1991), 72–82. On the use of Isaiah generally in the Book of Mormon, see Joseph M. Spencer, "Prolegomena to Any Future Study of Isaiah in the Book of Mormon," *Claremont Journal of Mormon Studies* 1, no. 1 (April 2011): 53–69.

21. See Joseph M. Spencer, "Nephi, Isaiah, and Europe," in *Reading Nephi Reading Isaiah*, ed. Joseph M. Spencer and Jenny Webb (Salem, Ore.: Salt Press, 2011).

> of limitation is characteristic of the [false] gods, not of God. . . . [D]o not expect to box [God] into some system that you have devised by observing him in the past; that is for idols.[22]

The desire Oswalt aptly describes, "to bring our diverse environment under control . . . through manipulation of the environmental elements," pervades modern thinking in both economics and politics.

Economists try to "manipulate the environment" by designing policy with economic incentives such that human behavior can be predictively shaped in a way that is conducive to maximal human flourishing. In contrast to economists' working assumption that market agents act in rational, self-interested, utility-maximizing ways, scripture describes the righteous members of the church as "humble . . . not proud in their own eyes . . . impart[ing] the word of God, one with another, without money and without price" (Alma 1:20). If economists or other social scientists were to use assumptions that humans would act in ways that are humble and charitable, they would be criticized for being utopian and unrealistic. In this sense, scripture does not conform well to the values of the world of social science. The social sciences value prediction over prescription, whereas scripture is fundamentally prescriptive.

Politics suffers from a similar, though subtler, problem. In political thought, social identities are recognized by various political institutions. This recognition allows institutions to be legally monitored in a way that ensures equality of treatment—and, in many cases, equality in the distribution of actual political goods. Political efforts to oversee the delivery of political equality are essentially attempts "to bring our diverse environment under control," to repeat Oswalt's description above. Political engineering may establish a form of peace in the short term, it will not do so in the medium and long term unless the wills and desires of the polity are oriented toward a robust conception of the good.

Although most modern economic and political frameworks are horizontally oriented, more vertically oriented alternatives do exist. These alternative frameworks tend not to be modern, strictly speaking, but draw inspiration from pre-modern thinkers—or, in some cases, from postmodern thinkers unafraid to present a robust, positive account of the good. Nephi's admonition that "the laborer in Zion shall labor for Zion" (2 Ne. 26:31), for example, fits more comfortably in an Aristotelian, virtue-

22. John N. Oswalt, *The Book of Isaiah: Chapters 40–66* (Grand Rapids: Eerdmans, 1998), 267.

based approach to the good than in a consequentialist or deontological approach. This is because Aristotle has a concept of final cause, a *telos* (an end or a goal) for the sake of which something exists. For Aristotle, *eudaimonia* (happiness or well-being) is the *telos* of human life, and it can be realized by living virtuously.[23] In this sense, to talk about the laborer in Zion laboring *for Zion* (rather than *for money* or *for gain*) is to talk about a laborer who labors virtuously, generating *eudaimonia* for herself and for her community.[24]

Returning to the ideas of universality and equality, we can consider them from a less dogmatically horizontal approach by considering how God's word gives us the resources for a vertically inspired overcoming of the myriad problems plaguing modern thinking about equality. These problems are, of course, much larger than can be addressed in the criminally short sketch I offer here. Nevertheless, my hope is that this sketch might suggest paths that others within the Mormon community—covenantally bound to the universal, transformative power of God's word—might pursue in an effort to mobilize an intellectual exodus out of the currently bleak economic and political situation of the modern world.

---

23. See Alasdair MacIntyre, *After Virtue: A Study in Moral Theory*, 3rd ed. (Notre Dame, Ind.: Notre Dame University Press, 2007).

24. It must be said, in the end, that modern thought is not incommensurable with scripture. For example, serious adherents of deontological or consequentialist ethical theory do not ignore the kinds of problems I have discussed. There is, however, an important sense in which these modes of modern thought give priority to instrumental values or rule-based modes of thought in a horizontally focused way. This focus crowds out other, more vertically focused concerns, especially as the increasingly competitive pressures of the global marketplace make the pursuit of higher learning as an end in itself, rather than a means for getting a better job, a luxury. Hence, even if consequentialist and deontological approaches are supplemented to include what I am calling more vertical elements, it is important not to underestimate the hegemony the dominant approaches continue to exercise in modern ethical and political theory. Moreover, these priorities and values of modern theory tend to imbue everyday concepts with meanings that move in directions quite different from, and generally less compatible with, the world of scripture. Navigating the differences represented by these distinct conceptual worlds requires careful attention to, on the one hand, the language, context, and concepts employed in scriptural texts and, on the other hand, modern concepts that permeate our thoughts, both consciously and unconsciously. Thus, to incarnate scriptural meanings *in* the modern world, in a way that is not *of* the modern world, requires great intellectual vigilance.

One alternative way to understand equality is in terms of the *active equality* we find in scripture rather than the *passive equality* we find in most modern thought. Political philosopher Todd May succinctly describes passive equality as positing a "subject of equality in the position of recipient rather than actor."[25] Active equality, in contrast, happens when all human beings are esteemed as equals, cable of acting rather than being acted upon (cf. 2 Ne. 2:26). The consequentialist logic used to criticize giving to the poor—discussed above—relies on a presupposition of passive equality in the following way. The poor do not deserve to be given to because they are judged to be mere passive possessors of an idle, undeserving disposition. Adhering to a presupposition of active equality, in contrast, entails an active belief or hope that the recipient, regardless of past mistakes, will act responsibly. Of course there is considerable risk that the recipient might act irresponsibly; nevertheless, as King Benjamin forcefully taught, we are all beggars, depending on God for forgiveness of our own sins (Mosiah 4:19–20), so we should give others a chance. Without presupposing active equality, we would all be slaves to carnal desires that compete within whatever the existing political governance system happens to be, without hope of a real or lasting peace.

Another, related way to understand equality is in terms of change: whereas economic and political thought tend to flatly assume that human nature is fixed and irredeemable, scripture maintains that, thanks to the Atonement, real change is always a possibility. This difference is tied inextricably to the questions of objectivity and subjectivity discussed above. The social sciences aspire to be objective in an effort to ensure that explanations are robust across time. The hope is that universal laws can be uncovered that make it possible to explain social phenomena in such a way that political and economic institutions can be developed that control the problems of human nature. The humanities, in contrast, do not aspire to this kind of objectivity or control; rather, subjectivity is a crucial presupposition. Subjective interpretation is required in the humanities because there is no absolute, fixed meaning to (non-scientific) texts. Interpretation

25. Todd May, *The Political Thought of Jacques Rancière: Creating Equality* (University Park: Pennsylvania State University Press, 2008), 4. For a fuller treatment of these ideas, see Jacques Rancière, *Disagreement: Politics and Philosophy*, trans. Julie Rose (Minneapolis: University of Minnesota Press, 2004). Also, for a theological application of Rancière's thought to the question of eschatology, see Bradley Johnson, "Doing Justice to Justice: Re-Assessing Deconstructive Eschatology," *Political Theology* 12, no. 1 (2011): 11–23.

thus requires subjective involvement of a reader, or a reading community. This subjective involvement is itself the catalyst for change since the act of subjective reading forces readers to exercise their agency and actively engage in an interpretive process linking the text, the world, and the subjectivity of the reader.

When God's word is distributed "without money and without price," change is made possible. In Alma 1, the generosity of the church members is itself an act that breaks with the carnal desires of human nature to share only when a definite return from sharing can be calculated. This unselfish act of sharing is itself evidence that economic self-interest and politically divergent wills do not fully govern human behavior. These acts attest to the fact that "new things" (Isa. 48:6; 1 Ne. 20:6) are in fact possible. This possibility of change effected by God's word is, moreover, precisely why, I propose, Nephi quoted the Isaianic phrase "without money and without price" just before launching into a vision of the change effected by the coming forth of the Book of Mormon in the last days (see 2 Ne. 26–29).

Inequality is rampant in this world—in our economies, in our polities, and in our churches. Although some of this inequality can be avoided, much of it cannot. Children, for example, inhabit an unequal, inferior position relative to their parents. But, then, Jesus teaches that "whosoever therefore shall humble himself as [a] little child, the same is greatest in the kingdom of heaven" (Matt. 18:4). Similarly, King Benjamin recounts the words of an angel announcing that, as saints, we are to "submit to all things which the Lord seeth fit to inflict upon [us], even as a child doth submit to his father" (Mosiah 3:19). Christ, as the typological Son, sets the example by allowing his own will to be "swallowed up in the will of the Father" (Mosiah 15:7). And Paul admonished church members to esteem others "better than themselves" (Philip. 2:3), like Christ submitted to the Father, even as he taught that Christ "thought it not robbery to be equal with God" (v. 6). This equality/inequality tension might appear paradoxical, but the paradox is resolved by seeing that present inequalities do not undermine the gospel's fundamental presupposition of equality, namely that God esteems all humankind equally. The ironic implication is that if this kind of scriptural equality is actively presupposed, by turning away from a resentful focus on the absence of such equality in the world as it is, then we find the greatest hope for such equality to in fact become actualized.

None of this is to say that economic and political programs do not have a positive role to play in the world, or that such programs could not be prudently used to complement the scriptural project of incarnating active equality. However, putting hope in a political or an economic program to establish passive, distributional equality is not the kind of hope offered by scripture. What is offered instead is a vision in which the word of God transgresses the boundaries of economics and politics by a logic that is beyond or without economic and political bounds, where the meaning, significance and possible implications of God's word are subjectively and transformatively enacted in accordance with the universal presupposition that God esteems all of his children equally.

THREE

"Take No Thought"

Adam S. Miller

They call it Christianity. I call it consciousness.
—Emerson

You are going to miss it.[1] You're distracted. You're not paying attention. God does not come and go, your attention does.

All sins are just variations on that same desire to do something else when you're already doing something. Multitaskers are children of the devil. You can't serve two masters. Divided attention is just dressed up inattention. "Hear, O Israel," the Shema begins, "the Lord our God is one Lord!" (Deut. 6:4). But are you one? Or do you keep getting shucked, splintered, and spread by every distraction that wanders by?

Put your phone away. Recent studies agree with Jesus. In their distressing 2009 paper "Cognitive control in media multitaskers," Ophir et al. found that heavy media multitaskers (or HMMs) "have greater difficulty filtering out irrelevant stimuli from their environment." They are "less likely to ignore irrelevant representations in memory." And they are "less effective in suppressing the activation of irrelevant task sets."[2]

Does this remind you of anyone? Do you know anyone who can't filter out irrelevant stimuli? Do you know anyone who keeps getting sucked down black holes of memory and fantasy? Do you know anyone who can't suppress the impulse to do something other than what they're supposed to be doing?

---

1. The first part of this essay has appeared also in Adam S. Miller, "Take No Thought," *Dialogue: A Journal of Mormon Thought* 44, no. 1 (Spring 2011): 115–22.

2. See Clifford Nass, Eyal Ophir, and Anthony Wagner, "Cognitive Control in Media Multitaskers," *Proceedings of the National Academy of Sciences of the United States of America* 106, no. 37 (September 15, 2009): 15583–87.

Do you know anyone who *doesn't* fit this description?

Such is the human condition: unable to filter stimuli or shunt impulses, everyone sins. "There is none righteous, no, not one" because sin beds down in the distraction of our daydreams (Rom. 3:10).

Multitasking, you fit yourself for distraction. You train yourself to never quite commit, to never quite settle in, to keep at least one eye on what you're not doing, on the people you're not with, on the things you don't have. With every email update, push notification, and status change—ding!—you prime your mind to wait on diversion. You train yourself to be displeased with the given and to hold out for whatever has not yet come.

Attention, by nature, is a matter of selective focus. But when you multitask, focus is never won because no selection is ever made. Instead, your mind spends itself in a buzz of anxious reservation. Your days oscillate between stress and boredom, two poles equally far from the poise of mindfulness. By turns lost or fretful, you brownout.

Jesus's canonical take on multitasking looks like this: "No man can serve two masters: for either he will hate the one, and love the other; or else he will hold to the one, and despise the other. Ye cannot serve God and mammon" (Matt. 6:24).

When Jesus says that "no man can serve two masters," I understand him to mean that no one can pay attention to two things at the same time. Serving means paying attention. You serve by *attending*, by giving your full attention to even the least little thing at hand. And, when you attend to the least among these things, it is the same as attending to God himself. "Inasmuch as ye have done it unto the least of these my brethren, ye have done it unto me" (Matt. 25:40).

How freely Jesus allows you to substitute even the least little thing for himself! Jesus doesn't worry about these substitutions. He encourages them. He doesn't worry about you serving mammon because "mammon" just names your avoidance of service. "Serving mammon" is oxymoronic because serving mammon is just a way of serving yourself and serving yourself isn't actually service.

It is impossible, then, to serve both God and mammon *because it is impossible to serve mammon.* Mammon names that bifurcation of attention that follows from your failing to serve and attend. To serve is, by definition, to serve God.

When Jesus says that no one "can serve two masters," which two masters does he have in mind? The particulars of the first may vary—doing it unto the least of these is the same as doing it unto God—but the second always seems to be the same: you. *You* are mammon. You can either serve God by attending to others or in attending to others you can try to serve yourself.

Self-interest is this second master that halves your attention. You double your interest in every least little thing with an interest in yourself. Before it even pops up you've already started to ask: How might this little thing either harm or benefit me? Will I love it or hate it? What does it have to do with me? Often, your double vision is so bad that you can barely even *see* that little thing because you're so intent on seeing yourself. Then, having failed to see the least among these, you inevitably fail to see God. And you're sad.

Trying to serve two masters, attention falters. When attention falters it bifurcates into love and hatred. "No man can serve two masters: for either he will hate the one, and love the other; or else he will hold to the one, and despise the other." Instead of serving things in terms of what they need from you, you end up judging them in terms of your own preferences, in terms of your own likes and dislikes. This bifurcation of attention into modes of preference—that is, into modes of loving or hating—is the root of sin because it turns attention back on itself.

Attention neither loves nor hates. It serves. And, in serving, it even loves what it hates by serving it.

"Okay," you may say, "but reading love and hatred as what *follows* from trying to have two masters rather than as the *cause* for its impossibility is a bit unconventional."

"And while we're at it," you may add, "I highly doubt that Jesus actually had multitasking in mind when he claimed that no man can serve two masters."

To be honest, I don't know what Jesus had in mind. But I do know something about what this saying of his *did to me*. And what it did led me to say what I said.

I take it as axiomatic that Jesus's saying is not a static picture upon which I ought to reflect. It is not (in any straightforward way) a transparent representation or object of contemplation. Rather, my assumption is that the text is itself an agent, an actor, a will—something more like a computer program than a still cut from a movie reel. Jesus's saying is meant to do something, to make something happen, to change something. The text is an operation. It's a bit of open-source code. It's a plug-in that needs to be run.

But, strangers in a strange world, we've got compatibility problems, cross-platform issues that require the text to be translated and then reatively recompiled. If we want it to run—rather than sit there like a museum piece—then we're going to have to port the text onto the kinds of platforms *we've* got available. We're going to have to render the text sufficiently pliable to cross that gap. En route, patches will have to be rigged and foreign material spliced. Ways of hashing the code will inevitably fork, and then, though multiple paths may be workable, we'll have to settle, for the moment, for one.

But once it's up and running the text should work more like an aggressive virus than a frozen PDF and it, in turn, will exapt, reformat, and repurpose *our* operating systems to meet *its* ends. This Jesus-text is an applet for viral inception.

In the end, the measure for success in creatively porting a text from one platform to another is just this: when we finally run the program, does it output charity? Does it repurpose my vanity? Because whatever else the text does, it is nothing without charity. If it doesn't show charity, it is only so much sounding brass and tinkling cymbals (cf. 1 Cor. 13:1–2).

The advantage, then, of how I've thus far ported this text from Matthew is twofold: even if it appears unconventional, even if it is only one possible reading among others, my reading (1) responds directly to the experience induced by the text, and (2) opens the door to reading this saying as deeply intertwined with the details of the verses that follow. Good readings ought to do both. They ought to bluntly connect with our lives and they ought to light up surrounding passages like Christmas trees. As readers, we must faithfully attend to both the least little thing the text does to us and the least little thing it does to the passages around it.

Taking into account the surrounding verses, I think it is crucial to read Matthew 6:24 together with 6:25–34 as one operational unit. I take 6:24 as the unit's thesis and 6:25–34 as an extended explanation of that thesis. The initial explanation of verse 24 is given in 25, and then repeated, by way of conclusion, in 34. The middle section, verses 26–33, elaborates on that explanation.

Here's the full King James Version of Matthew 6:24–34, formatted in such a way as to diagram the structure I've just outlined:

> [24]No man can serve two masters: for either he will hate the one, and love the other; or else he will hold to the one, and despise the other. Ye cannot serve God and mammon.
>
>> [25]Therefore I say unto you, Take no thought for your life, what ye shall eat, or what ye shall drink; nor yet for your body, what ye shall put on. Is not the life more than meat, and the body than raiment?

> [26]Behold the fowls of the air: for they sow not, neither do they reap, nor gather into barns; yet your heavenly Father feedeth them. Are ye not much better than they?
> [27]Which of you by taking thought can add one cubit unto his stature?
> [28]And why take ye thought for raiment? Consider the lilies of the field, how they grow; they toil not, neither do they spin:
> [29]And yet I say unto you, That even Solomon in all his glory was not arrayed like one of these.
> [30]Wherefore, if God so clothe the grass of the field, which to day is, and to morrow is cast into the oven, shall he not much more clothe you, O ye of little faith?
> [31]Therefore take no thought, saying, What shall we eat? or, What shall we drink? or, Wherewithal shall we be clothed?
> [32](For after all these things do the Gentiles seek:) for your heavenly Father knoweth that ye have need of all these things.
> [33]But seek ye first the kingdom of God, and his righteousness; and all these things shall be added unto you.
>
> [34]Take therefore no thought for the morrow: for the morrow shall take thought for the things of itself. Sufficient unto the day is the evil thereof.

Jesus's advice about *how* to pay attention—that is, about how to serve just one master—is repeated five times in these ten verses. He pounds the point home: "take no thought."

This is straightforward advice. To pay attention to the least little thing, you have to stop thinking about other things. When you play with your four-year-old, stop thinking about the book you could be reading. When you go to bed at night, stop thinking about the credit card you have yet to balance. When you're out with your wife, stop thinking about the waitress you aren't impressing. Be where you are, do what you're doing. Stop holding out. Make a choice, commit, and shoulder the attendant responsibility.

Matthew 6:25 captures the gist of Jesus's charge. Advising that we take no thought, Jesus specifies: "Take no thought *for your life*." How would taking no thought for your life help you to serve and pay attention? To begin with, in order to serve and attend to others you will have to stop thinking about *your* life. Drop the possessive. If you're thinking about *your* life when you're supposed to be attending to someone else's life, then your attention will bifurcate into preferential judgments and that familiar, second master (you!) will end up running the show.

For example, you might think: "I really should be paying attention right now to how well I wipe my baby's bottom so that she won't get a rash, but *I hate* this smell so I'm going to think about checking my email instead." Here, attention that should be wholly focused on bum-wiping gets bifurcated by your preference for non-stinky smells and then slips off into daydreams about fantasmatic emails.

This telling is complicated, of course, by the fact that attention is finite while its streaming objects are legion. Again and again, choices must be made and focal points selected. Some things will inevitably be left aside. But if time is fleeting and attention limited, then why attend to the smell of a baby's diaper? Why not slip off into plans or memories? For starters, because the diaper is *real* in a way that your daydream is not. But also because the test for every selection is simply this: *why* select this over that? Or, better: *who* does it serve? If the answer is "you" rather than "them," then see how your dodge preferentially splits rather than supports attention. See how, with a smooth sleight of hand, you've substituted one master for another and, thus, failed to attend.

But, with respect to "taking no thought," Jesus also has something more in mind. Verse 25 goes on to specify what he means by life. Taking thought for your life, Jesus says, amounts to taking thought for what you are going to eat, drink, and wear: "Take no thought for your life, what ye shall eat, or what ye shall drink; nor yet for your body, what ye shall put on." Shouldn't we "take thought" for these things? No. This is a frank imperative. And Jesus is clear about his reason: "Is not the life *more* than meat, and the body than raiment?"

What is this "more"?

Verse 34 recapitulates, by way of conclusion, what Jesus means when he says that you should take no thought for your life: "Take therefore no thought for the morrow: for the morrow shall take thought for the things of itself." Taking no thought for your life means taking no thought for tomorrow.

What, then, is this "more" to which Jesus re-directs our attention? What is more than tomorrow? This more is now.

Life is more than your distracted thoughts about what you'd like to do next. It is more than your thoughts about what you plan to eat, more than your thoughts about what you plan to drink, more than your thoughts about what you plan to wear. It is more than your preferences. It is more than you. Life includes *all* those least little things that metonymize God. More than your thoughts about tomorrow, life is the overflow of this unchosen moment, a moment whose current is too strong to be parlayed and, instead, can only be served.

Why do you prefer the distraction of your thoughts to the flood of the present? Because your thoughts are thin enough to mold and manipulate.

Building sand castles in your head, you play master of the house. But this is one too many masters. "Which of you by taking thought can add one cubit unto his stature?" Sand castles in your head will not make you taller.

Seek first to serve. Seek first to pay attention. Seek first "the kingdom of God, and his righteousness; and all these things shall be added unto you" (Matt. 6:33). If you attend to the least little things, then these least little things will add *themselves* to you. Instead of wrapping yourself in idle conceits, the lilies will clothe you. Instead of clouding your heart with worry, Solomon's sun will shine down on you. Instead of stuffing your belly with cardboard morale, the grasses will feed you.

When Jesus tells you to "take no thought," he's not advising that you re-pot yourself as an absent-minded vegetable. Nothing grows in the soil of apathy. Rather, taken together with Matthew 6:24, this apparently irresponsible advice to "take no thought" is nothing of the kind. Nothing is more demanding than "taking no thought." Nothing is harder than the work of paying attention. Nothing is more essential to service. And nothing is more productive. Forget yourself, go to work, and the kingdom will add *itself* to you. You will not need to take it.

"Take therefore no thought for the morrow: for the morrow shall take thought for the things of itself. Sufficient unto the day is the evil thereof." Paying attention depends on our faith in this sufficiency. It depends on our willingness to trust that what is given will be enough, that if—on God's behalf—you feed the fowls of the air, they will feed you. The grace of each day's "evil," of each day's trouble, of each day's need for our full attention, will be sufficient. You should not ask for, nor will you get, more. Tomorrow will give its own little things. As for today, there are already too many.

The kingdom of God is distressingly near. If you find yourself far from the Master's face, it is not because he has hidden it from you. It is because you, in a fever of existential multitasking, are addled and distracted.

Lay down your distraction. Rather than taking thought, give it.

No man can have two masters.

God does not come and go, your attention does.

Addendum

What are we doing when we read scripture? In particular, what are we as Mormon scholars doing when, in the context of a prophetic and authoritative tradition, we dare to read and interpret scripture? My thesis is that we are helping to build a world just as literally as if we had brick and mortar in hand.

I take it for granted that reading is itself material and that reading unfolds as a kind of "material semiotics." But my approach to this semiotic materialism gives it a twist. The twist is that I understand the relationship between the "material" and the "semiotic" as something that works in *both* directions at the same time. Signs must be understood as material but matter must also be understood as semiotic. This reciprocity is crucial to my understanding of what we're doing when we read and interpret scripture.

In contemporary theory it is common practice to point out that signs are themselves material and, thus, have a kind of life and independence of their own. Signs never quite do what we want them to do, never quite say what we want them to say, never quite go where we want them to go. There is always some gap between what we thought we meant to say, what the sign does, and what the other person receives. There is always a bit of "creative" translation involved as these gaps are negotiated. Meaning is the concrete result of this ad hoc material process of semiotic compromise and negotiation.

But the materiality of signs is only half of what I mean by "material semiotics" and, I think, the more familiar half. It is true that signs must be qualified by matter—we must recognize their material autonomy and, hence, their capacity for errancy—but, I'm claiming, it is perhaps even *more* important to recognize the semiological character of matter itself. If we recognize the material character of signs but not the semiological character of matter, then we'll remain stuck within a representational notion of signs. That is to say, we'll end up thinking that the gap between me, the sign, and the recipient is an *epistemological* gap. This, in my view, is not the way to go.

If the gap is fundamentally epistemological, if it is a mark of *our* inability to ever really know or articulate the solid and unified reality of the world as it actually is, then every negotiation and compromise necessitated by the stubborn, material character of the sign will indicate a failure on our part. If the job of our compromised words and signs is to represent the uncompromising reality of the world, then they will always fail. This is the postmodern pickle: postmodernity is an aborted semiological materialism that takes the relationship between "meaningful" signs and "brute" matter to be unidirectional.

But what if we extend the point and claim not only that signs are material but that matter is itself semiotic? In this case, when we think and speak and use signs, we are no longer engaged in a practice foreign to the materials of which we speak. If matter is semiotic, then signs are not a way of "overlaying" material reality with a representational system that will, fingers crossed, more or less fit the way things actually are. Rather, linguistic signs would be just another variation on the way that *all* material things interact with and relate to one another. Making the relationship between matter and signs reciprocal amounts to saying that any entity relating to any other entity in any conceivable way is doing something essentially semiotic: it is crossing a gap and creating a relationship through a process of compromise, translation, and negotiation that links the parties in question even as it fails to exhaustively unify them.

Here, the gap between a sign and a thing is not a representational or epistemological gap. Rather, the gap between signs and things is ontological in character. The gaps between *signs* and things are continuous in character with the ontological gaps between *things* and things. Signs are just another kind of material thing.

It follows that this brand of material semiotics breaks with a classical understanding of the "material" world on a key point. Where a classical materiality assumes the automatic, underlying, and substantial compatibility of all material things, this approach assumes that material objects themselves (not just our representations of them) are fundamentally multiple, fragmentary, and heterogeneous. Nature is no longer taken as an already unified field that our linguistic representations can only weakly, fragmentarily, and unsuccessfully hope to mimic. On the contrary, it is taken for granted that material objects can be brought into relationship with other material objects only through a process of ontological translation, compromise, and negotiation that mirrors the work done by signs. When carpenters build houses, when trees make sap, when bacteria reproduce, they must each engage in the *same* difficult work of compromise and negotiation as do signs. On my account, reading scripture is not qualitatively different from photosynthesis.

The upshot of this position is that if matter is itself semiotic, then when we negotiate and translate by way of signs *we are not betraying reality but engaging in the very same work that makes anything that is real be real.* Here, hermeneutic compromise does not indicate that we've failed to successfully represent the real world, it indicates that we're hip deep in just one more way of more or less successfully engaging it. Because reality itself is a broken and fragmentary network of heterogeneous matter, the incomplete and fragmentary character of signs positively confirms rather than negatively denies the legitimacy of the interpretive endeavor.

With respect to the work of reading scripture, the consequences of this position have heft. First, it entails that all interpretive work be understood as inherently creative and productive. There are no clean conversions or transparent revelations. Signs don't just innocently represent something that is already there because nothing is innocently already there. When a leaf translates light, this modifies both the leaf and the light. In bridging gaps and gathering objects, translations and interpretations inevitably make something new—and, crucially, this making something new must now be understood as a way of being *faithful* to the heterogeneous nature of reality. The translation doesn't ineffectively copy a preexisting unity, it creates a partial unity where none existed before.

Second, interpretive work should be understood as real ontological work, not just as representational, epistemological work. The work of reading scripture is as actively constructive as the work of building a house or running telephone wire. It gathers, collects, collates, aligns, and translates. It negotiates differences, creates alliances, defines oppositions, sets up tensions, lays out networks, and requires perpetual upkeep, just like any other building project.

Third, the measure of an interpretation's success is no longer its representational "correspondence" with an already smoothly connected reality, but its ability to *create* stable and durable (though not perfect or effortlessly permanent) connections between heterogeneous and naturally fragmentary groups of stuff. The larger the scale of the assemblage and the more durable and self-reinforcing its connections, the more successful, real, and truthful the interpretation is.

A key caveat to this third point is that the success of an interpretation is not just dependent on the number of humans that it is able to effectively convince and corral but also on the number of *nonhumans* that it is able to effectively gather and persuade. Because material relations are themselves semiological, as many as possible of the pertinent nonhumans must also be persuaded by the reading. For instance, someone may offer a brilliant, popularly supported reading of Genesis that requires the Earth to be just six thousand years old, but if 4.5 billion years worth of rocks and weather disagree, then that reading is seriously hamstrung. The opinion of a fossil matters. A reading is only as good as the number of Gods, angels, people, flowers, *and* riverbeds that it is able to persuade. The quantity and diversity of the persuaded population determine the quality of a reading.

In summary, I like this approach because: (1) it removes from the interpretive endeavor the stain of any *original* sin of representational betrayal or prophetic overstepping, (2) it takes interpretive work seriously as real ontological work, (3) it takes seriously and *positively* the need for ongoing interpretive network building, (4) it doesn't arbitrarily insulate our interpretive work from the real world but, instead, construes it as just another variation of the only kind of work there is, (5) it offers a clear (though laborious) standard for evaluating the quality of an interpretation, and (6) it allows us to view this ongoing, interpretive work of persuading, building, and gathering larger and larger networks of human *and* nonhuman things—whether with books, shovels, or copper wire—as potentially part of God's own divine work of persuading, building, and gathering both people and worlds.

FOUR

Jesus on Jesus: John 5 and 7

Eric D. Huntsman

Among the distinguishing features of the first half of the Gospel of John, the so-called "Book of Signs" (John 1:19–12:50), are seven discourses that Jesus delivers, either as dialogues with individuals or as public speeches to groups. They are, in order: The New Birth (3:1–36), The Water of Life (4:1–42), The Divine Son (5:17–47), The Bread of Life (6:35–58), The Life-Giving Spirit (7:16–52), The Light of the World (8:12–59), and The Good Shepherd (10:1–18). Like the seven signs (*sēmeia*), selected miracles that John uses to illustrate not just what Jesus can do but who, in fact, he is, the seven discourses reflect the extraordinarily high christology of John. The Johannine discourses are significant for discussions of christology because they are placed in the mouth of Jesus himself. Unlike in the Synoptic Gospels (of Matthew, Mark, and Luke), where Jesus is rarely forthright about his identity during much of his ministry, leading to the so-called "Messianic secret" in the Gospel of Mark, in John—as in the Doctrine and Covenants and select passages of the Book of Mormon—Jesus himself discusses his identity, his relationship to the Father, and his mission.

Reading the New Testament as a Latter-day Saint

Considering "Jesus on Jesus" of course raises any number of questions regarding sources, composition, and redaction, and it also leads us to think about how we understand and apply the principles of this text in our own time and faith community. As such, it causes us to differentiate between strict exegesis (that is, trying to understand the original meaning of the text) and exposition (or how we understand and apply the text to ourselves).[1] Examining the Gospel of John as a text, as a literary artifact,

1. Exegesis consists of a close reading of a scriptural text that seeks to "lead out" its original meaning by understanding its historical, literary, and theological

as well as a document of faith forces us to ask how accurately the received text that we have represents word for word what Jesus said. A comparison to the well-known programmatic statement of Thucydides regarding his composition of speeches may be telling. In it the Greek historian acknowledged that he was writing speeches for his characters that were what was appropriate for the situation while keeping as close as possible to what was actually said.[2]

To be sure, Latter-day Saints, institutionally and certainly as a body, tend to be rather conservative in their reception of biblical texts, the "as far as it is translated correctly" clause of the eighth article of faith notwithstanding. In particular, the writings of John—at least the Book of Revelation and to a lesser extent the gospel—seem to enjoy the support of passages from the Book of Mormon, the Doctrine and Covenants, and the *Teachings of the Prophet Joseph Smith*.[3] Further, from a personal, subjective perspective, the Spirit of God regularly bears witness to me of the truth, power, and beauty of the Johannine literature.

Still, the compositional and editorial history of the Book of Mormon—which attests to sources, original documents, redaction, editing, transmission, and translation—has surprising parallels to some of the very theories of Johannine composition that some Latter-day Saints might otherwise view as liberal or revisionist. But that very Book of Mormon model attests to me of God's care for the preservation and transmission of scripture: prophetic editing and translation in the case of the Book of Mormon and the superintending role of the Holy Spirit through the ages in the case of the Bible. With this in mind, I see room on the one hand for the creative role of the Beloved Disciple as either source or evangelist, as well as for the possibility of subsequent editing and even later tampering and some loss on the other (see D&C 93:18; 1 Ne. 13:28, 14:23).

Accordingly, my approach to "reading" the New Testament, and these specific Johannine Discourses by and about Jesus in particular, tends to be eclectic. Because I treat the text as a literary artifact, my method is,

---

context. For a basic review of the exegetical method and how Latter-day Saints may consider using it, see Huntsman, "Teaching through Exegesis: Helping Students Ask Questions of the Text," *Religious Educator* 6, no. 1 (Winter 2005): 107–26.

2. Thucydides, *History of the Peloponnesian War*, trans. Martin Hammond (New York: Oxford University Press, 2009), 1.22.

3. Consider 1 Nephi 14:18–27, Ether 4:16, D&C 7, D&C 77:1–15, and D&C 88:141; as well as Joseph Fielding Smith Jr., comp. and ed., *Teachings of the Prophet Joseph Smith* (Salt Lake City: Deseret Book, 1977), 247, 287–94.

at first, a blend of textual analysis (e.g., the literary structure of John), historical background (e.g., discussion of Jewish feasts), and contemporary, non-Mormon New Testament scholarship. But because I accept each text as scripture and have a personal conviction of its role as one facet of a diamond reflecting truth, I also mine it for "transhistorical" doctrine. Then, following its exegesis, my subsequent exposition finds it useful to see how the teaching of Joseph Smith and restoration doctrine might nuance or influence my interpretation of the New Testament. Thus my approach takes an academic understanding of biblical (i.e., not specifically Mormon) scriptural texts and then considers these texts to bear on Restoration texts and doctrines. This apparent privileging of the biblical texts is partly the result of temperament and partly an effort at "leveling the playing field," since just the opposite is, I think, the norm in our community. But ultimately my intent is not to privilege one body of scriptural thought over the other or to use one to proof-text the other. Rather it is to find *parallels* in the thought of, say, the Gospel of John and the teachings of Joseph Smith that reinforce each other. In other words, one should do exegesis first, exposition second.

Johannine Christology and Restoration Thought

Established from the onset in the prologue or "Logos" Hymn (John 1:1–18), Johannine christology maintains that the man Jesus was in fact the divine Christ from the beginning.[4] The high christology of John has much in common with Book of Mormon christology, where the title page identifies Jesus as "the Christ, the Eternal God" and the Lord describes himself as "the God of Israel, and the God of the whole earth" (3 Ne. 11:14).[5] Throughout the first half of the Book of Mormon, the promised Jesus is as often as not identified simply as God. For instance, the angel through King Benjamin prophesies that "the Lord Omnipotent, who reigneth, who was, and is from all eternity to all eternity, shall come down from heaven among the children of men, and shall dwell in a tabernacle

4. Raymond E. Brown, *An Introduction to New Testament Christology* (New York: Paulist Press, 1994), 103–41; Eric D. Huntsman, "'And the Word Was Made Flesh': Latter-day Saint Exegesis of the Blood and Water in the Gospel of John," *Studies in the Bible and Antiquity* 1 (2009): 52–53.

5. See Krister Stendahl, "The Sermon on the Mount and Third Nephi," in *Reflections on Mormonism: Judaeo-Christian Parallels*, ed. Truman G. Madsen (Provo, Utah: BYU Religious Studies Center, 1978), 139–54.

of clay" (Mosiah 3:5). In addition to this similarity in christology, Blake Ostler has suggested that the revelations in the Doctrine and Covenants reflect "a major shift from Pauline to Johannine categories of thought."[6] Consequently, it is not surprising that Joseph Smith found so many theological points of contact in the Gospel of John.

All the Johannine Discourses—not just those in the Book of Signs but also, and especially, the Farewell Discourses (John 13–17) of the Book of Glory—provide rich material and provocative launching points for discussions of Restoration theology. Two have particular resonance with Mormon thought: The Divine Son (5:17–47) and a single section from The Life-Giving Spirit (7:16–52). Although Jesus acknowledges his identity not just as "the Messiah, which is, being interpreted, the Christ" but also as "the Son of God" as early as his interchange with Nathanael in John 1:47–51, and while he certainly alludes to his divinity and salvific role in his dialogues with Nicodemus (3:1–36) and the Samaritan Woman (4:1–42), the Discourse on the Divine Son is his first, unmistakable public assertion of his divinity and status as God's Son.

John 5: Jesus as the Divine Son

Raymond Brown characterized much of the Book of Signs as "Jewish Feasts and Their Replacement by Christ."[7] The text only establishes the setting of chapter 5 as "a feast of the Jews" (John 5:1). Because many Byzantine manuscripts read "*the* feast," commentators used to assume that the feast in question was the Passover, although this is by no means clear. Another possibility is "the feast of the Trumpets," or Rosh Hashanah, which is attractive because of allusions to the creation of the world: Rosh Hashanah is often associated with "the birthday of the world" and thus commemorative of creation.[8] This is first evident in the sign, or miracle, of the Healing of the Lame Man at Bethesda (vv. 2–16). Here the multitude of invalids waiting for "the moving of the water" at the pool, the name of which may mean "House of Mercy or Grace," resonates with the spirit

6. Blake T. Ostler, "The Development of the Mormon Concept of Grace," *Dialogue: A Journal of Mormon Thought* 24, no. 1 (Spring 1991): 57.

7. Raymond E. Brown, *The Gospel according to John* (New York: Doubleday, 1966), 201–4.

8. In the end, however, it is not possible to identify the feast with any certainty. Leon Morris, *The Gospel according to John* (Grand Rapids, Mich.: Eerdmans, 1995), 265.

of God moving over the primordial waters at the outset of creation in Genesis 1:2. Then, in the discourse itself, Jesus's references to "his father working," alludes to the six days of creation, after which God ended his work (Gen. 2:2).

The idea is that just as God created in the first instance, Jesus now re-creates—or heals, on this occasion. The fact that the healing of the lame man occurs on Shabbat fits the standard motif known from the Synoptics of Jesus's compassion causing him to ignore then-contemporary Sabbath restrictions, but John 5 implicitly connects the incident with God completing his creative work in Genesis. As a result, Jesus's pronouncement at the beginning of his discourse that "My Father worketh hitherto, and I work" (John 5:17) associates him with his Father's divine creative efforts. But as we shall see, while the Father's initial creation was finished (*shabbat* meaning "to make complete, to finish, to stop"), Jesus's creative (or perhaps re-creative) efforts continue.

The response of "the Jews" (evidently John's standard way of referring to Jesus's opponents among the aristocratic, ruling class) to Jesus's proclamation that he, like the Father, "works," was to seek all the more to kill him "because he not only had broken the sabbath, but said also that God was his Father, making himself equal with God" (John 5:18). Jesus's next statement is pivotal, not only for Johannine christology, but also for Restoration theology: "The Son can do nothing of himself, but what he seeth the Father do: for what things soever he doeth, these also doeth the Son likewise" (v. 19). Although Joseph Smith does not seem to have publicly taught or commented on this passage until the Nauvoo period, when he did it was part of a stunning Restoration declaration during the King Follett Discourse of April 7, 1844:

> I wish I was in a suitable place to tell it, and that I had the trump of an archangel, so that I could tell the story in such a manner that persecution would cease forever. What did Jesus say? (Mark it, Elder Rigdon!) The Scriptures inform us that Jesus said, As the Father hath power in Himself, even so hath the Son power—to do what? Why, what the Father did. The answer is obvious—in a manner to lay down His body and take it up again. Jesus, what are you going to do? To lay down my life as my Father did, and take it up again. Do we believe it? If you do not believe it, you do not believe the Bible. The Scriptures say it, and I defy all the learning and wisdom and all the combined powers of earth and hell together to refute it.[9]

---

9. Joseph Fielding Smith, comp., *Teachings of the Prophet Joseph Smith* (Salt Lake City: Deseret Book, 1977), 346.

Joseph Smith's teaching here seems to have not only John 5:19 behind it but also John 10:17–18: "Therefore doth my Father love me, because I lay down my life, that might take it again. No man taketh it from me, but I lay it down of myself. I have power to lay it down, and I have the power to take it again." This last passage actually reflects a unique Johannine doctrinal insight. In the other Gospels, in the speeches of Peter and Paul in Acts, and also in the epistles, the Jews and Romans *take* the life of Jesus and then God raises him from the dead. But the Johannine Jesus, uniquely divine, cannot be killed: he must lay down his own life. Likewise, he has life in himself to take it up again.

That in laying down his life Jesus may have in fact been imitating his Father presents an intriguing doctrinal possibility, but we are not concerned here with what this statement might suggest about the Father; instead we are concerned with the segue it provides for this discourse's discussion of the role of the Son. The fact that John 5:19 can be understood with later reference to John 10:18 explains why the next part of chapter 5 turns to a discussion of resurrection: "For as the Father raiseth up the dead, and quickeneth them: even so the Son quickeneth whom he will" (v. 21). Jesus's role in raising the dead is connected with the judgment that the Father commits to him (vv. 22–27), laying the groundwork for another doctrinal concept that the Lord unfolded to Joseph Smith as early as 1832.

After teaching that he would quicken those whom he would and that all judgment was committed to him, Jesus proclaimed: "Marvel not at this: for the hour is coming, in the which all that are in the graves shall hear his voice, and shall come forth; they that have done good, unto the resurrection of life; and they that have done evil, unto the resurrection of damnation" (John 5:28–29). The fact that Jesus had earlier said that he "quickeneth whom he will" ("quick" being an older English word for "alive" and an antonym for "dead") may have contributed to the notion of some Christians that only the saved or righteous would be resurrected. Yet verse 29 makes it clear that all are resurrected, the righteous "unto life" and the evil "unto damnation." This passage, of course, proved to be the catalyst for the great revelation that we now know as Doctrine and Covenants 76. When Joseph and Sidney Rigdon came upon these verses in the course of their "new translation," the ideas in them led to an open vision in which the different degrees of post-resurrection glory were described.[10]

---

10. Joseph Smith, *History of the Church of Jesus Christ of Latter-day Saints*, ed. B. H. Roberts, 7 vols. 2nd ed., rev. ed. (Salt Lake City: Deseret Book, 1948), 1:245–52.

The way to understand Jesus's earlier statement in John 5:21 about quickening only those whom he would, as opposed to the accepted truth of a universal resurrection, may be to recall the prevalence of realized eschatology in the Gospel of John. In this very discourse, for instance, Jesus taught: "he that heareth my word, and believeth on him that sent me, hath [present tense] everlasting life, and shall not come unto condemnation; but is passed [perfect with present meaning] from death unto life" (v. 24). Here, life and death seem not to refer to just physical, that is, biological, life, but to spiritual life, which believers can attain to even in this life. Yet the fact that "the hour is coming" when the physically dead shall come forth "alive" makes it clear that John also contains future eschatology. With the judgment, however, both senses of "life" seem to obtain: all, good and evil, are resurrected with spiritual bodies, but only the righteous will continue to enjoy true spiritual life (which D&C 76:50–70 equates with exaltation in the celestial kingdom). This feeds again into Joseph's observation in the King Follett Discourse:

> Here, then, is eternal life—to know the only wise and true God; and you have got to learn how to be gods yourselves, and to be kings and priests to God, the same as all gods have done before you, namely, by going from one small degree to another, and from a small capacity to a great one; from grace to grace, from exaltation to exaltation, until you attain to the resurrection of the dead, and are able to dwell in everlasting burnings, and to sit in glory, as do those who sit enthroned in everlasting power. And I want you to know that God, in the last days, while certain individuals are proclaiming his name, is not trifling with you or me.[11]

John 7: Jesus and Rivers of Living Waters

In the centuries before Jesus's birth, Sukkot, or the Festival of Tabernacles, had taken on a number of ritual additions, including the drawing of water from the Gihon spring, which was poured on the altar as part of the autumnal prayers for rain, and the lighting of great lamps in the temple courtyards. Both of these practices gave occasions for symbolic statements by Jesus, namely that he was the source of living waters or life-giving spirit in John 7:37b–39 and the light of the world in John 8:12.[12] In the first of these, Jesus echoed his earlier words to the Samaritan woman at the well, saying, "If any man thirst, let him come unto me, and

---

11. Smith, *Teachings of the Prophet Joseph Smith*, 346.
12. Brown, *The Gospel according to John*, 326–29.

drink. He that believeth on me, as the scripture hath said, out of his belly shall flow rivers of living water" (John 7:37b–38).

This passage has notable difficulties. The first involves punctuation and affects the antecedent of the genitive of possession in "out of his belly (*koilia*)," which some translations render as "heart." What is uncertain here is whether the Greek should be read to mean "Let anyone who believes in me come and drink! As scripture says, 'From *his* [i.e., Jesus's] heart shall flow streams of living water'" (as in the New Jerusalem Bible), or "and let the one who believes in me drink. As the scripture has said, 'Out of *the believer's heart* shall flow rivers of living water'" (as in the New Revised Standard Version).[13] The problem is that no extant Old Testament text describes streams of water flowing from anyone's heart, either from the Lord's or a believer's. However, if "the scripture" that Jesus alludes to is taken not as a direct citation but rather as a broad reference to the Mosaic story of water flowing from the rock (see Ex. 17:6; Num. 20:11; Deut. 8:15; Ps. 105:41), then the first rendering, which holds that living water will flow from Jesus's heart, is more likely. This is because Paul took the rock as a type of Christ (see 1 Cor. 10:4), thus making Jesus the source of the streams of living waters. This passage then parallels the earlier pericope of the woman at the well, where the water Jesus gives becomes "a well of water, springing up into everlasting life" (John 4:14).[14]

Another difficulty arises in the next verse, which connects this living water closely with the spirit: "But this spake he of the Spirit, which they that believe on him should receive: for the Holy Ghost was not yet *given* because that Jesus was not yet glorified" (John 7:39).[15] The meaning of this verse has caused considerable discussion, both within and without LDS circles, although in this instance the King James rendering may have complicated the question unnecessarily. The Greek text *oupō gar ēn pneuma*, literally rendered, simply states, "there was not yet spirit," without specifying that it was the Holy Ghost that was absent or that it was somehow not yet "given."[16]

---

13. Ibid., 374–78; Francis J. Moloney, *The Gospel of John* (Collegeville, Minn.: Liturgical Press, 1998), 256; Morris, *The Gospel according to John*, 374–78; Huntsman, "'And the Word Was Made Flesh,'" 61.

14. Brown, *The Gospel according to John*, 321–23.

15. Craig R. Koester, *Symbolism in the Fourth Gospel*, 2nd ed. (Minneapolis: Fortress Press, 2003), 201.

16. Huntsman, "'And the Word Was Made Flesh,'" 62.

In LDS theology, resurrected, glorified beings are not only tangible bodies of flesh and bone, they are also in a sense "spiritual" bodies because they are animated, sustained, and quickened by spirit rather than blood, the symbol of mortality. According to former LDS Church president Joseph F. Smith,

> After the resurrection from the dead our bodies will be spiritual bodies, but they will be bodies that are tangible, bodies that have been purified, but they will nevertheless be bodies of flesh and bones . . . they will not be blood bodies, they will no longer be quickened by blood but quickened by the spirit which is eternal and they shall become immortal and shall never die.[17]

In this sense, prior to the death of Jesus's mortal body and his subsequent resurrection, there was not yet any animating, life-giving, or even resurrecting spirit for those to whom he would give eternal life.

A final, possible aspect of Jesus's role in "giving life" might be discerned in the image of living water flowing *ek tēs koilias*, or "from his belly." While *koilia* generally refers to organs of nourishment, particularly the stomach, commentators have usually taken it in its metaphorical sense as the seat of emotions, feelings, and desires that were anciently placed in the viscera or bowels but for which modern English generally prefers "heart."[18] Nevertheless, there is another possibility, since *koilia* can refer to the womb or uterus,[19] as is the case in Luke 1:41, 44; 2:21; 11:27; 23:29; and especially in John 3:4. In these instances, of course, it is applied to a woman, but we may be able to say that as a woman gives birth to a child, so Jesus gives new birth to the believer.[20] Indeed, the sense that not only Jesus can pass on this eternal life but so can those who receive it in its fullness from him, which is suggested by the alternate punctuation and reading of John 7:38, is supported by Restoration scripture—particularly Doctrine and Covenants 132:19, 24, which speaks of "a continuation of the seeds forever and ever" and "eternal lives" (plural) in those who become candidates for exaltation.[21]

17. Joseph F. Smith, *Report of the Semi-Annual Conference of the Church of Jesus Christ of Latter-day Saints*, April 8, 1917 (Salt Lake City: Church of Jesus Christ of Latter-day Saints, semi-annual), 63.

18. Brown, *The Gospel according to John*, 323; Moloney, *The Gospel of John*, 257.

19. W. F. Arndt, et al, *A Greek-English Lexicon of the New Testament and Other Early Christian Literature*, 3rd ed. (Chicago: University of Chicago Press, 2000), 550–51.

20. Matthew G. Ancell, "Blood and Water: Unity in the Gospel of John" (master's thesis, Brigham Young University, 1998), 20.

21. Huntsman, "'And the Word Was Made Flesh,'" 62–63.

Blood and Water

The streams of living water flowing from Christ's belly in John 7 have an important echo in the blood and water flowing from Christ's side at the end of the crucifixion scene in John 19. While we have seen here that flowing water represents both the divine, life-giving spirit that flows from Christ, elsewhere I have written about the symbolism of blood and water that I discern throughout the Gospel of John—namely that water represents the divine spirit while blood represents mortal life.[22] While there is no discourse of Jesus in John 19—that is, there is no "Jesus on Jesus" where he tells us about who he is and what he does—the symbolism of blood and water comes to fruition at the end of the crucifixion scene: "But one of the soldiers with a spear pierced his side, and *forthwith came there out blood and water*. And he that saw it bare record, and his record is true: and he knoweth that he saith true, that ye might believe" (vv. 34–35; emphasis mine). The importance of this symbol is patent, as seen by John's eagerness to bear witness of it and stress that he is sharing this sign so that the reader might believe.[23]

While scholarly exegesis has at times associated the water and blood here with "the water of baptism" (John 3:5) and "the blood of the Eucharist" (6:53, 54, 55–56),[24] there has been a recognition that the symbols are best viewed in accordance with John's use of the terms elsewhere, notably with talk of the believer "not being born of blood" (1:13), of those who are born "of water and the spirit" (3:5), of "living water" as the gift of Christ (4:10–14), and of living waters as the spirit flowing from believers or from Christ (7:38–39).[25] If blood indeed does represent the source of mortal life (see Gen. 9:4), and if water symbolizes the life-giving spirit that is the source of eternal life,[26] then this sign in fact reflects the dual nature

22. Ibid., 56–59.

23. Moloney, *The Gospel of John*, 505.

24. Ibid., 506.

25. Morris, *The Gospel according to John*, 724–25.

26. To be sure, ancient physiology posited that in addition to blood, the body contained other important fluids or "humors," including a clear liquid called *ichōr*. A divine form of this fluid, however, was also believed to be the special substance of the gods, which flowed in their veins *instead* of blood (see Homer, *Iliad*, trans. Anthony Verity [New York: Oxford University Press, 2011], 5.340; Plutarch, *Moralia*, trans. Frank Cole Babbitt et al. [Cambridge: Harvard University Press, 1927–1969], 180E, 341B; and the brief discussion in Koester, *Symbolism in the Fourth Gospel*, 203). Given that resurrected bodies are bodies of flesh and bone

of the Incarnate Word as both the mortal son of Mary (blood) and the Divine Son of God (water).

However, the blood and water may have represented not just *who* Jesus was but *what* he did: as the sacrificial Lamb of God, his atoning blood flowed on the wood of the cross to save his people even as the blood of the paschal lambs stained the wooden doorframes of the Israelites to deliver them from death on the first Passover. Nevertheless the water from Jesus's side suggests that the cross, a dead tree and symbol of cursing, also became a type of the Tree of Life and a source of blessings. Thus, just as Old Testament visions featured rivers of healing, life-imbibing water issuing from millennial Jerusalem and its temple, which was the place of sacrifice (Ezek. 47:1–12; Zech. 14:8), so now living waters flow from Jesus on the cross.[27]

But the flowing of water and blood from Jesus's "side" (*pleura*) in John 19:34–35 may have further significance that parallels the rivers of water flowing from the *koilia* in John 7:38. Originally, *pleura*, usually in the plural, referred to "ribs,"[28] and here John may be recalling the singular use of *pleura* in the Greek text of Genesis 2:22, where it referred to God forming Eve out of one of Adam's ribs, the idea being that somehow woman was born from man.[29] The idea that the atoning death of Jesus somehow "gave birth" to the eternal life of those who believe in him is supported by the presence of blood and water, which are elements that accompany the physical birth of a child.[30] These, together with spirit, are mentioned together in restoration scripture in Moses 6:59–60, where they are the means by which believers "are sanctified from sin, and enjoy the words of eternal life in this world, and eternal life in the world to come, even immortal glory." Thus, Jesus's unique status as the Divine Word made Flesh enabled him to "give birth" to his own, providing them life both on earth and in the next.

The idea of the fatherhood of Christ is particularly supported by another passage of LDS scripture, Mosiah 5:7: "ye shall be called the children of Christ, his sons, and his daughters; for behold, *this day he hath spiritu-*

---

and not flesh *and blood*, if symbolically water = spirit, the flowing water could, in fact, represent the quickening spirit that animates immortal beings.

27. Huntsman, "'And the Word Was Made Flesh,'" 63–64.

28. H. G. Liddell and R. Scott, *Greek-English Lexicon* (Oxford: Clarendon Press, 1996), 1416–17.

29. Brown, *The Gospel according to John*, 935.

30. Ancell, "Blood and Water," 17.

ally begotten you; for ye say that your hearts are changed through faith on his name; therefore, *ye are born of him and have become his sons and his daughters*" (emphases mine). This understanding gives Jesus's promise in John 14:18 new meaning: "I will not leave you comfortless [*orphanous*, literally 'orphans']: I will come to you," suggesting that he will become a father to us. According to LDS theology, God is the spiritual father of all men and women, just as our earthly parents gave us biological life. Through his infinite and eternal Atonement, Jesus becomes yet another father for his saints, giving them eternal life. The image of water—or spiritual, eternal life—streaming from his belly or pouring from his side graphically illustrates this point with symbolism that is consistent with the use of blood and water throughout the Gospel.[31] Thus, this final sign eloquently illustrates what Jesus himself has said about Jesus.

31. Huntsman, "'And the Word Was Made Flesh,'" 64–65.

FIVE

I, Nephi

Claudia L. Bushman

I wonder if Nephi had the power to return to life to influence human affairs. If so, I wonder if he was responsible for the disappearance of the ill-fated 116 original first pages of the manuscript that became the Book of Mormon. Those pages would have contained his account of his father Lehi's life in the wicked city of Jerusalem, his prayers and sacrifices for repentance and aid, the Lord's answers to his personal pleas, his withdrawal into the wilderness, the beginning of a new life in the Promised Land, and the friction that developed between his descendants. The Book of Mormon should have begun that way, with Lehi's instructions from the Lord and his plans and attempts to carry them out. This would have been a soft narration, full of belief and pleading for mercy for the people.

But we don't get that. The potent Nephi, perhaps returning from the beyond, has snatched that story and replaced it with another of his own stories, a much darker account, written thirty to forty years later, kept on a second set of plates by the Lord's command, as directed in 2 Nephi 5:18–34. In this second account, I suggest, Nephi negotiates back and forth between the account he wrote when he was young, the one of the lost 116 pages, and the account he wrote of the same period thirty to forty years later. In the later account, he recalls the action of the first account, but his narrative reflects the passage of time, the developments that have occurred in the meantime. Lehi's goodness and his effectiveness as a prophet are downplayed. The older brothers, though grudgingly obedient, are portrayed negatively, foretelling the complete break that came later. And the Promised Land has already lost its luster.

The older Nephi recalls his fearless youth. He tells how as a young man, by swearing allegiance to the Lord and to his father, he swept aside his older brothers, and how, uniting physical strength, daring, and acuity, he audaciously carried out an impossible assignment: procuring the precious family records to justify the escape of a single, small family branch. These records were a symbol of authority as palpable as a scepter. With the records, Lehi's small family, the chosen remnant of Joseph, had the learning and the law of the past. The pen was indeed mightier than the sword here, as Nephi, the pen's possessor, inscribed himself as his people's leader. But Nephi also laid claim to the sword, stolen along with the plates, which he carried along and preserved. He valued this sword for its materials and fine workmanship more than for its power to kill. But the point is that in utilizing the double roles of keeper (and provider) of the record along with the ability to subdue his enemies violently, he took on two of his society's power roles.

The Book of Mormon opens with this strong, action-filled, conflict-ridden story. Nephi, a powerful narrator, who lives in the mythic world of obedience to divine command, immediately takes control and speaks with the authority of his visionary father and of the Lord. He brooks no objections. His brothers, who live in the reasonable, observable world, are wrong. Although scorned by his elder brothers, he surpasses them. The Lord has endowed him with authority and with intellectual and physical power. He is the great man. How do we know? He tells us so.

He greets us imperiously as "I, Nephi," not identifying himself, for all the fuss about his father's record, as the son of Lehi (1 Ne. 1:1). The goodly parents are gone now. He does not identify himself by them. He is talking about himself. He recalls himself as a boy, but chronologically, at the time of writing the record, he is a mature man. This is his second time through this material.

The literary quality of the first chapters of First Nephi is very high. Whatever may have been in the lost 116 pages of Joseph Smith's translation, pages somehow lost by Smith and his friends, could scarcely be of more interest to the reader than the section which now begins the book. Nephi, with much to prove in these first six chapters, convinces us that he speaks for deity through his father's influence, that he justifies violence and crime in the name of the Lord, that a familial and spiritual record—even one with unknown content—is essential, that people who oppose him by choosing the wrong side will suffer, and that if they do not shape up they will perish. He assumes authority. He lays down the law. In this second version of the generational conflict, the characters are polarized from the beginning; Nephi is older and speaks even more severely than he must have done in the earlier account.

As must be clear to all readers by this time, I am speaking about this beginning section of the Book of Mormon in a cool, non-worshipful way. I am reading this account as literature, not as scripture. I am accepting the complicated history as it is available to us, assuming that this text comes to us as its creators, Nephi, Joseph Smith, and the Lord, want us to have it. (There are, moreover, few substantive differences between the earliest text of the Book of Mormon and the text as it now stands.)[1] So, accepting the words and the history, I am giving this scripture the kind of close reading I would to any other text, one in literature or history for instance. I am looking for tone, themes, internal tensions, style, character, and personality.

I am trying to stay within the text as I apply "the willing suspension of disbelief" that Samuel Taylor Coleridge defined to justify a reader's acceptance of fantastic, hard-to-believe stories with non-realistic literary elements. Although there is much room to doubt Nephi's story, his approach to us is straightforward and believable. We can take him seriously, even if we do not always approve of his behavior. I do not question Nephi's story as generally true and factual, but I do suggest that he, like every other writer, has manipulated the record. Even after accepting the truthfulness of his version of the record I see that there is much more to say about it. What I am writing here is revisionist history. I am writing against the grain of the usually accepted meaning of this text.

I long for those first 116 pages, and I want to read them against our First Nephi, to compare the youthful and probably ambitious and optimistic Nephi to the wounded and resentful man who writes two generations later. What did he repeat in his second version of the story? What did he leave out? What did he reemphasize? I'd like to line up the two accounts, to trace the decline of the "Promised Land" to the poor inheritance described in Jacob's eloquent vision of a hostile world: "Our lives passed away like as it were unto us a dream, we being a lonesome and a solemn people, wanderers, cast out from Jerusalem, born in tribulation, in a wilderness, and hated of our brethren, which caused wars and contentions; wherefore, we did mourn out our days" (Jacob 7:26).[2]

---

1. See Royal Skousen, ed., *The Book of Mormon: The Earliest Text* (New Haven: Yale University Press, 2009).

2. According to Nibley, "there is only one direction from which any ancient writing may be profitably approached. It must be considered in its original ancient setting and in no other." Hugh Nibley, *An Approach to the Book of Mormon* (Salt Lake City: Deseret Book Company, 1964), 6. That may be true if the aim is

Authority

Lehi is apparently a merchant from a wealthy and distinguished family. He lives in Jerusalem, but is comfortable traveling in the desert, a safer place for his family than the city under both the leadership of the "Jews of Jerusalem" and the threat of destruction. Hugh Nibley has described the background of Lehi's isolation in and departure from Jerusalem. Lehi has distanced himself from the "elders of the Jews," the pro-Egyptian group in power. He feels no loyalty to these people, being himself a part of the prophetic pro-Babylonian party. Although Lehi is of the old aristocracy—rich, well-educated, with a noble ancestry and an ancient family—he is unpopular. Lehi is not a villain, but he was an unfriendly member of the opposing party.[3]

Lehi, driven from Jerusalem, has lost his authority. Therefore, Nephi must establish his own authority before he begins his story. He writes our version of First Nephi after the death of his father, an event that causes the final breakup between the two camps of Lehi's sons (2 Ne. 4:12–13). Given that, Nephi needs to establish his authority, leaving no hope of retrieving the lost group. When Nephi lists his credentials, he writes in anger and sorrow. He is experienced. He has suffered. He has seen many afflictions which he does not describe. Nevertheless, he has been highly favored by the highest power, the Lord. He suggests that his knowledge and favor have bypassed Lehi's. He presents himself as a chosen one. Indeed, the Lord is not a figure of fear and dread to Nephi. He has great knowledge of the goodness and the mysteries of God. Nephi, with direct access, has made a record of his proceedings in his days (1 Ne. 1:1).

Nephi goes on to explain that he writes with the learning of the Jews and the language of the Egyptians (1 Ne. 1:2), showing his erudition and moving his record into a new linguistic plane. He stamps his record with authority, saying that it is true, written by himself, and from his own knowledge (v. 3). In three verses, then, and without actually saying very much, Nephi establishes himself as a person of experience and authority with excellent connections. He knows a lot, he knows how to do things,

---

to test the document's claim to be ancient, in which case its weaknesses will be revealed by comparison with contemporary documents. But there are many other ways to read a text than to test its ancient authenticity. Here I just accept the ancientness of the text, even as I cast a jaundiced eye on the heroic narrator.

3. Skousen, *The Book of Mormon*, 55, 76–77, 85–86, 96, 99, 201.

and he acts with impeccable credentials. When he says his record is true, he says so with some justification.

But is this the only way to tell the story? Nephi could have told another story. We could have had the narrative of Lehi, told by his son Nephi: Lehi, the trusted prophet of the Lord, received insider information about bad days to come; he devoted himself to the Lord's work and spread the word. Though we can imagine this story, it's not the one we're given. Instead Nephi, writing from the perspective of his later experience, displays (without explicit statement) a Lehi who is an ineffective leader. He shows his mild father suffering from visions of destruction and praising God with humility and rejoicing. He shows Lehi failing to convince the people of their coming destruction. Even when Lehi manages to get his family away into the wilderness, they hold back. Nephi portrays his father as wise, good, and obedient to the Lord, but as anything but a strong leader. Lehi receives much faint praise, and Nephi's authority is therefore all the clearer.

Other Available Narratives

Poor Laman and Lemuel. They would have done better to return to Jerusalem and perish or be driven into captivity by the conquering Babylonians than to oppose Nephi. Then they could have been forgotten in their laziness and sin. Instead, they are skewered forever in Nephi's record as "the bad boys." They are the young Mormons who chose the wrong. From their first appearance they are difficult, disobedient naysayers. Lehi first mentions them as lacking righteousness and steadiness. Nephi upgrades those sins to murmuring and stiffneckedness, but these remain rather minor offenses (1 Ne. 2:8–11). In our First Nephi, these poor boys are never shown as the beloved sons of Lehi and Sariah which they certainly must have been in the first version. Laman and Lemuel complain, but they come along on the journey, generally do what they are told to do, and regularly repent. They were not that bad. But Nephi makes them look as bad as he can: always the other, the undifferentiated bad boys. I propose this as evidence of rewriting after the final family break, after the debilitating battles and wars between the two branches of the family. Nephi shows his resentment against them. All this is sad and ironic because we know that in the final accounting, the bad boys are victorious.

Laman and Lemuel are not allowed to tell their own tale. Damned from the beginning by their arrogant, pen-wielding brother, they get no respect, and considerable denunciation. They did not want to leave their pleasant lives in Jerusalem. They see their father as old and foolish (1 Ne. 1:11). But, as Nibley notes, they never question his ability to lead them through the wilderness.[4] We know that by the time Nephi writes his second narrative, Laman and Lemuel are not just troublesome boys; they have come to be his sworn enemies. They have repeatedly fought life-and-death battles. I wish that Nephi had played fair with their earlier actions—as well as with those of their mother Sariah. They must have had things to say, cases to make. I wish that these had been included in their own voices. When Nephi speaks to us, he has to be right. According to Nephi, the brothers acted as they did because "they knew not the dealings of that God who had created them" (v. 12). Had they not gotten the teachings and experience that Nephi did? What was the difference between their early educations? Why are they not more alike? They didn't begin as hardened enemies, but as still-malleable boys. When Lehi, "being filled with the spirit," denounces the brothers, he is quite able to scare them silent, or so he says, so that "their frames did shake" (2:14). But shouldn't they have been handled in a more kindly way? The other older brother Sam, persuaded that Nephi truly speaks by the Holy Spirit, believes him. But Sam, another good boy, gets very little mention or quotation. It is all "I, Nephi." The wounded and sorrowful scribe has frozen his discontent and theirs, his righteousness and their otherness, into the record forever.

The Other Other: The Women

What can we say of the invisible women in this text? We do not expect much attention to be given to females, and they do not get much. In the heading at the beginning of First Nephi, likely the work of Mormon rather than Nephi, we get several mentions of women. The "account of Lehi and his wife Sariah" shows both equality and possession in the marital pair. They are named together, but Lehi owns Sariah. Elsewhere, women are not important enough to name. The "daughters of Ishmael" who will provide half of the genes of the chosen people in the Promised Land are always identified by their father. We know they had individual names and a mother, but in the introduction to the book where it says, "they take the daughters of Ishmael to wife," the men appropriate all action, ownership, and identity. Not that Ishmael himself gets much attention. He is not introduced and

4. Ibid., 61.

does not even get his exclusive invitation to the wilderness to intermarry from Lehi, but from the boy Nephi. He seems, however, ready enough to come and moves into the desert as easily as Lehi's family had.

Nephi mentions his father Lehi several times before he is named in the fourth and fifth verses of chapter 1 and then becomes central to the narrative. Sariah is the only female character mentioned by name in Nephi's writings at all. Although Sariah is certainly engaged in such housewifery as is required for a pair who dwell in a tent—the business of food, clothing, cleanliness, caring for animals, and keeping order—she is given only a single scene, that of the household shrew in chapter five when she berates her visionary husband for the loss of her sons and her Jerusalem home. Only her complaints are given space in the narrative. She doubts her husband's visionary nature and blames him for the likely fatal result of following his direction, namely, that the whole family will perish in the wilderness. Nephi indicates that there are more complaints "after this manner" (1 Ne. 6:8).

In her unhappiness and doubt, Sariah serves as a foil for Lehi's faith. The safe return of the sons persuades her that Lehi has been right all along, and she testifies of the Lord's protection of her sons. This "conversion" of Sariah's unifies the family, who all rejoice, sacrifice, burn offerings, and give thanks "unto the God of Israel" (1 Ne. 6:9). Sariah, who had been murmuring along with Laman and Lemuel, serves a didactic purpose, returning to obedience and belief. When the boys return, her conviction and testimony get a full hearing. She is honestly overjoyed and dismisses her doubts as unfounded. But having served her purpose, she does not appear again. One strongly feels that she is given this space only to further Nephi's didactic purposes, to show repentance for her doubt.

No family sisters are mentioned at this point, although a later passage suggests that some might have married Ishmael's sons prior to departure from Jerusalem (see 2 Ne. 5:6). Had there been daughters present, how would they have been treated? They would likely have been quiet and obedient, like Sam, but also like Sam, they would have been scarcely mentioned, if mentioned at all. Women, required to bear the children for the Promised Land, are important enough to authorize a special journey to fetch them. But they are also shown to be an afterthought.

Although this is the section of the Book of Mormon most heavily populated with females, they are largely invisible. What are women to make of this exclusion? Perhaps the New World, like heaven before it, had no female inhabitants. If the men are locked into mortal combat mostly by generational divides, the women who accompany them are scarcely involved at all.

Three Journeys

In considering Nephi's two accounts, the return journeys take on additional significance. The sons of Lehi make two major journeys and one partial journey back to Jerusalem before they leave for good. These are extensive trips. The boys took their tents with them. How long are they on the road? Grant Hardy suggests that Jerusalem is about a two week journey away from Lehi's tent in the desert.[5] Their first trip is to retrieve the all-important record. The narrative shows Laman, who has been chosen by lot to wrench the record from Laban, its protector, failing twice. These accounts show how very difficult the task is. His failure opens the way for Nephi, on the second journey (they have returned to the wilderness, but not to the family's camp), to save the day in desperate, violent, God-approved behavior. Here is the fairy-tale archetype. The older sons fail before the youngest, strongest, and most noble son succeeds. Nephi did not need to include the first failed efforts in his story this second time through, but again he uses his brothers' behavior to valorize his own remarkable success. We have not only the events, but Nephi's self-serving representation of the events.

The third journey was to acquire wives. Lehi's triumphant prophecies concerning his seed and the record they will keep seem to remind him and the Lord that something else is required to produce the future generations. In considering the value of women here, shouldn't this absence of future mates have been acknowledged in the narrative before? Shouldn't wives have been recruited before leaving Jerusalem the first time? Couldn't they have been picked up by Laman and Lemuel while Nephi was engaged with Laban? Apparently some decision had already been made that Ishmael's daughters were to be married to Lehi's boys. Perhaps prior arrangements had been made. But the boys bring back another family larger than their own. Ishmael and his wife bring two of their sons and their families, and five daughters, allowing wives for the four sons of Nephi and for Zoram. Ishmael's larger family does not seem to challenge the leadership of Lehi and Nephi at all.

5. Grant Hardy, *Understanding the Book of Mormon: A Reader's Guide* (New York: Oxford University Press, 2010), 16.

The Expansion and Compression of Time

Time in the story as Nephi tells it is compressed, likely because what Nephi once considered important probably wasn't as important when he looked back. The wars between the Nephites and the Lamanites are not even recounted in the second version of the story. Battles and tactics diminish in importance once victory is achieved. As we know that Nephi has compressed at least some stories, we must give greater attention to the things he has expanded.

Nephi furthers his own interests with this cavalier treatment of time. This many-scened narrative takes place over several years. Nephi draws out the time with much detailed superior lecturing to the elder brothers when they are on the road back to Jerusalem. He details the incident when Laman and Lemuel beat their younger brothers, Nephi and Sam, with a rod (1 Ne. 3:28–29), and the virtuous youngsters are saved by divine intervention. All this is an old story by the time Nephi revisits the incidents and the lectures, but Nephi tells it in detail so that he can set up the climax. The older boys, who have reason and likelihood on their side, are crushingly told, "Know ye not that the Lord hath chosen [Nephi] to be a ruler over you, and this because of your iniquities?" (1 Ne. 3:29). That speech is enough to convince any older brothers that peaceful cohabitation is unlikely.

We see another dramatic example of Nephi's compression and expansion of the narrative in chapter 7. Lehi's sons are returning to the wilderness with Ishmael's family when many of them have second thoughts. They want to go back. Although this account is strongly compressed before this point, Nephi slows down the clock here and expatiates on the lessons to be learned about hearkening "unto the word of the Lord" (1 Ne. 7:9). For more than half of the chapter, we have Nephi's sermon to his brothers. Have they not seen an angel? Didn't they get the record from Laban? Don't they know that faithfulness to the Lord will bring them to the Promised Land? Can't they believe in the future destruction of Jerusalem where the prophets have been rejected and Jeremiah imprisoned? Do they not realize that a return to Jerusalem will result in their deaths? It's well worth asking why Nephi needs to repeat all these arguments at such length.

Nephi's tone here is persuasive. He is reasonable and kind. Yet he stirs his brothers up to wrath and violence. "They did lay their hands upon me, for behold, they were exceeding wroth, and they did bind me with cords, for they sought to take away my life, that they might leave me in the wilderness to be devoured by wild beasts" (1 Ne. 7:16). This reaction is too strong for the sermon that Nephi has preached to them. What's going on here? My own innocent reading of this section is that in retelling the story Nephi has extended and softened his own words to his brothers, making them sound reasonable to us while he actually irritated his brothers beyond reason. The result is a narrative that further demonizes them. He makes himself look good and them bad. Thus, even as they tie him up, he prays and is freed from his bonds. His brothers, still wroth with him, attempt to retake him and are only dissuaded by the pleas of Ishmael's fair wife, daughter, and son. Defeated again, the brothers "bow down" before Nephi and plead for forgiveness. Nephi, the good, "frankly forgive[s] them," (vv. 20–21), exhorting them to pray to the Lord for forgiveness as well. The chapter ends with uneasy harmony, sacrifice and burnt offerings (v. 22).

My point here is again to mark the power of the record and the recorder to shape events for a certain purpose. Nephi convinces us, especially at first, to see events through his eyes and to accept his story. I suggest that Nephi purposely extends his account of this speech, even while making it less offensive than it probably was, to dramatize his confrontation with his brothers and his successful escape and victory over them.

The Murder

Where else do we see Nephi's cunning hand at work? Surely it is tempting to consider Nephi's fearsome murder of Laban and the story that surrounds it. While Hugh Nibley considers this act of murder completely commonplace within the tradition of the East, it remains shocking to us.[6]

Nephi needs the potent authority that he has established—his obedience to his father and his close communication with God—to explain and justify the bloody and horrifying murder of Laban. Nephi tries to prepare us by carefully setting up the scene. He tells us that Lehi had told only him of the dream in which he is commanded to get the brass plates. Nephi is to tell his brothers and take them to Jerusalem. Lehi may have actually asked the brothers first and been refused because he suggests that the murmuring of the brothers will prevent them from being successful, setting the stage for Nephi's great "I will go and do" speech. This is the speech with which untold young Mormons have attempted to gird up their loins

6. Nibley, *An Approach to the Book of Mormon*, 88.

to do the impossible: "I will go and do the things which the Lord hath commanded, for I know that the Lord giveth no commandments unto the children of men, save he shall prepare a way for them that they may accomplish the thing which he commandeth them" (1 Ne. 3:7).

We know from the thrust of the narrative that Nephi will succeed. But first we see poor Laman suffering the wrath of Laban and the loss of Lehi's treasure to the greedy kinsman. Nephi thus characterizes Laban as a bad man. Nephi's angry brothers are badly scared of the mighty Laban who "can slay fifty" (1 Ne. 3:31). They see the impossibility of this quest. In response to their doubts, Nephi again expands the time of the narrative with a long faithful speech, reminding his brothers that the Lord "is mightier than all the earth" (4:1). He likens them to Moses doing the impossible. He reminds them of the angel. He doesn't really persuade them, but he has written his speech into the record.

Then we come to the awful scene. The setting is night. Think how dark it must have been. I see it as pitch black (though there could have been moonlight). Somehow, Nephi, near Laban's house, comes upon Laban himself, drunken, "fallen to the earth" (1 Ne. 4:7). Here again Nephi stretches out the time, chronicling his gradual decision to do the frightful deed, Laban cooperatively remaining insensible during all these deliberations.

Nephi, having been the mover and shaker, is now led at every step by "the Spirit" (1 Ne. 4:7–18). Who or what is this spirit? Is this the Holy Spirit he mentions above? Is this the Spirit that speaks to Lehi in chapter 1? Is this the Spirit that interprets Lehi's dream to Nephi? That Spirit came in the "form of a man; yet nevertheless, I knew that it was the Spirit of the Lord" (11:11). No identification or description is given here, yet this inner voice or impulse, rather than Nephi himself or the Lord, is credited with the coming violent actions. Although Nephi argues with the Spirit about slaying Laban, saying that he "shrunk" from the task because he had never "shed the blood of man" (4:10), he had already drawn forth Laban's beautiful sword. The narrative time stops as Nephi examines, in the dark, this treasure: "And I beheld his sword, and I drew it forth from the sheath thereof; and the hilt thereof was of pure gold, and the workmanship thereof was exceeding fine, and I saw that the blade thereof was of the most precious steel" (v. 9). Nephi's attention is more fixed on this sword than it is on the record that he has come to get. The inclusion of this description of the sword of Laban in the dramatic murder scene jars the reader. Nephi has been directed to kill a drunken man he comes upon, yet he pauses in the action to describe the beauty of the chosen weapon, of "pure gold" and the "most precious steel." Nephi's artisanal skills are aroused by the "exceeding fine" workmanship (v. 9). But this pause to look at the sword breaks his concentration and ours.

The Spirit argues for the murder. The Lord has delivered a vulnerable Laban to Nephi. Laban had tried to kill the boys. He wouldn't listen to the commandments of the Lord. Laban had taken Lehi's property. The Spirit tells Nephi that the "Lord slayeth the wicked to bring forth his righteous purposes" and that "it is better that one man should perish than a nation should dwindle and perish in unbelief" (1 Ne. 4:13). Persuaded, Nephi begins to justify the deed on his own. The Lord promised prosperity to his seed for obedience. They need the plates. Laban had been delivered into his hands so he could get the records. Nephi again stresses that he is following authority: "I did obey the voice of the Spirit, and took Laban by the hair of the head, and I smote off his head with his own sword" (v. 18).

Nephi repeats this last phrase twice. Beheading a man with his own sword multiplies the power of the defeat. The sword gives ritual importance to this political murder. This is a ceremonial sword, meant to show authority, to be worn with court dress, not a battle weapon. As this sword was for ritual purposes, it was not likely to have a keenly sharpened blade. In that case, even the powerful Nephi would have had to do more sawing than smiting. And that raises the question as to whether the murder was also a ceremony. Nephi changes clothes with the corpse—remember the darkness and imagine the gushing blood—and sets out for the treasury where he impersonates Laban, persuading the servant Zoram to give him the brass plates and to follow him. Nibley describes this scene as "an authentic bit of Oriental romance and of history." He likens Nephi's exploit to Sir Richard Burton's "amazingly audacious masquerades in the East, carried on in broad daylight and for months on end with perfect success."[7] Could Nephi have been playing out some swash-buckling adventure story? Perhaps Nephi's writing is a tale told rather than an actual experience. The inevitability that blood would be everywhere suggests that this might have been a ritual murder, a complete overpowering of one person by another, climaxing with subduing the enemy and the sword moving into the hands of the victor. The decapitation seems particularly theatrical.

What really happened? Nephi might have stripped the drunken Laban before the fatal event. Such smart thinking under pressure is certainly his style. Perhaps he knocked the hapless drunkard on the head and dragged

7. Ibid., 95.

him into an alley. Laban would have been quiet until morning. However, canny as he is, with no witnesses, he is able to make his own story of his obedience to the Spirit immeasurably stronger with this report of his violent, faith-driven action. Whether the event actually happened as he describes it or not, his description gives us the impression of victory for himself and total humiliation for Laban. We have a hearkening back to a primitive and therefore sacred world.

Nephi's skill in writing this scene is much to be admired. Having shown the difficulty of the task, having shown his hesitation, having persuaded himself to kill Laban, being physically large and up to the task, following directions without implicating the Lord, his father, or even himself, Nephi reports that he smote off the head of Laban and got the plates. But how valorous is it to kill a defenseless, unconscious man in this brutal way? Grant Hardy notes here that when Nephi returns to his father's tent, he claims no credit for the deed. The boys do not swagger in triumph. Lehi does not praise them. The murder is not even referred to in the text. The scene switches immediately to Sariah's modest rebellion, berating the visionary Lehi for taking her boys into the desert to die. Their return means that she joyfully forgives Lehi and praises the Lord, allowing for a legitimate celebration. Laban's execution is apparently left out of their rejoicing.[8]

The Brass Plates

We know that Nephi loved the sword of Laban. His description of the sword of Laban stands out in this otherwise barren narrative. It is his strongest declaration of affection in this section. Nephi values this sword, this precious religious artifact, more than he values the record that he kills Laban to possess. The "plates of brass" merit little praise for their looks, their cunning technology, or their handsome metal. In the narrative, the plates serve mainly as an excuse for Nephi to confront and overpower the enemy, establishing his superiority. The brass plates do have, however, religious and historical value. The plates will "preserve unto our children the language of our fathers" (1 Ne. 3:19). They will provide the law of Moses to the people in the Promised Land. But they also provide lineage connections to valorize Lehi as a descendant of Joseph: "even that Joseph

8. Hardy, *Understanding the Book of Mormon*, 18.

who was the son of Jacob, . . . And thus my father, Lehi, did discover the genealogy of his fathers" (5:14–15).

Surely we are surprised that Lehi does not know his genealogy. He knew where to get the record, that Laban was a kinsman. Would he not have known that he was part of this family? Lehi's birth seems to have been included on those records. Perhaps the family had not been interested in or aware of this genealogy prior to their departure from the city. Nephi tells us that they did not know the value of the record and had not felt that it was necessary until "the Lord had commanded us" to obtain the record (1 Ne. 5:20). After they had searched the plates, they found that "they were desirable; yea, even of great worth unto us, insomuch that we could preserve the commandments of the Lord unto our children" (v. 21). The records were valuable, then, for genealogy, for doctrine, and for culture.

Perhaps more important, the presence of these plates allowed Lehi to prophesy, perhaps in the way that the golden plates of Nephi themselves, later exhumed from burial, allowed Joseph Smith to see, prophesy, and write scripture. The presence of the plates allowed Lehi, "filled with the spirit," to "prophesy concerning his seed" (1 Ne. 5:17). Lehi says many things, but two dramatic ones that Nephi quotes are that "these plates of brass should go forth unto all nations, kindreds, tongues, and people" who were of his seed, and that the plates "should never perish; neither should they be dimmed any more by time" (vv. 18–19). These prophecies about what were early books of the Bible have certainly come to pass, although the dissemination of information did not come from the plates of brass but from other early writings of the Bible.

So Nephi justifies the theft of the plates of brass which allowed his seed access to this early record of his people. He asserts that it was "wisdom in the Lord that we should carry [the plates] with us" (1 Ne. 5:22). But couldn't Lehi have gotten the plates while he was a great man in Jerusalem, or, not unreasonably, had them copied? An example of Nephi's changing values between his two narratives is that Nephi does not copy the genealogy of his fathers into his own record. His descent from Joseph is enough for him. The genealogy being available somewhere else, the plates recede in value. To get the plates with the genealogy, the family has risked all. But when Nephi comes to copy material into his second record, he chooses to copy Isaiah rather than genealogy.

Conclusion

In my reading of this important first section of the Book of Mormon, I consider, and accept, its purported history. Having done so, I consider the implications of how a man engaged in a harrowing and life-threatening enterprise might write his story differently over a period of thirty or forty years, how the passage of time might have modified the way he told his story. These people act in history, even as they record their own stories. People frequently retell their stories differently as time passes, selecting, revising, and justifying their accounts. Particularly when the years have passed and other witnesses have disappeared, written accounts tend to become bolder. Writers exaggerate. People make the stories they remember smoother and cleaner. They appropriate the experience of others. Historians privilege contemporary accounts over those written many years later, knowing that while even contemporary accounts are generally told to the benefit of the narrator, later accounts are less reliable. I am proposing that Nephi's intervention in American history to replace his earlier boyish account with a more mature, if disillusioned account of his youthful adventures, changes the Book of Mormon as we might have known it.

I am thus trying to imagine the differences there might be in the two accounts and why changes have been made. I am envisioning the trying experiences the family might have had, even as they attempted to do their best and act in accordance with instructions from Deity. I am trying to envision the mature leader in his wounded state.

Finally, I am paying homage to the writer and the written text. Power follows the author. He can shape and describe his account as he wishes. He has the last word. His is the version that will live. Even if, as is always the case, he has a different agenda than the reader who comes centuries later to his account, his are the words that must be reckoned with. I have been hard on Nephi, but I salute him as our guide through a God-directed world of the past.

SIX

Alma's Wisdom-Poem to Helaman (Alma 37:35–37)

Bruce W. Jorgensen

Occasions

For about three years, 1998–2001, I served on the High Council of a BYU student stake, and on November 18, 2000, my assignment was to speak for about ten minutes to an Elders Quorum on the scriptural theme for a ward conference, Alma 37:35–37. I don't recall how much advance notice I had. Those verses, when I re-read them, struck me as a small poem like the ones familiar in English translations of some parts of Proverbs. I copied out the verses in parallel clauses and wrote a few interpretive notes for my talk. A couple years later, when I transcribed the notes I expanded them into a brief essay draft, which I revised and enlarged over the next three years, thinking I might sometime try to publish it.

Not all of the occasions for my efforts at scriptural interpretation are as specifically "pastoral" or "ecclesial" as this one was, nor as were the occasions for the two dozen sermons I wrote notes or texts for during those three years. But all in some way, to some degree, are rooted in my community at the time, respond to a call within or from that community, and are offered to that community. That is the first thing that "Mormon scriptural hermeneutics" means to me. Were I not a member of a Mormon community and thus an heir of the texts it regards as holy scripture, I'm not at all sure I would have read, or would continue to read, those texts, nor that I would feel any impulse to write about them, much less publish anything I write about them. But I am a member and I read the scriptures, and I often respond to an explicit or implicit call to interpret and write about them. My published readings, so far, have all arisen in academic contexts that, because I teach at a Church-sponsored university, are strongly inflected by my community's care for its sacred texts and its habits of using them.

As an undergraduate English major at BYU, I took the required religion courses, some of which encouraged close reading of scripture, and I took a Bible as Literature course that made me wonder if the Book of Mormon also might be read "as literature." As a graduate student at Cornell, I taught a once-a-week Institute class for a year, and, because I'd learned something of typology from courses I took or audited in Old and Middle English literature, began to think about typological patterns in the Book of Mormon. One eventual published result of this was "The Dark Way to the Tree."[1]

About 1986 I taught the second semester of the Book of Mormon course required of all BYU students, and noticed (with a mild shock) that nowhere in Alma 39 does Alma charge his son Corianton with fornication, the sin Mormons usually, and too casually, convict him of, and often, on the basis of one verse (Alma 39:5, which uses the plural "these things"), regard as "*the* sin next to murder." Out of that perplexity I eventually wrote "Scriptural Chastity Lessons."[2] A year or two later, in an Honors Colloquium, trying to help students distinguish "didactic" stories (told to illustrate a "message") from—for want of a better term—"mimetic" stories (told to move an audience by engaging them imaginatively with the lives and feelings and deeds of characters), I found myself spontaneously retelling the three stories Jesus tells in Luke 15, where the third story differs sharply in its form and detailed development from the first two; and sometime later I realized I had an essay to write about that: "'This Man Receiveth Sinners': Moral Storytelling in Luke 15."[3]

This is to say, among other things, that my forays into scriptural interpretation have never amounted to steps in any "research agenda"; they were not part of any "plan" of "professional development." After "The Dark Way to the Tree" I did map out three related essays that might join

1. See Bruce W. Jorgensen, "The Dark Way to the Tree: Typological Unity in the Book of Mormon," *Encyclia* 54, no. 2 (1977): 16–24. Reprinted with a "Postscript 1980" in *Literature of Belief: Sacred Scriptures and Religious Experience*, ed. Neal E. Lambert (Provo, Utah: BYU Religious Studies Center, 1981), 217–31.

2. See Bruce W. Jorgensen, "Scriptural Chastity Lessons: Joseph and Potiphar's Wife; Corianton and the Harlot Isabel," *Dialogue* 32, no. 1 (Spring 1999): 7–34.

3. See Bruce W. Jorgensen, "'This Man Receiveth Sinners': Moral Storytelling in Luke 15," *Sunstone* 20, no. 4 (December 1997): 18–26.

it and work toward a small, useful book. I presented "The Figure of the Vineyard" at the Mormon History Association meetings in Canandaigua, New York, in 1980, and "Violence in the Book of Mormon" in a "conjoint" session of The Association for Mormon Letters at the Rocky Mountain Modern Language Association in Las Cruces, New Mexico, in 1988; I've not yet finished these to my satisfaction. Nor have I finished "The Good Story Mark Tells," a narrative commentary, presented in fragmentary form in 1995, and initially provoked by the neglect of Mark in the LDS Sunday School curriculum. And still not in an ecclesial setting, though very much in a Mormon community, invited to give a plenary "keynote" speech at the Association for Mormon Letters conference in 2004, I wrote and presented "What If the Book of Mormon Were a Novel?—Which of Course It Is Not," urging and starting to explore the notion that the sacred text might usefully be read not "monologically" but "dialogically."[4]

My Mormon scriptural interpretations, then, mostly came when their occasions came, however long after the occasions it took to think them farther (not likely think them "through," whatever that might mean) and, as far as I could, to write them out. They have all been "amateur" efforts in the better and worse senses of the word: done for love, and done without "professional" qualifications, training, or (as far as I can tell) rewards. I have used whatever skills and habits of attention—to texts and their contexts—I've acquired as a lifelong reader of prose and poetry and, formally, as an undergraduate and graduate student of literature. The present essay is one more of this kind.

Principles (If I Have Any)

Is all hermeneutics general hermeneutics, particular only when and as it engages a particular text? Can it be tagged adjectivally—as "Mormon" or "Freudian" or "Marxist" or any "-ist" or "-ian"—only in terms of the interpreter's ideological or doctrinal allegiances and pre-texts (the texts and understandings used to "translate" the understandings of the target text)? Maybe so. And does ideological or doctrinal allegiance seldom or never prescribe or in some degree guide any series of steps in any specific act of interpretation? Maybe so. Questions like these may keep me from ever getting off the ground as a possibly "Mormon" interpreter of anything.

---

4. See Bruce W. Jorgensen, "What If the Book of Mormon Were a Novel?—Which of Course It Is Not," *Irreantum* 6, no. 2 (October 2004): 13–32.

I have supposed that every interpretive practice and every hermeneutic act have both an ideological aspect and a methodological aspect. Maybe "doctrinal" would be a better word than "ideological" (though the latter rhymes better with "methodological"); I don't think I want to use the word "ideological" in its strongest (Marxist) sense, yet perhaps I should not be over-cautious about that. Anyway, is it true that every interpretive act is both ideological and methodological? Does an ideology or a doctrine of some sort lie behind, or operate within, even so seemingly primary or elementary an act as "close reading," or as consulting a dictionary or parsing a sentence? Maybe so. But what would such an ideology or doctrine look like if articulated?

As a "Mormon interpreter," minimally an interpreter who also happens to be a (practicing) Mormon, am I *necessarily* bound by *any* "Mormon doctrine" to any specific ideas or to any specific maneuvers to satisfy my interest in a text, to understand it better? I can't say that I am; I can't say whether my being a Mormon and having some set of "Mormon doctrines" or "Mormon ideas" in my head makes any substantial difference in my interpretive practices or acts. So far, I feel myself hard-pressed—or as Candide says of Pangloss, *bien embarrassé*—to demonstrate that it does. But I might be wrong, and would gladly attend to any arguments that would demonstrate I am.

Might it be the case that, just as plumbing is plumbing and the only distinctions that matter are those between more and less competent jobs of plumbing, based on criteria such as whether joints and valves do not leak and drains do not clog, so with hermeneutics: all hermeneutics is general hermeneutics, and the only meaningful distinctions are among more and less competent hermeneutic acts, based on criteria internal to hermeneutics itself? Will an analogy between plumbing jobs and hermeneutic acts hold, or will it leak or clog? How deep are the differences between plumbing and interpreting? At least as deep as the differences between pipes and valves and liquids and words and sentences and genres and meanings? Can there be clog-proof paragraphs? Leakproof syntactic joints? A lifetime warranty on the reliable delivery of hot or cold meanings at so many gallons per minute, with *x* degree of softness?

It seems critical that hermeneutics—interpretation, understanding—is a transaction between persons, however separated by distance, time, cultural and linguistic difference, not to mention personal difference; that, because it is conducted in a language (of some kind or other, whether lexical-syntactic, gestural, or what-have-you), language is at once the matter of the interpretation and its means and manner. As if plumbing plumbed itself! (Don't we all wish! Unless plumbing plumbed itself in ways as leaky and clogging as the hermeneutics of so many scholars in the humanities.)

This seems to be getting me farther away from my question. Yet it doesn't seem entirely irrelevant either. If the pertinent criteria for hermeneutic acts are internal to hermeneutics itself, to its functionality or usefulness, what difference can it make in any of my hermeneutic acts that I happen to be a Mormon? My distinction between methodological and ideological aspects of hermeneutic acts may be purely conceptual; the aspects might be inseparable in the acts themselves. Still, would a Mormon ideology or doctrine or cultural attitude or traditional practice be discernible not so much in the moves of a Mormon interpreter's interpretation as in the objects he selects for attention or excludes from it (crude example: R-rated films), and in the outcomes of his acts—a detectable preference, say, for the "uplifting" or for readings that support Mormonism's current image of the "traditional family" or man-woman monogamous marriage, or that do not question what any general authority has ever said about a scriptural text? Deck-stacking instances, I know. But isn't the very phrase "Mormon interpretation" at least covertly deck-stacking? It seems to me that if this is where one might locate the "Mormon" in "Mormon hermeneutics," then that is not hermeneutics itself but a set of prejudices, pre-judgments, about its proper objects and preferable outcomes, which may well have influenced or guided some of the moves during the hermeneutic act.

And yet again, because both the objects and the acts of interpretation are enacted or produced by human agents, by persons, and because every person is situated in time, space, culture, language, communal and personal history, and ideology, there is no way to rule such prejudices out; or perhaps they may be called "fore-understandings." Moreover, it matters very much that these prejudices or fore-understandings be given play, because it is highly likely that they will disclose hitherto unnoticed meanings in the objects of understanding. Let interpretations multiply. If they conflict, they conflict; if they agree, they agree. Either way, as they multiply they multiply understandings. As Gadamer wrote, "we understand in a *different* way, *if we understand at all*."[5] Then let differences multiply and differ and flourish and interact to generate more differences. For in any case we shall not be able to close them down. No two interpreters can occupy the same hermeneutic locus or read a text from exactly the

5. Hans-Georg Gadamer, *Truth and Method*, trans. Joel Weinsheimer and Donald G. Marshall, 2nd ed. (New York: Continuum, 2004), 296.

same angle, and thus every interpreter may see something no other sees, however minuscule the difference, and every interpretation will offer some part of the "whole truth" (if there is such a thing).

I have preferred to limit myself to textual hermeneutics, and mostly to "literary" and "narrative" texts at that. Partly because narrative texts, short stories, novels, narrative poems, scriptural stories, are often, if not always, about what I call interpersonal hermeneutics. They are about the ways their characters (their lexical-syntactic representations of persons in relation) understand or fail to understand one another. (Read Robert Frost's "Home Burial," for instance.)

But one could take up any act of interpersonal hermeneutics in daily life. It is Thursday evening, May 8, 2008, and between stints at drafting an essay on Mormon hermeneutics, as I stand in the kitchen warming leftover rice and refried beans for my supper, my wife tells me that the shoes I wore on Sunday and am now wearing are "no longer church-worthy" because the left upper is visibly split in three places. It is hard for me to imagine a more "Mormon" object and act and context of interpretation. The previous summer I attended an Episcopal service in California, and in that religious context and occasion, although it was Sunday and I wore a jacket and tie and good shoes (these same shoes, before the left upper started to split), it seemed clear from the variability of attire in the congregation that no one was likely to care what I had on my feet. Tonight I question my wife's interpretation of my left shoe: Why do the splits in the upper make it not "church-worthy"? Because people will notice. But will they? I don't notice what people at church have on their feet, and if I did, I doubt I would make any judgments of that kind about their footwear. She hopes that makes me happy. Yes, on that point, it does; I admit I prefer not to trouble myself, if I can help it, with judging others' footwear, or my own, provided it is serviceable, comfortable, and not filthy (for the context, of course; for yard work I wear a very old, worn, broken-down, often mud-caked pair of shoes that I would rather not wear to church or the office or the classroom). What was "Mormon" about my wife's hermeneutic acts in that exchange? Or about my own hermeneutic acts in response to hers? How did our differentially-shared "Mormonism" make a difference in the conduct or the content of that compound-complex hermeneutic enactment?

Or what about dog hermeneutics? It's clear there is something of the sort. Later this same evening in May 2008 as I roll open the bedroom closet door to hang up some freshly laundered shirts and pants, our dog trots up the short stairs into the upstairs hall that is officially off-limits to her and from which we repeatedly scold her away. She takes the sound of the sliding door as a sign that I might take her for a walk. In colder weather, at least once per evening, she would be right: I'd be getting out my jacket and putting it on. But she is wrong far more often than she is right, because she is less of a contextualist than I am, or than most human beings are. She seems not to remember, or not to care, that we already had our walk this evening, and not to have connected the armload of shirts and pants she saw me carry up from the laundry room with the rumble of the sliding hollow-core closet door. She does have certain prejudices, and these render her interpretation false this time, though of course her interpretation does disclose a possibility in that sound and in my opening the door that is quite real to both of us, and always desirable to her and sometimes to me, though it is not on my agenda in this instance. Done with the evening's load of laundry, I intend to get back to writing my essay.

My dog hermeneutics example is not entirely frivolous—after all, Socrates' figure in the Republic for the guardians is a dog who has learned correctly to distinguish, to interpret, who's friend and who's foe. Our dog's "prejudice," her narrow one-track fore-understanding of the noise of our closet door, offers a brute instance, a sort of paradigm, of the problem inherent in the inescapable ideological or doctrinal aspect of any hermeneutic practice; especially of practices admitting an explicit and systematic set of doctrinal ideas. Freudianism, Marxism, Jungianism, Christianity, Mormonism: won't all doctrinal systems, admitted into the interpretation of texts, behave in much the same way—mapping susceptible details of the text onto the pertinent terms and relations of the doctrine or ideology? The literary critic Austin Quigley has put the problem soberly in highly general terms: "What so often happens . . . is that 'seeing something in terms of X' degenerates into 'seeing something as X' and finally into simply 'seeing X.' The . . . mode of orientation becomes not the means of discovery but the thing to be (re)discovered."[6] The same sees the same and not the other. So the devout Catholic writer Flannery O'Connor counseled would-be fiction writers, "Your beliefs will be the light by which you see, but they will not be what you see and they will not be a substitute for seeing."[7] In another context she remarked that "There is no reason that

6. Austin E. Quigley, "Wittgenstein's Philosophizing and Literary Theorizing," in *Ordinary Language Criticism: Literary Thinking after Cavell after Wittgenstein*, ed. Kenneth Dauber and Walter Jost (Evanston: Northwestern UP, 2003), 20.

7. Flannery O'Connor, *Mystery and Manners: Occasional Prose*, ed. Sally and Robert Fitzgerald (New York: Farrar, 1970), 91.

fixed dogma should fix anything that the writer sees in the world. On the contrary, dogma is an instrument for penetrating reality."[8]

Even Flannery O'Connor's figure for the relation of belief to "seeing" poses a problem. We all know how certain lights change the apparent color of the objects they fall on, or how the angle of incidence of light will highlight some features of the object and cast others into shadow, and even compose a deceptive image from highlights and shadows: a giant sculpture of the face of Jesus on the surface of Mars; a ledge on Maui that, from a certain angle, is John F. Kennedy's profile.

Granting the difficulty of separating ideological from methodological aspects of hermeneutic acts, even if ideology does not prescribe method, could there be some sort of uniquely "Mormon way" of interpretation? I doubt it. One good candidate I can think of would be the inspiration of the Holy Ghost. Yet although I think I receive rather frequent gifts from that source in my hermeneutic acts, I do not cite the Spirit in my endnotes, and I give thanks as privately as I receive the gifts. And while faithful Mormons may hope to enjoy the constant company of the Holy Ghost, and likely need that company in their everyday hermeneutic acts, they surely have no exclusive privilege in this respect. "The Spirit giveth light to every man that cometh into the world" (D&C 84:46). And "the wind bloweth where it listeth, and thou hearest the sound thereof, but canst not tell whence it cometh, and whither it goeth" (John 3:8).

Could there be some use or application of uniquely Mormon doctrines in hermeneutic acts—supposing there are uniquely Mormon doctrines—even if none specifically address the interpretation of texts? If so, which doctrines? My own first candidates would be an embodied God, the agency of embodied persons, and the eternality of family relationships. But can you show me how such concepts play in actual hermeneutic acts, especially interpretations of non-Mormon texts, perhaps especially of resolutely secular and atheistic texts? Won't this be a necessary test? If there is a Mormon hermeneutics, will it not have to demonstrate its usefulness on any text at all? And then what of the obvious danger in the doctrinal aspect of any hermeneutic act, if we must concede that every interpreter, by being an interpreter at all, being historically and culturally situated, carries some doctrinal baggage or other?

The obvious danger in the ideological aspect would be to see the object of interpretation as simply an instance of one's ideology. Make a

8. Ibid., 178.

Freudian of Woolf, a Marxist of Austen, a Mormon of Milton. But is that almost too easy, and would more rigor and scrupulosity of method tend to correct the errors of ideological and methodological excess, which have been so abundantly parodied (as in Frederick Crews's *Pooh Perplex* and *Postmodern Pooh*, or in Harold Kaplan's collection *The Overwrought Urn*), perhaps because they so often parody themselves? And how would one possibly ban all ideology from acts of interpretation?

The Mormon temptation to doctrinal distortion in interpretation comes obviously from the belief that we have the Real Truth, ultimate and absolute and eternal, from which standpoint anything else may be confidently criticized. This sounds like a parody, a cartoon of a hermeneutic posture and conduct that no actual interpreter, no concrete act of interpretation, could ever quite fit. Still, the doctrinal temptation runs that way. Yet, "ye shall know the truth, and the truth shall make you free" (John 8:32). This could mean—ought to mean, I think—that, as an interpreter, one who knows "the truth" might be free to understand what he does not know, to understand it *as* something else, other, not one more instantiation of what he already knows; also free to be generous to that other, not to distort or to dismiss but to behold patiently and attentively "in order" (in Simone Weil's formulation) that the soul may "receive into itself the being it is looking at, just as [it] is, in all [its] truth."[9]

Does that truth look alien (and why not? how not?), does it look separate, disconnected from the truth I think I already know, even contrary to it? If so, am I not called to faith and to longer patience, to longsuffering, to hope that somehow and sometime I will learn how all the many and disparate truths may hold together?

It has seemed to me that, rather than a "method," interpretation is an exercise of *phronesis*, of know-how derived from experience (however much or little guided at any stage by a master or mentor), of tact and taste. And likely also a matter of the interpreter's location and participation in (usually) an already ongoing conversation about a text. Or conversations, plural, and rather often conversations that include interlocutors both of and not-of the interpreter's nearest community: Frank Kermode is not a Christian, as far as I know, yet partakes in the conversation on the Gospel of Mark; Harold Bloom is a gnostic Jew, yet partakes in the conversation on the Book of Mormon. Often an interlocutor might not be aware of the conversation he or she is taking part in, by way of quotation or other

9. Simone Weil, *Waiting for God*, trans. Emma Craufurd (New York: Harper, 1973), 115.

uses: Grant Hardy has remarked that Meir Sternberg's *Poetics of Biblical Narrative* "may be one of the best books ever written about the Book of Mormon";[10] and like Hardy and others, I've often had Robert Alter and some of his moves or habits in mind as I read the Book of Mormon (not to mention all the literary critics who've affected how I read poems, stories, novels). More recently, as in this essay, I've brought in James Kugel and J. P. Fokkelman.

One implication here seems to be that no interpreter—at least not I as one—is ever purely this or that sort of interpreter. It's all a kind of bricolage; we're all some kind of bricoleur, taking up whatever seems handy for the task at hand. Interpretation falls somewhere within the domains of the technical (but does it have techniques?) and the ethical/political; maybe on the borders of the technical and the ethical/political. To me it seems less like playing an instrument or throwing a pot than like understanding what to do in some exigency of family life or friendship (though usually granted more leisure than these allow).

Are interpreters, then, people without principles; more likely without pre-scribed procedures, but with habits and savvy and presumptions and (perhaps shifty) allegiances? Maybe so. In any case, it's hard for me to see how, if they have principles, those principles prescribe any procedures, especially a sequence of them, A, B, C, D, and so on, that could be guaranteed to work in any particular case. T. S. Eliot once wrote (in a context praising Aristotle as a literary critic) that "there is no method except to be very intelligent."[11] I think by "intelligent"—which, after all, etymologically suggests a capacity to "choose among" options, as in any concrete situation, in which, as Aristotle said, the judgment lies with perception—he meant something like what I point toward with words like *phronesis*, know-how, taste, tact, etc.

Are there any general hermeneutic principles, any habits, any moves or methods, that could be called "Mormon"? I'd like to think, for instance, that a Mormon hermeneutics would not be a hermeneutics of suspicion, though I guess at times that might be in order. I'd like to think that, on the contrary, it would be a hermeneutics of charity. But charity is hardly a doctrine or habit peculiar to Mormons. The literary critic Alan Jacobs got there way ahead of me in *A Theology of Reading: The Hermeneutics of Love* (2001),

---

10. Grant Hardy, *Understanding the Book of Mormon: A Reader's Guide* (New York: Oxford University Press, 2010), 277.

11. T. S. Eliot, "The Perfect Critic," in *Selected Prose of T. S. Eliot*, ed. Frank Kermode (New York: Harcourt/Farrar, 1975), 55.

which draws together many of the thinkers who've guided my thinking along these lines (notably Martha Nussbaum, Iris Murdoch, Simone Weil, and Mikhail Bakhtin).[12] And the French Catholic theologian and phenomenologist Jean-Luc Marion got there even sooner in his 1992 *Communio* essay "Christian Philosophy and Charity," in which he wrote that

> the Christian outlook exercises a radically new hermeneutics vis-à-vis the world only insofar as it sees or facilitates therein the appearance of phenomena that are themselves radically new. The Christian outlook facilitates the resurgence and appearance in the world of phenomena that have up until then remained invisible, on the basis of which a new interpretation of already visible phenomena becomes thenceforth legitimate. What is this new given and this new interpretation? The answer is charity, which gives itself and allows itself to be seen by those who love it.[13]

Thus for Marion, "only those who love see the phenomena of love. Loving becomes a theoretical exigency."[14] To which I must give my belated and wholehearted Amen. But when Marion sums up finally that "There is . . . a specifically Christian outlook on the world. It is an outlook instructed by charity, a radically new phenomenon, which permits the discovery, by a radically new hermeneutics, of other new phenomena, and in the end renders all things new,"[15] my Amen carries with it the admission that I cannot claim a hermeneutics of charity as anything unique to Mormonism or to me as a Mormon interpreter. Indeed, I'm not sure Marion can claim a hermeneutics of charity as uniquely Christian. Can it be demonstrated that Buddhist compassion does not permit the discovery of new phenomena that might be the same as those discovered by Christian charity? (Jacobs's disparagement of "a kind of hermeneutical Buddhism" does not take into account the "compassionate Buddha.")[16]

Perhaps the most authentically—or "essentially"—Mormon or Christian interpretive acts will be acts in which the interpreters do not know—and thus do not show—that they are Mormon or Christian. Like the "blessed of my Father" in Jesus's late parable of the sheep and goats, amazed to be told that they had clothed and fed and visited the Lord

---

12. See Alan Jacobs, *A Theology of Reading: The Hermeneutics of Love* (Boulder: Westview Press, 2001).

13. Jean-Luc Marion, "Christian Philosophy and Charity," trans. Mark Sebanc, *Communio* 19 (Fall 1992): 469.

14. Ibid., 470.

15. Ibid., 472.

16. Jacobs, *A Theology of Reading*, 34.

Jesus: it had not occurred to them. "Lord, when saw we thee . . . ?" (Matt. 25:31–46, especially 34, 37–39).

Poems in the Scriptures

The Hebrew Bible, J. P. Fokkelman estimates, is "roughly one third" poetry.[17] Does the Book of Mormon, which claims kin with (a "traditionary" relation to) the Hebrew Bible, include poems? If it does, where, what kinds, how does each poem poetically work, and how are they related to the prose narratives and other prose forms in which they occur? Those would be the largest and longest questions any approach to "poems," or to "poetry" (to me these terms differ), in the Book of Mormon should try, however provisionally, to offer some answers to.

There are large obstacles in the way. The Book of Mormon includes no "books" largely or entirely composed in verse, as does the Bible (Job, Lamentations), no collections of songs like those in the Bible (Psalms, Song of Songs), and no collection of proverbs in verse. Virtually all of the Book of Mormon's sizeable prophetic poems present themselves as quoted from Hebrew prophetic books, overwhelmingly Isaiah, which means in turn that most of the poems, or most of the poetic lines, so far discerned in the Book of Mormon (by, for example, Donald Parry and Grant Hardy) were written by Isaiah (and mostly match the translations of the committee that produced the Authorized Version). This would leave us to look for poems unique to the Book of Mormon distributed within the prose of the book's historical narrative, exhortation, and didactic exposition. Do such poems in the Book of Mormon (supposing we find them), as Fokkelman says of those in the Bible, "articulate the mass of narrative prose, throughout the entire 'history' track"?[18] Or what do they do?

Like English translations of the Bible until the mid-twentieth century, the Book of Mormon comes to us printed throughout as prose, whether in its first edition of 1830 or as later formatted in columns and numbered in verses; and its numbered "verses" (for convenience of citation), just like verses in English Bible translations, often do not coincide with the verses (lines) of poems. But the problem of distinguishing poems in our books of scripture is not just an unfortunate consequence of print culture. Robert Alter reminds us that "poems are not set out as poetry in the traditional

17. J. P. Fokkelman, *Reading Biblical Poetry: An Introductory Guide*, trans. Ineke Smit (Louisville: Westminster John Knox, 2001), 1.

18. Ibid., 2.

Hebrew text."[19] Apparently, many ancient systems of writing simply did not develop visual or spatial conventions (lines, stanzas, etc.) for presenting poems as poems, or signs for marking verse lines as lines. Nonetheless, philologists for centuries have discerned the "rules" for "verse," and the poems, in various traditions and manuscripts (e.g., the continuing recoveries of *Gilgamesh* from clay tablets and shards, or the Old English heroic poem *Beowulf*, which comes down to us by way of a single manuscript that might just as well not have survived a fire). It helps us late modern print-culture readers to hear a poem *as* a poem (especially one that does not use end-rhyme) if we can see it on the page; ancient hearers and readers (who normally read aloud) seem not to have needed such aids, or at any rate they did not have them.

So it's not surprising that different readers of the Book of Mormon in its standard printed format have not all discerned the same poems. Few LDS readers now would question the designation of 2 Nephi 4:17b–35 as "The Psalm of Nephi." That this poem starts in the middle of a numbered verse nicely illustrates the problem of discerning poems without the aid of typographic or spatial conventions; that Parry sets just less than half of its numbered verses in his "parallelistic patterns" may be an even stronger demonstration.[20] Or does the "psalm" start at verse 15b, then lapse into prose at verse 17a and restart at verse 17b, as Hardy prints it in his *Reader's Edition*?[21] The brief "wisdom-poem" I propose to discuss here, Alma 37:35–37, has not been uniformly recognized: R. Dilworth Rust[22] and Grant Hardy[23] do set it as a poem (though they set its lines slightly differently), but Parry sets only vv. 35–36 as verse (dividing the first lines differently from Rust and Hardy to display their chiastic pattern).[24] Both Parry (partially)[25] and Hardy (entirely)[26] set Alma 37:33–34 as verse lines (with different lineation); yet those same numbered verses do not strike

19. Robert Alter, *The Art of Biblical Poetry* (New York: Basic Books, 1985), 5.

20. Donald W. Parry, *The Book of Mormon Text Reformatted According to Parallelistic Patterns* (Provo, Utah: FARMS, 1992), 58–60.

21. Grant Hardy, *The Book of Mormon: A Reader's Edition* (Urbana: University of Illinois Press, 2003), 71–72.

22. R. Dilworth Rust, *Feasting on the Word: The Literary Testimony of the Book of Mormon* (Salt Lake City and Provo, Utah: Deseret Book and FARMS, 1997), 86–87.

23. Hardy, *Reader's Edition*, 360.

24. Parry, *The Book of Mormon Text Reformatted*, 284–85.

25. Ibid., 284.

26. Hardy, *Reader's Edition*, 359–60.

me as a poem with anything like the clarity that vv. 35–37 do. It appears that even among readers on the *qui vive* for poems or parallelisms, not all look out at the text with the same formal traits in mind, or they look out differently. Royal Skousen in *The Book of Mormon: The Earliest Text* does not seek to distinguish prose and poetry; yet he does set off Alma 37:35–37 as a paragraph,[27] and his "sense-lines" (most of them visibly shorter than others in the immediate context) do allow this text to be perceived as a poem.

Such different discernments of poems in the Book of Mormon surely reflect the continuing lack of full or exact consensus even among the most poetically attentive readers of the Hebrew Bible. The big problem has been, and still is, in James Kugel's title phrase, "the idea of biblical poetry": "what," Kugel asks, "is the difference between what is called biblical poetry and biblical prose?"[28] This turns out to be less simple than one might wish or suppose. Kugel traces the effort to discern and define biblical poetry, and especially to discover a "meter" for it, from late antiquity to our own time. And as Robert Alter sees it, he "comes perilously close to concluding that there is no poetry in the Bible, only a 'continuum' from loosely parallelistic structures in what we think of as the prose sections to a more 'heightened rhetoric' of parallelistic devices in what we misleadingly label verse."[29]

Though Alter does at times concur with Kugel, I find Kugel's rigorously cautious and circumspect, not to say skeptical, arguments on this major critical point harder to get around than Alter does. The lack of an inclusive word in biblical Hebrew for "poem" or "poetry" seems especially telling. Though the Bible has, and names, many recognizable genres (hymns, prayers, curses, proverbs, blessings, genealogies, laws, etc.), biblical Hebrew has no words that can be accurately translated with our words "poem" and "poetry." Our terms derive from Greek, and like the Greeks we include various genres—from lyric to epic and more—within the broad category "poem." So we should never forget that when we use the words "poem," "poetry," and especially "poet," we are applying terms and concepts apparently quite foreign to the language, tradition, and culture that produced the Hebrew Bible.

---

27. Royal Skousen, *The Book of Mormon: The Earliest Text* (New Haven: Yale University Press, 2009), 413–14.

28. James L. Kugel, *The Idea of Biblical Poetry: Parallelism and Its History* (Baltimore: Johns Hopkins University Press, 1981), 76.

29. Alter, *The Art of Biblical Poetry*, 4.

Still, from ancient times to the present, many biblical texts, especially the psalms, have been regarded as "poems," and Jewish and Christian interpreters have attempted to elucidate the "system" of "Hebrew poetry" as something analogous to the more or less regular metrical and strophic patterns used in western cultures from the Greeks and Romans on down. And down to our own time, what almost no one seems inclined to dispute is that something we can call (since the English Bishop Robert Lowth's "discovery" in the mid-eighteenth century) "parallelism"—or something like it—is the first thing to attend to. But what does "parallel" mean, and what aspects of the language in a passage may be said to be "parallel"?

Lowth in his *De sacra poesi Hebraeorum* (1753) called it *parallelismus membrorum*, parallelism of the "members" or clauses; yet in many cases the parallel "members" are less than full clauses (sometimes, for instance, a full clause subjoined by a second predicate or complement, with a subject or subject and verb doing duty for both). James Kugel begins by saying that "the basic feature of biblical songs . . . is the recurrent use of a relatively short sentence-form that consists of two brief clauses" with a "slight pause" between and a "full pause" at the end.[30] He notes that "here and there ternary sentences . . . also occur, but the binary form is definitely the rule in Hebrew and ternary the exception."[31]

Lowth offered three categories of "parallelism": "synonymous," "antithetical," and "synthetic." Kugel, for one, argues persuasively that synonymous parallels are almost never synonymous, antithetical is "a distinction without a difference," and synthetic is a "catchall."[32] Since Lowth the categories have been subdivided and supplemented and multiplied, but all that taxonomic ingenuity seems mostly wasted. Fokkelman basically repeats Kugel's arguments, and calls Lowth's third category, the "synthetic" or "complementary," a "basket term" and "a counsel of despair."[33] "In the end," Kugel writes, "the most significant long-term result of Lowth's presentation has been the equation of 'parallelism' with poetry." And he regards the continued discovery of poetic fragments in the prose books of the Hebrew Bible as "right and . . . wrong, for the whole notion of biblical poetry is both right and wrong."[34]

30. Kugel, *The Idea of Biblical Poetry*, 1.
31. Ibid.
32. Ibid., 12–13; cf. 57–58.
33. Fokkelman, *Reading Biblical Poetry*, 26.
34. Kugel, *The Idea of Biblical Poetry*, 286.

This is not an easy conclusion to feel comfortable with, yet it seems hard to avoid. And perhaps, if we once accept Kugel's central claim that "Biblical parallelism is of one sort, 'A, and what's more, B,' or a hundred sorts; but it is not three,"[35] we can settle down to read sentence by sentence, line upon line, and thus begin at least, whether it suits our notions or not, to discern and display the artistry and the meanings that are there.

The single most useful thing I've learned, so far, toward reading biblical poems, and thus toward discerning poems in the Book of Mormon, is Kugel's simple, just-mentioned formula, "A is so, and what's more, B." That is, this kind of biblical text is (mostly) based on a two-part (or much less often three-part) sentence form consisting of a first part, A, then a slight pause, then a second part, B, then a full pause. Kugel represents this sentence form as

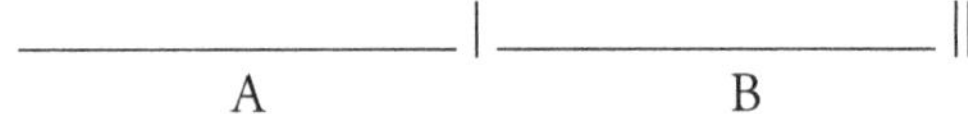

where A and B are often, but not always, full clauses, and where the slight and full pauses indicated by | and || , respectively, function somewhat like commas (or semicolons) and periods. Kugel generally refers to these clauses or "members" as A and B (using C when a three-part sentence calls for it). Diverging from Lowth and his successors, Kugel stresses that because B follows A, it is both broken from A and (in one way or another) continues or "seconds" A; B is "subjoined" to A, and thus always adds something to A. What Kugel and Alter and Fokkelman do at their best is to help me (and, I would think, anyone who spends time with them) hear how a reader of Psalms or Job or Proverbs or the prophets can track the dynamic movements from A to B (and sometimes to C) through longer series of these biblical sentences that, however wary we should be of our term, do seem to compose something like what we call "poems."

Reading One Poem in the Book of Mormon

Poems in the Book of Mormon have received far less attention than doctrinal and narrative content, and (outside the frequently discussed "Psalm of Nephi" in 2 Nephi 4:15b–35) even less close reading (the best I know is Steven Sondrup's "Lyric Reading" of the Psalm of Nephi).[36] One large recent

35. Ibid., 58.

36. See Steven P. Sondrup, "The Psalm of Nephi: A Lyric Reading," *BYU Studies* 21, no. 3 (Summer 1981): 357–72.

exception, R. Dilworth Rust's lengthy chapter 4, "By the Spirit of Prophecy," in his *Feasting on the Word*, ranges over at least a score of examples with helpful lineations.[37] Yet even Rust's perceptive discussion seldom attempts really close reading. The present verse-division and two-column prose format of the Book of Mormon have naturally obscured many occasional poetic passages, though the first edition's long chapters and paragraphs would have obscured just as many or more. Still, a reader, especially reading aloud, may occasionally strike a few sentences or verses in the Book of Mormon that, in their cadenced syntactical and semantic parallelism, sound startlingly like the Hebraic poetry of Psalms, Proverbs, Job, or the Prophets.

So I hear these three verses, printed as prose, as a small poem (I should mention that I'm using the 1981 LDS edition, and that Skousen's *Earliest Text* differs substantively at a few points and amends the 1830 typesetter John Gilbert's punctuation):

> 35 O remember, my son, and learn wisdom in thy youth; yea, learn in thy youth to keep the commandments of God.
> 36 Yea, and cry unto God for all thy support; yea, let all thy doings be unto the Lord, and whithersoever thou goest let it be in the Lord; yea, let all thy thoughts be directed unto the Lord; yea, let the affections of thy heart be placed upon the Lord forever.
> 37 Counsel with the Lord in all thy doings, and he will direct thee for good; yea, when thou liest down at night lie down unto the Lord, that he may watch over you in your sleep; and when thou risest in the morning let thy heart be full of thanks unto God; and if ye do these things, ye shall be lifted up at the last day. (Alma 37:35–37)

Verse-division here corresponds to sentence punctuation, though periods could replace any of the semicolons in the passage (as indeed Skousen does replace all but the first, as well as one comma, and as the first two periods here replace semicolons in the 1830 edition). Yet the prose format cannot entirely obscure the parallelistic rhythms of the clauses. And although some lines here are often used separately (e.g., the first two clauses of verse 37), it's also easy to sense these lines as a coherent unit of expression, of heartfelt and heart-thought exhortation, continuous with yet separable from what precedes and follows them.

I'm not the first or only reader to notice a poem here: I'd not read his chapter when I first discussed Alma 37:35–37 as a poem, but Rust also presents these verses as an instance of Book of Mormon poetry, "Alma's Instructions to Helaman," printing them in two strophes of seven and

---

37. Rust, *Feasting on the Word*, 65–100.

eight lines and italicizing some key words and phrases.[38] I want to give closer and more extended attention to what he remarks on very briefly (a dozen lines). And beyond that, I want to suggest that readers of the Book of Mormon might well have a richer and more memorable experience of its language and its religious insights if its poems were printed as poems (as Grant Hardy also prints these verses in his *Reader's Edition*, and as Skousen's "sense-lines" and line-spaced paragraphing let them appear)—at least if we learned to read them as poems.

These verses occur in Alma's "commandments" (or instructions, or charge) to his eldest son Helaman, who did not accompany Alma, Shiblon, and Corianton on the mission to the Zoramites, and specifically just after Alma has charged Helaman as his successor in keeping and continuing the Nephite records. Apparently Mormon includes these "commandments" to Helaman, as well as the briefer instruction to Shiblon and the much longer discourse to Corianton, at this point in his abridgement of Alma's record because this is where they occurred: after the Zoramite mission and just before a Lamanite invasion starts a long war. Mormon calls this "an account . . . according to [Alma's] own record" (35:16), which I take to indicate that chapters 36–42 are a (largely) verbatim transcript, or an insertion, of Alma's own writing into Mormon's abridgment.

It may strike a reader as odd that Alma says "in thy youth" to Helaman, who is his eldest son and perhaps a mature man with responsibilities that prevented him from leaving Zarahemla for the Zoramite mission. Alma's entrusting the records to Helaman (37:1–2) would also suggest Helaman's readiness for a sacred responsibility. Yet still Alma has said "thou art in thy youth" (36:3). "Youth" for Alma may be not so much a matter of age as of experience, of whether one has yet begun to "learn wisdom" (37:35). But the call to attention, "O remember, my son," also evokes the standard situation of ancient near-eastern wisdom poetry, in which a member of the older generation, a father (or at many points in Proverbs, the personified Lady Wisdom), addresses "my son," a "youth" of the younger generation. "Wisdom-poetry" itself is a modern category, though it usefully designates an identifiable "family" of texts in ancient near-eastern literature, including many texts in the Hebrew Bible.

Alma 37:35–37, then, comprises a "wisdom-poem" set into the midst of a (mainly) prose discourse. In fact these verses occur as a kind of hinge between Alma's discussion of the sacred records and his typological inter-

38. Ibid., 86–87.

pretation of the Liahona, which he is also entrusting to Helaman. It would be interesting and instructive to study the relations among these segments of chapter 37, but I want to concentrate only on the wisdom-poem itself.

To disclose the poetic (and even, it seems to me, rather musical) structure of this passage, I will re-set it in lines or "versets" (Benjamin Hrushovski's term, adopted by Alter and Fokkelman, who uses it alternately with "colon," plural "cola"[39]). My lineation differs from Hardy's and Rust's, and from Skousen's "sense-lines," at only a few points, the most salient being my assignment of the initial call to attention as a separate line. The near-congruence of our independent lineations suggests the relative stability and "legibility" of poetic form in this passage. I've set each "verset" as a separate line, but also grouped them in sets of two and three which would correspond to binary and ternary "lines" in Kugel's, Alter's, and Fokkelman's analyses of Biblical poems.

> O remember, my son,
>
> and learn wisdom in thy youth;
> yea, learn in thy youth to keep the commandments of God.
>
> Yea, and cry unto God for all thy support;
> yea, let all thy doings be unto the Lord,
> and whithersoever thou goest let it be in the Lord;
>
> yea, let all thy thoughts be directed unto the Lord;
> yea, let the affections of thy heart be placed upon the Lord forever.
>
> Counsel with the Lord in all thy doings,
> and he will direct thee for good;
>
> yea, when thou liest down at night
> lie down unto the Lord,
> that he may watch over you in your sleep;
>
> and when thou risest in the morning
> let thy heart be full of thanks unto God;
>
> and if ye do these things,
> ye shall be lifted up at the last day. (Alma 37:35–37)

It's generally not hard to recognize the parallel phrases or clauses of biblical "poems," and that is what we can hear in this passage, after the introductory call to attention, "O remember, my son." That call itself looks like a standard formula in wisdom-poetry; consider "My son, hear the

39. Benjamin Hrushovski, "Prosody, Hebrew." *Encyclopaedia Judaica* (New York: Macmillan, 1971), 16:595–623.

instruction of thy father" (Prov. 1:8), "My son, forget not my law" (3:1), "Hear, ye children, the instruction of a father" (4:1), "My son, attend unto my wisdom" (5:1), "My son, keep my words" (7:1), or Alma's own more expansive "And now, O my son Helaman . . . I beseech of thee that thou wilt hear my words and learn of me" (Alma 36:3). Alma's poem, in fact, seems to be an "instructional" expansion of his testimony in Alma 36:3b: "for I do know that whosoever shall put their trust in God shall be supported in their trials, and their troubles, and their afflictions, and shall be lifted up at the last day." James G. Williams, in his article on "Proverbs and Ecclesiastes" in *The Literary Guide to the Bible*, explains that one subcategory of wisdom-poetry is "instruction," characterized by imperative verbs,[40] which dominate these verses.

The parallel phrases or clauses or versets of biblical poems occur commonly in pairs, sometimes in threes, with the second (or second and third) verset continuing, amplifying, or focusing the first, sometimes reversing the order of its key terms ("chiasm"), as in the first pair here (I'll mark what I hear as primary stresses, to call attention to rhythmic parallels and differences, here the doubling, in terms of stress-count, of the amplifying clause):

> and leárn wísdom in thy yoúth;
> yéa, leárn in thy yoúth to keép the commándments of Gód.

This suggests either that wisdom *is* keeping the commandments, or that keeping the commandments is the *way* to learn wisdom, or that we need wisdom *in order to* keep the commandments, or perhaps all of the above.

In biblical poetry (particularly as Hrushovski, Alter, and Fokkelman read it), semantic and syntactic parallelism are often joined and reinforced by rhythmic parallelism, a balancing, or sometimes off-balancing, of stress-count, sometimes even syllable-count, between versets. Of course the rhythms of biblical Hebrew cannot exactly carry over in translation, yet English renderings of biblical poems often achieve something like this balance or off-balance with the stress-patterns of English. We have no access to the "original" language of the Book of Mormon (presumably a colonial dialect of biblical Hebrew, but any back-translations would be suspect as either speculative or biased); for all practical purposes, English is the original language of the Book of Mormon, an "origin" we cannot

---

40. James G. Williams, "Proverbs and Ecclesiastes," in *The Literary Guide to the Bible*, ed. Robert Alter and Frank Kermode (Cambridge: Belknap/Harvard University Press, 1978), 270.

go behind. So it makes some sense to attend to the English rhythms and sounds of poems in the Book of Mormon.

From the standpoint of rhythmic parallelism, Rust's lineation, taking "O remember, my son, and learn wisdom in thy youth" as the first verset, yielding two versets with six stresses each, makes better sense than my separation of the call to attention. Yet all the examples of the call that I quoted above from Proverbs are separate versets, each completed by a semantically and syntactically parallel verset. In both my lineation and Rust's, the second verset here approximates a very loose English iambic pentameter (with an initial spondee and three anapests). To my ear, most of the lines in Alma's poem sound nearly (and often exactly) iambic, with occasional notable departures from that norm.[41]

After Alma's opening line or lines, I think, we have a line (or set) of three versets, with the second and third again reversing the order of key terms in the first, and also urging habits of action that complement the petition recommended in the first:

> Yéa, and crý unto Gód for áll thy suppórt;
> yeá, let áll thy dóings bé untó the Lórd,
> and whíthersoéver thou góest lét it bé in the Lórd;

I hear these as one iambic pentameter and two hexameters; the first line begins with two reversed (trochaic) feet and ends with an anapest, the second is catalectic (lacking its initial unstressed syllable), and the third is not only longer but also loosened by three anapests. Notice how the sense of *unto* changes (along with a contextual shift in its stress-contour): it's one thing to "cry unto God," but something else to "let all thy doings be unto the Lord"; one petitions, the other offers or submits.

Then in the third, longest verset (lengthened by syntax and by syllable-count), *unto* is replaced by *in*. All three versets urge a complete reliance on, and dedication to, God (in whom, as Paul told the Athenians in Acts

41. This raises the interesting question of where Joseph Smith got his ear for iambic meter in English. My first hunch would be, from the verse prologue of Bunyan's *Pilgrim's Progress*, which is quite skillful, if homespun-sounding, iambic pentameter. But it's also the case that iambic meter in much early and modern English rests on an older Germanic stratum of accentual or strong-stress versification, normally four primary stresses per line, distributed as two per half-line and usually marked and linked by alliteration. Distribution of strong stresses in English also tends to be "isochronous," with roughly the same intervals of time between any two primary stresses. Stress markings other than the ones I offer here are possible without distorting "natural" speech rhythm; some that I've marked as primary might be marked as secondary.

17:28, "we live, and move, and have our being"): "all thy support," "all thy doings," "whithersoever thou goest." (James Kugel points out how the Hebrew *kol*, "all," often occurs in the second or B segment of a sentence as "one of the most characteristic ways that B is made to go beyond A," "a reinforcement" that "brings with it a feeling of inclusiveness";[42] but that normal pattern does not seem to govern the uses of "all" in these lines.)

Given the development here, which is underscored or expressed in the syntactic and rhythmic enlargement of that third verset, it's easy to notice a similar progression or intensification of focus as the next pair of parallel versets shifts inward from doings and goings, first to "thy thoughts" and then to "the affections of thy heart":

> yeá, let áll thy thóughts be dirécted untó the Lórd;
> yeá, lét the afféctions óf thy heárt be pláced upón the Lórd forévér.

Again the syntactic and syllabic and (thus necessarily) rhythmic expansion of the second, focusing or intensifying verset supports or indeed creates the emphasis; with nine stresses, it's half again the length of the first, and takes a noticeably longer breath to speak. The "affections of [the] heart," the moving powers of habit and action, are to be "placed upon the Lord forever": the unexpected post-positioned adverb *forever* (after four versets have ended with "God" or "the Lord") extends the categorial and spatial inclusiveness of the previous set of three versets into the dimension of human and divine temporality, perhaps with a subtle reminder that "the Lord" *is* "forever." ("Endless," as he declares in D&C 19:10, is one of his names.) The use of "forever" here might also recall its recurrence in the second verset of every line of Psalm 136 as part of an antiphonal refrain (though that psalm is regarded as post-exilic and, if so, would not have been available in Alma's literary tradition): "for his mercy endureth forever" (where the Hebrew *hesed* may also be rendered "kindness" and always implies, as Alter points out, "steadfast faithfulness").[43]

Next comes what Williams calls an "instruction proverb":[44] an imperative clause, "Counsel with the Lord in all thy doings," followed by an indicative clause of result or consequence, "and he will direct thee for good," in which the future tense "will direct" makes an implied conditional promise—*if* you counsel, he *will* direct. These versets (a trochaic pentam-

42. Kugel, *The Idea of Biblical Poetry*, 47–48.

43. Robert Alter, *The Book of Psalms: A Translation with Commentary* (New York: Norton, 2007), 469.

44. Williams, "Proverbs and Ecclesiastes," 270.

eter followed by a loose trimeter) also embed a chiasm: you "counsel with the Lord" / "he will direct thee." Perhaps it's worth noticing here that "for good," which (like "in all thy doings") stands outside the chiastic pattern to complete the sense of the verb *direct*, also stands in the end-position earlier occupied by "God" and "the Lord" and, just previously, "forever." For speakers of English the sound-resemblance—almost a pun—between "good" and "God" is inescapable (in Old English the words sound identical, and are spelled identically, though they diverge etymologically). And also, at least in English, "for good" may carry the sense of "forever" or "permanently."

The next line (or set) of versets, is also an instruction proverb in very similar form, and it also makes another move of focus or specification:

> yeá, when thou líest dówn at níght
> lie dówn untó the Lórd,
> that hé may wátch óver yoú in your sleép;

Perhaps I should treat this as two versets, as Rust and Hardy do, but to emphasize its syntax and its cumulative rhythm, and the chiastic pattern of its imperative and result clauses, I've given each clause a separate line (identical with Skousen's "sense-lines," though he adds a comma after the first): a tetrameter with a reversed first foot (not uncommon in English iambic lines), a regular trimeter, then a pentameter with dramatically reversed third and fourth feet. We move here from "all thy doings" to one kind of doing, and a largely passive kind at that: how we lie down at night, and what we may hope for if we "lie down unto the Lord"—that, when we are not awake or "watching," He will keep "watch over" us. (For English-speaking readers, this may recall the first couplet of the bedtime prayer that millions of English-speaking children used to learn, "Now I lay me down to sleep; / I pray the Lord my soul to keep," which appeared in the 1784 edition of the *New England Primer*. Though, having noticed that, I should perhaps also note that "unto the Lord," as it were, replaces "to sleep.")

The next line or verset-pair begins as a parallel to, and a sequential continuation from, this one, yet it lacks the result-clause. Here, a trochaic "counterpointed" rhythm set up in the first verset (iambic tetrameter with one hypermetrical syllable) by "risest" and "morning" plays through the second (pentameter) verset until its last foot returns to iambic:

> and whén thou rísest ín the mórning,
> lét thy heárt be fúll of thánks unto Gód;

Thanks, evidently, for God keeping "watch over you in your sleep," and that you do rise "in the morning" to a new day's light, God's first creation and earliest, most constant gift. This pair of lines, in fact, might also call to our minds that ancient poem of the days of creation itself, in Genesis 1, which reiterates "the evening and the morning." And noticing this, we might also notice how many of the imperatives in Alma's wisdom-poem echo (the English translation of) the Creator's first imperative too: "Let there be light."

But this admittedly faint echo of Genesis 1 is not all. For Alma appears to be working in—and strongly alluding to—a poetic tradition he inherits from the brass plates he is turning over to Helaman with this very discourse. The paired (and opposing) verbs *lie down* and *rise*—a merism which, like "high and low" or "heaven and earth" or "the evening and the morning," maps a totality by marking its extreme parts—occur together elsewhere in scripture only twice in Deuteronomy (unless we count a likely despairing echo of Deuteronomy in Job 7:4): in the *Shema Yisrael* (6:4–9) and in a later echo from it (11:13–21). "Hear, O Israel: the Lord our God is one Lord," it begins (the *shema* proper). And it includes the injunction that "these words, which I command thee this day, shall be in thine heart: And thou shalt teach them diligently unto thy children, and shalt talk of them when thou sittest in thine house, and when thou walkest by the way, and when thou liest down, and when thou risest up" (Deut. 6:6–7; cf. 11:19). These are two of the most important prayers in Judaism and in ancient Israel, the centerpiece of morning and evening prayer service, which parents would teach their children at bedtime. We may begin to guess what resonances Helaman could hear in his father's words.

I noted the apparent absence of a result-clause in this penultimate line, the absence of a parallel to "that he may watch over you in your sleep." But the result-clause in the last line of the text (another "instruction proverb" combining a conditional with a future indicative) does perform that function, even as it sums up the entire poem in a single encompassing conditional promise:

and íf ye dó these thíngs,
ye sháll be lífted úp at the lást dáy.

The final spondee here, stopping an otherwise steady iambic movement, gives emphatic closure to the whole poem. In the initial regular trimeter, "these things" must surely refer back not only to lying down and rising "unto the Lord," but to the entire series of imperatively commended habits and actions, after which, and as a gracious result of which, the son who "learn[s] wisdom in [his] youth" "shall be lifted up."

The language of this poem, compared to that of the best wisdom-poems in the Hebrew Bible, is generalized and abstract, almost entirely bare of concrete imagery or of the witty "sharpness" that marks the best of Proverbs.[45] Even lying down at night and rising in the morning are routine or generic actions—which may be partly Alma's point. If he knew some of the finest work in his poetic tradition, Alma might well have confessed, with Nephi (2 Ne. 33:1) and Moroni (Ether 12:23), his comparative "weakness in writing," his lack of the best poets' gifts for keen imagery and metaphoric wit. Still, he does exercise something like their skill with parallelistic structure and development. And in his "own record" he does show us how one kind of wisdom-poem might have arisen from, and been embedded in, the lived and recorded history of a particular father and son.

Ancient Hebrew wisdom-poetry is persistently concerned with actions and results, with, as Robert Alter puts it, "dynamic process moving toward some culmination."[46] In these lines constructed on ancient models and perhaps echoing the primal song of creation itself, Alma is instructing Helaman how to shape and conduct his life, from his "youth" (whatever age he is when he begins to "learn wisdom") to his "last day," when to rise in the morning will be to be "lifted up": a life lived in wisdom or in the learning of wisdom, which for Alma is a life lived "unto the Lord" and "in the Lord," will finally, "at the last day," be a life "lifted up" unto that same Lord, who was himself "lifted up" in order that he might "draw all men" unto him (John 12:32; cf. 3 Ne. 27:14).

---

45. Kugel, *The Idea of Biblical Poetry*, 11–12.

46. Robert Alter, "The Characteristics of Ancient Hebrew Poetry," in *The Literary Guide to the Bible*, ed. by Robert Alter and Frank Kermode (Cambridge: Belknap/Harvard University Press, 1978), 620.

SEVEN

"Seek Ye Earnestly the Best Gifts"

P. Jane Hafen

In my junior year at Brigham Young University, I was a member of the 46th ward. The ward had a number of traditions, including its own homecoming weekend when former ward members returned. One of the previous bishops, music professor Rendol Gibbons, had composed a fight song ("We Are the Members of the Fighting 46th") and had also composed a hymn with the words about spiritual gifts from the 46th section of the Doctrine and Covenants. Singing together, having a sense of origin or history, participating in church activities that invoked covenants, such as sacrament meetings and temple ordinances—all this gave us a sense of community. As young students our eyes were turned toward the future, our hopes and dreams were yet to be realized. We had a sense of belonging and confidence, and an indelible impression of Doctrine and Covenants section 46.

Joseph Smith received several revelations on March 7–8, 1831, in Kirtland, Ohio, revelations that are now sections 45–49 of the Doctrine and Covenants. The heading to section 45 explains that these revelations responded to false reports circulating in the area. These sections clarify the role of and relationship with Jesus Christ and discuss the Second Coming (45); announce the appointment of John Whitmer as scribe (47); direct obtaining property (48); and refute some Shaker beliefs which convert Leman Copley had not forsaken (49). Section 49 also has the iconic statement that the "Lamanites shall blossom as the rose" (verse 24).

For its part, section 46 gives general directions about conducting meetings and defines the participants in such meetings. This revelation comes early in the history of the Church when some fundamental ideas and practices were being revealed and developed. Moreover, Mark Lyman Staker outlines a cultural setting where prior to the "Mormonite" takeover of the Kirtland area, members of Christian congregations experienced "ecstatic manifestations" of the Spirit and "enthusiasm consist[ing] of impulses, feeling and a variety of physical manifestations expressed in the body through the Holy Spirit."[1] Thus, section 46 additionally lists the gifts of the Spirit and adds the crucial element of priesthood authority in discerning those gifts: "And unto the bishop of the church, and unto such as God shall appoint and ordain to watch over the church and to be elders unto the church, are to have it given unto them to discern all those gifts lest there shall be any among you professing and yet be not of God" (D&C 46:27). This priesthood authority was important in establishing the young, restored Church.

In reading scripture—and this text in particular—I am myself concerned more with how the revelation establishes community in diversity and among people with disparate spiritual gifts than with merely historical questions. Helpful in highlighting this theme, as I will show, is the constant recurrence of the word "profit" in this revelation. Moreover, as I will also show, these themes are concretized in the actual work of teaching—of teaching section 46, for instance. After discussing these themes and by way of conclusion, I will turn to the question of how section 46 addresses epistemological questions about knowledge and belief. At that point, I will say more about what it means to read scripture, and, in particular, say something more about the personal connection I feel with this section.

Community and Diversity

The first verses of section 46 are about the meetings of the Saints. As pointed out in the dated but still useful commentary by Smith and Sjodahl, this revelation answers a concern about who should be allowed to attend public meetings.[2] Verse 3 summarily commands "never to cast any one out." In sacrament meetings, all are to be included "who are earnestly seeking the kingdom." The only restrictions on this injunction are not a matter of who can attend, but of ensuring that someone who has "trespassed" should not "partake [of the sacrament] until he makes reconciliation" (v. 4).

---

1. Mark Lyman Staker, *Hearken, O Ye People: The Historical Setting of Joseph Smith's Ohio Revelations* (Salt Lake City: Greg Kofford Books, 2009), 12.

2. Hyrum M. Smith and Janne M. Sjodahl, *Doctrine and Covenants, Containing Revelations Given to Joseph Smith, Jr., the Prophet, with an Introduction and Historical and Exegetical Notes*, rev. ed. (Salt Lake City: Deseret Book, 1972), 271.

The revelation also instructs that meetings should be directed by the Spirit. James Faulconer makes the following observation:

> Verses 2–8 do not form a chiasm, but they do form a related rhetorical form, "inclusion," in which there is a sandwich of material, beginning and ending with parallel themes or phrases and the filling of the sandwich between them:
>
> a Verse 2: Conduct meetings by the Spirit.
> b Verses 3–6: No one should be excluded from your public meetings.
> a' Verses 7–8: Ask God in all things.[3]

Faulconer then asks: "What is the point of this inclusion?" The rhetorical enveloping of "inclusion" parallels the content of the verses with its focus on inclusion in community. Directed by the Holy Ghost (the Spirit) and by God, as outlined in the text, no one is to be excluded; all are as one. The scriptures are replete with instructions regarding oneness. For example, Paul taught "one Lord, one faith, one baptism" (Eph. 4:5), and Alma taught that "there should be no contention one with another, but that they should look forward with one eye, having one faith and one baptism, having their hearts knit together in unity and in love one towards another" (Mosiah 18:21). (Indeed, under "Unity" in the topical guide there are nearly fifty scriptural references.)

My question, to which the answer may be obvious, is this: If we are one—if we are all alike who come unto Christ, male and female, black and white, bond and free (see 2 Ne. 26:30)—in what ways are we different, and do such differences distract from the sense of community?

One answer, outlined by Victor Turner in *The Ritual Process*, is structuralist. Simply put, for a collective community or oneness to exist, hierarchy must be balanced by liminality:

> Communitas has an existential quality; it involves the whole man in relationship to other whole men. . . . Communitas breaks through the interstices of culture, in liminality; at the edges of structure, in marginality; and from beneath structure, in inferiority. It is almost everywhere held to be sacred or "holy," possibly because it transgresses or dissolves the norms that govern structured or institutionalized relationships and is accompanied by periods of unexpected potency.[4]

---

3. James E. Faulconer, "Sunday School Lesson 15," Times and Seasons, April 3, 2005, http://timesandseasons.org/index.php/2005/04/sunday-school-lesson-15/ (accessed June 15, 2010).

4. Victor Turner, *The Ritual Process: Structure and Anti-structure* (Chicago: Aldine Publishing, 1969). Excerpted in *A Reader in the Anthropology of Religion*, ed. Michael Lembbek (Malden, Mass.: Blackwell, 2002), 372.

So that all are alike who come unto Christ, all partake of the communal, eucharistic body and blood of Christ. Under the hierarchy of priesthood authority, as sinners (liminals) we bind together through sacramental covenant, while nonetheless remaining distinct individuals. However, if we are truly all alike, one community without distinctions, how can we learn, serve, and meet the challenges of mortal existence? How can we love one another as a community when love faces challenges, when love requires occasionally—often, even—the most difficult gesture of the heart?

Section 46 answers these questions in two ways. First, in verse 7 the Lord instructs:

> But ye are commanded in all things to ask of God, who giveth liberally; and that which the Spirit testifies unto you even so I would that ye should do in all holiness of heart, walking uprightly before me, considering the end of your salvation, doing all things with prayer and thanksgiving, that ye may not be seduced by evil spirits, or doctrines of devils, or the commandments of men; for some are of men, and others of devils.

God knows our imperfections and knows that we must depend on him with "prayer and thanksgiving." If God gives (and forgives) me liberally, must not I also give and forgive? Second, these questions are answered by the enumeration of spiritual gifts, making up the bulk of section 46. Such gifts are also mentioned in 1 Corinthians 12:4–11 and Moroni 10:8–18. Pertinently, Paul avers in his letter to the Corinthians that "there are diversities of gifts, but the same Spirit" (1 Cor. 2:4), thus reiterating the idea that there are differences within union—anti-structure in diversity and unity in spirit. In turn, Moroni's listing of spiritual gifts follows the claim in Moroni 10:5 that "by the power of the Holy Ghost ye may know the truth of all things," a claim not unlike the admonition to follow the Spirit at the beginning of section 46. Coming then to the question of diversity and unity, Moroni says: "And again, I exhort you, my brethren, that ye deny not the gifts of God, for they are many; and they come from the same God. And there are different ways that these gifts are administered; but it is the same God who worketh all in all; and they are given by the manifestations of the Spirit of God unto men, to profit them" (Moro. 10:8).

The gifts are for a *single* purpose—to serve the community of Saints—yet the *diversity* of gifts is necessary to fulfill the Lord's purposes. What foreign-language missionary has not needed the gift of tongues or of interpretation?[5] And why are some called to be priesthood and auxiliary leaders while others are called to be clerks and secretaries? Why is this person a scout leader and that person an organist? I have learned that I do not have the gift of administration, although I might have other gifts that serve the needs of the whole. "And all these gifts come from God, for the benefit of the children of God" (D&C 46:26).

These themes appear from the opening admonition of section 46: "Hearken, O ye people of my church; for verily I say unto you that these things were spoken unto you for your profit and learning." As in many other sections of the Doctrine and Covenants, the initial address establishes the relationship between the speaker and the listeners. Instead of the more common "I am God and you are X" formula, section 46 opens with a more general address to the people from the author of the Church. If these details speak to questions of unity and diversity, however, I want to look now at the introduction here, right at the beginning of the revelation, of the word "profit," specifically in the connection it apparently makes to learning.

Indeed, the repetition of the word "profit" throughout section 46 marks an interesting metaphor for the sense of spiritual progress that can come through our meetings and our seeking out of spiritual gifts. Among others, Webster's 1828 dictionary provides the following definition for the word "profit":

> Any advantage; any accession of good from labor or exertion; an extensive signification, comprehending the acquisition of any thing valuable, corporeal or intellectual, temporal or spiritual. A person may derive profit from exercise, amusements, reading, study, meditation, social intercourse, religious instruction, &c. Every improvement or advance in knowledge is profit to a wise man.

This definition makes the connection between profit and learning or gaining knowledge and wisdom explicit. The subsequent instructions about meetings in the revelation tie to an earlier admonition that when the Saints were "assembled together," they were to "instruct and edify each other" (D&C 43:8).

The word "profit" occurs a second time in verse 12 when the text outlines the purpose of various spiritual gifts: "To some is given one, and to

5. I have offered a modern interpretation of the gift of tongues. However, at the time of this revelation, 1831, there were church meetings where members, in prayer for the missionaries who were in Missouri preaching to the Lamanites, would fall on the floor and speak in "Indian" dialects. See Staker, *Hearken, O Ye People*, 82.

some is given another, that all may be profited thereby." This mention of profit restates a point familiar by now, namely, that individual gifts are for the good of the whole community. Four verses later, after defining the spiritual gift of "diversities of operations," the reader is again told that "the manifestations of the Spirit may be given to every man to profit withal" (D&C 46:16). As before, talk of profit seems to be a reaffirmation that the gifts of the spirit are diverse, particular, individual, and for the good (or profit) of the whole body of Christ. Some verses later, the list of spiritual gifts concludes by noting that "unto some it may be given to have all those gifts, that there may be a head, in order that every member may be profited thereby" (v. 29). But even here, where one person has many or all of the gifts of the Spirit, the gifts are to bless others, and the focus is on community. This recognition echoes Christ's admonition that the greatest is the one who serves—as well as Turner's structuralist conception of community.

While profit is usually defined in economic—and therefore almost inevitably divisive—terms, here the community as a whole is blessed, profited, by spiritual gifts. Individual spiritual gifts are intended to bless others.

These themes play out at the weekly level in Gospel Doctrine classes. That is, to teach scripture to an adult class of varying backgrounds and interests is to embody the concerns of section 46, where each member of the community of saints has his or her own spiritual gifts. Each student brings unique understanding and experience to the text. When assigned to teach, I try to follow the admonition in Doctrine and Covenants section 42: "and these shall be their teachings, as they shall be directed by the Spirit. And the Spirit shall be given unto you by the prayer of faith; and if ye receive not the Spirit ye shall not teach" (vv. 13–14). Sometimes teaching by the Spirit requires junking all my preparation and following the class. Teaching requires listening and encouraging constructive discussion. The spiritual gift of teaching is a matter of knowing when to cut off, kindly, a rambling class member with an agenda, when to listen to instructive comments, when to encourage class members to ponder the topics of the lessons, when to bear witness of principles, when to bear personal testimony.

So how would I go about teaching this revelation? Generally, I start by considering the very basics: Who is speaking? In section 46, it is the Lord. Who is the intended audience? Members of the Church, and all potential converts. Where is it taking place? Kirtland, Ohio. What context is important? The Church has been organized less than a year. Are the meanings of the words what we assume them to be?

With section 46, I would continue with questions related to specific verses. For example, verse 8 reads: "Wherefore, beware lest ye are deceived; and that ye may not be deceived seek ye earnestly the best gifts, always remembering for what they are given." What are the "best gifts"? How does one seek them? Why is it important to be earnest? How can seeking the best gifts help us avoid being deceived? A possible answer regarding the purpose of the "best gifts" follows in verse 9: "For verily I say unto you they are given for the benefit of those who love me and keep all my commandments, and him that seeketh so to do; that all may be benefited that seek or that ask of me, that ask and not for a sign that they may consume it upon their lusts." But this only raises more questions. We understand the admonition to love the Lord and keep his commandments, so how does seeking the best gifts benefit those who follow those admonitions? And what is the Lord's warning?

After such questions, I would go through the list of gifts and ask the class members to define them. I will postpone discussion of verses 13 and 14 for now, but consider the following in verses 17–21:

> And again, verily I say unto you, to some is given, by the Spirit of God, the word of wisdom. To another is given the word of knowledge, that all may be taught to be wise and to have knowledge. And again, to some it is given to have faith to be healed; and to others it is given to have faith to heal. And again, to some is given the working of miracles.

The listing of these gifts leads back to an earlier question: How do we seek after the best gifts? We do not, each of us, have all of these gifts, but it should be remembered that they are for the benefit and profit of all. We may not, moreover, have a gift for the whole of our life but only when we need it to bless others—perhaps in conjunction with a church calling. Do we look for a gift without giving back or without using it for the benefit of others?

Questions continue to proliferate. The "word of wisdom" mentioned in verse 17 seems to mean something different here from what it means in section 89. The phrase is an articulation of wisdom. How can we be wise? Is this a gift we should seek? How can wisdom benefit others? Moreover, how is knowledge different from wisdom? I have advanced degrees, so certainly I must have knowledge and be learned. Yet, as Nephi says:

> O that cunning plan of the evil one! O the vainness, and the frailties, and the foolishness of men! When they are learned they think they are wise, and they hearken not unto the counsel of God, for they set it aside, supposing they know of themselves, wherefore, their wisdom is foolishness and it profiteth

> them not. And they shall perish. But to be learned is good if they hearken unto the counsels of God. (2 Ne. 9:28–29)

And there is that idea of profit again, accompanied by an admonition to follow God. Knowledge, which begins the list of spiritual gifts, is reiterated in the context of wisdom.

Next comes talk of healing. Should we seek healing for wounds we feel? Having a chip on my shoulder is so much easier, after all. Do we have the faith to accept the healing love of Christ? And what is sin? Can my own experiences help others heal? And, then, what is a miracle? Is the working of miracles a gift we should seek? In a teaching situation, these questions would not be merely rhetorical, but would elicit answers from class members. I would also hope that class members who do not speak—as well as readers of this essay—would consider these questions.

The conclusion of the lesson would cover verses 28 and 30–32, all of which invoke the Spirit of the Lord:

> And it shall come to pass that he that asketh in Spirit shall receive in Spirit. . . . He that asketh in the Spirit asketh according to the will of God; wherefore it is done even as he asketh. And again, I say unto you, all things must be done in the name of Christ, whatsoever you do in the Spirit; and ye must give thanks unto God in the Spirit for whatsoever blessing ye are blessed with.

I read these verses as saying that we should submit ourselves to the will of God, do things for his purpose, and give thanks in the Spirit. If we do these things we will be blessed to become part of God's community (referring back to the beginning of the revelation). We will receive gifts of the Spirit to bless or benefit others, and as we benefit others the Lord will continue to bless us.

Likening the Scriptures unto Ourselves

Such are the communal themes of the revelation, both in the abstract and—hopefully—in the concrete. I want now to discuss how the verses in section 46 have impacted me personally, to offer some personal observations about reading scriptures.

Reading scriptures critically can be a challenge for me. As a Taos Pueblo American Indian, I am troubled by historicity and racial implications in the Book of Mormon. I do not want to be classed as a lazy or evil Lamanite. In conversations with Native colleagues, I have been asked if my skin is getting whiter or if I am blossoming like a rose. I have been reminded that for non-believers, the Book of Mormon seems a "fantasy origin myth" imposed on indigenous peoples of this hemisphere and is another manifestation of colonialism. Culturally, most indigenous communities have linguistic terms for people who do not fall into the pattern of heteronormativity, and those terms are often imbued with sacredness. For example, the Zuni have *lhamana*, the Navajo use *nádleehí*, the Lakota *winktje*, and so on. My tribe's language, Tiwa, uses *lhunide*. The closest English term is "Two-Spirit." Rather than focus on those difficulties, I have written in another essay about the affirmation of my personal experiences and my tribal background.[6] I have learned to live with paradox and cognitive dissonance.

Another difficult critical question is the silence of women in the standard works. I understand the historical privileging of male voices. Nevertheless, I appreciate instructors and writers who acknowledge this pattern and who are inclusive in their discussions. I anticipate meeting Sister Alma and hearing how she endured and encouraged her wayward son. However, because of scriptural traditions, I have to recognize that some historical language is gender specific, not gender neutral. In section 46, verses 11 and 16 state that "to every *man* is given a gift by the Spirit of God" and that "the manifestations of the Spirit may be given to every *man* to profit withal." I have to believe that every *woman* is also given a gift and that every person profits.

Despite these occasional obstacles, I find other critical applications useful in understanding the scriptures. As I tried to demonstrate earlier in this essay about section 46, I am interested in matters of definition of community and how diverse individuals create that community. In trying to follow Christ as a disciple, I look to favorite passages where all are alike unto God, where there are no "-ites"—such as the early chapters in Mosiah where we learn about ourselves and our relation to God and our responsibilities to others, or later in Mosiah where our commitment to bear one another's burdens and to comfort each other is explicit; also, where Christ says to love one another as he has loved us (John 15:12). My favorite story from the New Testament is when Christ meets the Samaritan woman at the well. She could not be more different from him and yet he treats her with compassion and love.

---

6. See Jane Hafen, "The Being and Place of a Native American Mormon," in *A New Genesis: A Mormon Reader on Land and Community*, ed. Terry Tempest Williams, William B. Smart, and Gibbs M. Smith (Salt Lake City: Gibbs Smith Books, 1998), 35–41.

Because of a major turn of events in my life (more on that later), I now violate the "James Faulconer model" I used to follow. Faulconer says:

> I prefer to do my best to look to the scriptures themselves and let them teach me their doctrines. The meaning of the word *doctrine* is, after all, "teaching." In this approach, I seek to be taught by scriptures without knowing in advance what they will teach. Rather than beginning by implicitly (or even explicitly) knowing what I will find—by assuming the doctrinal content of the scriptures—I hope to allow the scriptures to teach me.[7]

For my part, I now find I look for familiar texts where I know I will find consolation and affirmation—those scriptures that will strengthen my tenuous hold on my faith. I am not a linguist, so I do not look for original language translations or etymology of particular words in my personal reading. I confess to liking the biblical commentary of Robert Alter, but generally I do not consult outside sources. I prefer the Book of Mormon, so I cannot turn to verifiable cultural and linguistic context beyond Webster's 1828 dictionary. Call me a New Critic who stays with the primary text, but I also feel compelled to "liken all scripture unto [myself], that it might be for [my] profit and learning" (1 Ne. 19:23).

In preparation for this essay, I consulted with a number of people about how they read scripture. I spoke to Mormons and non-Mormons, academics and non-academics. With the smallness of my admittedly statistically unrepresentative examples, I found that a surprising number do not regularly read scripture. Some read prayerfully, some read topically, none reads commentaries (although one non-Mormon reads a scripture guide prepared by clergy). In considering why members of the Mormon Church in particular may not read academically or consult commentaries, I am brought back to the origin of our faith and the model of Joseph Smith reading the Bible independently and alone: "If any of you lack wisdom, let him ask of God, that giveth to all men liberally, and upbraideth not; and it shall be given him. But let him ask in faith, nothing wavering" (James 1:5–6). The foundation of our religion is that God personally answered Joseph's prayer. We believe in personal revelation, guidance and affirmation from the Holy Ghost, not the filtering of the gospel through institutions, translators, or rituals. Authority comes directly from God to Joseph Smith. Modern General Conference, moreover, including the talks I have looked at that discuss section 46, seems to aim to inspire rather

7. James E. Faulconer, *Romans 1: Notes & Reflections* (Provo, Utah: FARMS, 1999), xi.

than interpret. Gospel principles are explicated with anecdotes, personal stories, contemplations, and admonitions rather than with careful reading of scripture. (Of course there are exceptions, but the general topic of discourse in General Conference is far beyond the scope of this essay.)

I read scripture through the lens of my own experience. Nephi exhorts that to understand Isaiah we must "liken all scriptures unto us, that it might be for our profit and learning" (1 Ne. 19:23). (There is that phrase about profiting the community again!) I have faith that I will find personal understanding, affirmation, and hope as I read. When I started reading section 46 closely for this project, however, the "James Faulconer model" of being taught by scripture emerged unexpectedly. Rereading surprised me by teaching me what I had forgotten about the beginning of the section and the admonition for inclusion of all in sacrament meeting:

> Nevertheless ye are commanded never to cast any one out from your public meetings, which are held before the world. Ye are also commanded not to cast any one who belongeth to the church out of your sacrament meetings; nevertheless, if any have trespassed, let him not partake until he makes reconciliation. (D&C 46:3–4)

This inclusion is reiterated in verse five. The experience was immediately personalized for me because of my returned-missionary son who is homosexual and no longer attends sacrament meeting because he does not feel welcome. In his words, there is no place for him in the Church of Jesus Christ of Latter-day Saints. As I liken the scripture to my experience as his mother, I feel disjointed from the community. I acknowledge the gap between the recently-defined ideal—only chaste homosexuals being included in the gospel—and the reality of our practice.

Indeed, much of what I have discussed here and what I believed about community was shattered by my son's revelation. I have learned that there is a general antipathy—despite what Church leaders have said—toward homosexuality. Longtime friends became suddenly silent or inquired about our other children and obviously did not ask about our gay son. Certain church leaders were dismissive, misinformed, and even a beloved cousin made public and hurtful comments. I felt remorse over my own ignorance and over my son's lifetime in the Church where he was taught to loathe his orientation, his desires, and, ultimately, himself. Whatever feelings our son still carried for the Church as an institution were destroyed by the malevolent tone of the Proposition 8 campaign in California where he lives. How can we practice community in theory when the practice testifies to a range of attitudes, from compassion to intolerance and bigotry? I will not rehearse the Church's positions on homosexuality, but only observe how my own faith has been challenged, as has my comfort and complacency. My son's situation is not the only issue in my life, but it stands out and brings me into conflict with long-held beliefs. My son is gay and that will not change. He has his own story to tell. His circumstance, though, affects all in our family. Some wonderful friends and leaders have been constant and supportive with our family. More have not. I too have experienced the response of silence.

Throughout my discussion about reading scripture through the lens of my fractured faith, I have articulated *testimonio* as it is described by John Beverly in his essay "The Margin at the Center":

> The word *testimonio* translates literally as testimony, as in the act of testifying or bearing witness in a legal or religious sense. That connotation is important because it distinguishes *testimonio* from simply recorded participant narrative, as in the case of "oral history." In oral history it is the intentionality of the recorder—usually a social scientist—that is dominant, and the resulting text is in some sense "data." In *testimonio*, by contrast, it is the intentionality of the narrator that is paramount. The situation of narration in *testimonio* has to involve an urgency to communicate, a problem of repression, poverty, subalternity, imprisonment, struggle for survival, and so on, implicated in the act of narration itself.[8]

Because my experience falls outside the happy family narrative of Mormon culture, because there is a traumatic fissure between my Mormon traditions and my current experience, my faith has experienced a traumatic blow. The response of rejection or silence to *testimonio* is a failure to acknowledge and to confront very difficult issues without abstraction. And yet in discussions with other contributors to this collection, discussions that occurred as I prepared to write this essay, George Handley shared his experience of consolation in the temple regarding some of these same issues, as well as his thoughtful view of universal redemption through temple ordinances. Further, Claudia Bushman observed that "all political matters are personal," and in doing so she was reiterating Beverly's claim that *testimonio* "is an instance of . . . the personal [being] political."[9]

Reading and interpreting scripture through this personal lens is, because of my life situation, *testimonio*. I cannot think about community without considering who is truly excluded, without considering my own

8. John Beverly, "The Margin at the Center: On Testimonio (Testimonial Narrative)," *Modern Fiction Studies* 35.1 (Spring 1989): 14.

9. Ibid., 15.

position in the community, the ways I have been excluded, the ways I have been included, and the ways I am ignored or responded to with silence. In the twelve years since I have been aware of my son's homosexuality, I feel like I have transitioned from the gift of my own knowledge of the gospel of Jesus Christ to belief on the words of those who have that knowledge. I feel a rupture in the two spiritual gifts I neglected to discuss earlier: "To some it is given by the Holy Ghost to know that Jesus Christ is the Son of God, and that he was crucified for the sins of the world. To others it is given to believe on their words, that they also might have eternal life if they continue faithful" (D&C 46:13–14).

I have known many who have been blessed with this gift of knowledge. We hear the testimonies of apostles, like Elder Bruce R. McConkie in his famous and inspiring last testimony, or like President Thomas S. Monson who recently testified:

> Who was this "man of sorrows, . . . acquainted with grief"? Who is this "King of glory," this "Lord of lords"? He is our Master. He is our Savior. He is the Son of God. He is the Author of Our Salvation. He beckons, "Follow me." He instructs, "Go, and do thou likewise." He pleads, "Keep my commandments." Let us follow Him. Let us emulate His example. Let us obey His words. By so doing, we give to Him the divine gift of gratitude.[10]

The Brother of Jared, to take another example, had a "perfect knowledge" and "he could not be kept from within the veil; therefore he saw Jesus; and he did minister unto him" (Ether 3:20). In fast and testimony meetings, many bear witness of knowledge of the Savior. That expression of knowledge is part of the community of Saints and that is a blessing and gift of the Spirit.

However, Alma cautions us: "If a man [or woman] knoweth a thing [s]he hath no cause to believe, for [s]he knoweth it. . . . Faith is not to have a perfect knowledge of things; therefore if ye have faith ye hope for things which are not seen, which are true" (Alma 32:18, 21). Alma then relates the story of the seed of faith and how it requires constant nourishment and promises that "ye shall reap the rewards of your faith, and your diligence, and patience, and long-suffering, waiting for the tree to bring forth fruit unto you" (Alma 32:43). From these verses I would say faith seems more closely allied with belief and hope than with knowledge, as Mormon also tells us (see Moro. 7:42). Faith, as Alma illustrates in the

---

10. Thomas S. Monson, "The Divine Gift of Gratitude," http://www.lds.org/general-conference/2010/10/the-divine-gift-of-gratitude (accessed June 25, 2012).

story of the seed, requires action. It is not something that is static, like knowledge can be. I know certain facts that do not change—where I was born, the year and date, for instance. That factual knowledge is different from spiritual knowledge, which is a gift of the Holy Ghost. Discussing faith, Adam Miller has suggested that

> a stripping away of certainties may very well mark a decisive spiritual step forward. God is a master whittler and pruner. "Epistemological" pruning—which may feel like a step backwards—may be very much a step in the direction of deepened compassion and fidelity. And these things are what matter in the end.[11]

Losing the certainty of knowledge may actually lead to increased faith and faithfulness, and eternal life is promised to the faithful.

I feel like my life has moved from a personal faith of the Atonement of Jesus Christ to a belief and hope on the words of others—particularly on the words of my husband and on his faith in the sealing power of the temple. For years after my son's return from his mission, he and I would attend the temple together. We had some spiritual experiences there, for which I am grateful. However, when I attend the temple now, I hear its compulsory heteronormativity, and I hear my son's words about guilt and shame even though he had not acted on his homosexual desires. The temple is no longer a place of community for me. Quite frankly, my husband has more faith than I do that all will work out, that the sealing powers will transcend our limited understanding. I am left to believe on his words and his witness of the Holy Ghost.

I have been blessed with friends and sustained by their knowledge and their faith. When I used to think about the differences between knowledge and belief, I always assumed knowledge was better, that there was a hierarchical relationship between saying "I know" and "I believe." Through study and prayer, though, I have learned that faith is what leads to hope. Mormon states: "if a man [or woman] have faith [s]he must needs have hope for without faith there cannot be any hope" (Moro. 7:42). Reading the scriptures helps me find hope and belief.

I hope and believe my sins will be forgiven. I believe faith and hope lead to charity. I hope that the sealing powers in the temple will transcend my understanding. I believe Christ wants us to love everyone, regardless of our differences. I believe civil discourse is not only possible but necessary for us to love our neighbors. I hope my children know that I love them and

11. Adam S. Miller, email to Jane Hafen, November 2, 2010.

hope that they will forgive my shortcomings as a parent. I hope they will feel the Spirit in their lives. I hope my grandchildren will be safe and happy.

Verses 31–33 of section 46 have therefore become more meaningful and personal to me:

> And again, I say unto you, all things must be done in the name of Christ, whatsoever you do in the Spirit; and ye must give thanks unto God in the Spirit for whatsoever blessing ye are blessed with. And ye must practice virtue and holiness before me continually. Even so. Amen.

This reminds me to love my son. Despite the human unkindness of others, especially Church members, our whole family is part of the community of Saints and should not be excluded. My son has spiritual gifts that continue to bless others. I must seek the gifts of the Spirit so I may respond with love and patience to all. We all seek out our spiritual gifts so we may act on the Spirit and benefit others, so we may become one, meet together, and profit each other.

When I was young and singing the march song of the Fighting 46th, I knew life would have its challenges. I never anticipated that having a gay son would be my challenge as a member of the Church. Long gone are the days of fight song singing, youthful exuberance, and young faith in a covenant community. Gone are the simple beliefs. Here and now is my hope for a truly inclusive community of virtue and holiness, for spiritual gifts, and for eternal life. Those hopes, too, are spiritual gifts.

EIGHT

Records, Reading, and Writing in Doctrine and Covenants 128

Jenny Webb

A Brief Orientation

My purpose here is two-fold: to engage a scriptural text through reading (perhaps better put: through my own individual reading) and to reflect upon that engagement in order to consciously think through the underlying methodologies at work in my reading, with the ultimate goal of saying something about a possible Mormon scriptural theology. To begin, I offer a brief orientation regarding what I plan and hope to actually *do* as I read through the first half of Doctrine and Covenants 128.

1. I will begin with and strive to continually return to the text at hand, that is, Doctrine and Covenants 128. I will leave the text at times in pursuit of a particularly persuasive question, but the text itself will serve as the originary and orienting site around which my reading will pivot.
2. I will try to read carefully, thoughtfully, creatively, and faithfully. I do not believe that these are mutually exclusive goals. By faithfully, I mean both that I will strive to be faithful to the text and that in doing so I will also adhere in faithfulness to the doctrine presented therein.
3. I do not claim to read the text here completely, comprehensively, or in any manner that would serve to "exhaust" all possible meaning from the text. In dealing with a scriptural text, I believe we are dealing with an ongoing potentiality—a site for continuing revelation—and as such, any attempts to claim some type of interpretive mastery or textual totality would be problematic at best.

So that we all begin with the same understanding of the text, I offer the briefest of contextualizations. Doctrine and Covenants 128 was written by Joseph Smith in the form of a letter to the Saints while he was in hiding around Nauvoo during the late summer of 1842.[1] Its main theme is generally identified as baptism for the dead, although there certainly is (as we will see) additional thematic material of significance.

Reading Doctrine and Covenants 128

In considering this section, I have been struck time and again by the implicit ties between the themes of record keeping, ordinance, interpretation, and voice, all of which are generically related to questions of textuality. I had the feeling several times that Joseph was trying to lay out something as plainly as he could regarding these themes—trying to tell me how they are tied together, and why they are important—but that I was simply not hearing what he was saying. I'm sure we were both equally frustrated. Section 128 clearly deals with baptism for the dead, but I propose that we miss Joseph's intent if we stop there. Rather, I think that it is about baptism for the dead because that ordinance is an essential piece of a larger, incredibly beautiful, and important doctrine of the salvific relationship between our siblings and the Godhead, and the ways in which textuality witnesses that doctrine.

Joseph begins his letter with a very practical, even prosaic account telling us that he will "now resume the subject of the baptism for the dead," a subject he apparently cannot stop thinking about while he is apart from the saints and "pursued by [his] enemies" (v. 1). Verses 2–4 detail how said baptisms need to take place in front of an eye-witness who will then keep a record of the ordinance and that these recorders may then take their record to a general church recorder who will enter their records in a central record. Joseph then reassures us that copying and redistributing the original records in no way diminishes their truth, efficacy, or sanctity: "And

---

1. Section 128, along with section 127 (written the same week), were included in the original 1844 edition of the Doctrine and Covenants and were the only original inclusions not to conform to the more traditional revelatory format found throughout the rest of the text. That is, they were not revelations received and dictated by Joseph to another, but rather, they were letters intended for immediate and mass distribution to the Saints generally; their status as revelations is their self-identification as such within the letter form. Unless indicated otherwise, all shortened scriptural references in this chapter refer to verses in section 128.

when this is done on the general church book, the record shall be *just as holy*, and shall answer the ordinance *just the same* as if he had seen with his eyes and heard with his ears, and made a record of the same on the general church book" (v. 4; emphasis mine). There is also an interesting conflation between the record and the recorder here—the subject appears to shift seamlessly between the two, creating a sense both that the record itself has a witnessing voice and that the recorder himself is somewhat ontologically aligned with the record he produces.

After this detailed account, Joseph acknowledges that the preceding instructions might be "very particular," but then explains that they are so because they "answer to the will of God, by conforming to the ordinance and preparation that the Lord ordained and prepared before the foundation of the world, for the salvation of the dead who should die without a knowledge of the gospel" (v. 5). What is this "ordinance and preparation"? Its specific purpose is for salvation, but not for the salvation of everyone: it is for those who die without knowledge of the gospel. It is something that was initiated at a specific time and place. We do not know much regarding the time and place specified as "before the foundation of the world," but we do know that it was where at least portions of God's covenantal law were put in place (D&C 132:5), where God's love was felt (John 17:24), where people were chosen, foreordained, and ordained (Eph. 1:4; 1 Pet. 1:20; D&C 127:2), where Christ was prepared (Moses 5:57), and where the priesthood was found (Abr. 1:3). In locating this ordinance and preparation within this framework, Joseph thus radically recontextualizes these seemingly mundane details regarding record keeping—the work is not clerical, but sacral.

Given the stated topic under discussion (baptism for the dead), and the preceding reference to "the ordinance" in verse 4 (where it clearly refers in context to the ordinance of baptism for the dead), I think it is possible (and probably right) to read the "ordinance and preparation" as a specific reference to the ordinance of baptism for the dead. And, given its recontextualization, it is clear that this ordinance is not an afterthought, or a way to "make up" for a missed earthly experience, but rather something that has been fundamental to God's plan from the beginning in the sense that covenant, priesthood, and Christ are fundamental.

In verses 6–18, Joseph proceeds to expand and explain what, precisely, is at stake in this "ordinance and preparation." He does so by quoting scriptures that deal with the topic at hand and then providing his own interpretation.[2] He first turns to Revelation 20:12 and interprets it to mean that men are judged by the "records which are kept on the earth" while "the book of life is the record which is kept in heaven" (D&C 128:7). This arrangement is then called a "principle," and it is from this fundamental truth that Joseph will then extrapolate the logic behind the ordinance of baptism for the dead.

In order to explain baptism for the dead, Joseph first turns to its "nature." The innate quality of the ordinance "consists in the power of the priesthood" (v. 8). Note that "consists in" is a construction with a slightly different meaning from the more common "consists of": "consists in" means to have as an essential feature rather than to be composed of. Baptism for the dead *is* in an essential, intrinsic, and possibly even hereditary sense, "the power of the priesthood."

That power is first defined in terms of a binding and loosening that, while effected on earth, holds true in heaven. Joseph then provides what he terms "a different view of the translation": "whatsoever you record on earth shall be recorded in heaven, and whatsoever you do not record on earth shall not be recorded in heaven" (v. 8). It is this linking of "binding" with "recording"—of sealing with writing—that unites the images presented so far. The seemingly common act of keeping a record of an ordinance performed is, it appears, an essential part of the ordinance and an act of priesthood power. Or, read another way, the ordinance of baptism for the dead is itself a type of priesthood writing wherein the individual is "bound" to Christ as their name is written over and the name of Christ is "recorded" as their own. This writing goes beyond the mechanics of pen and paper; it is specifically an embodied writing wherein the *literal* submission of the flesh to guiding hands and created elements press upon the soul the saving name of Christ. There is a starkness here—a sense in

2. Throughout this section it appears that Joseph utilized a model of communication and instruction with which he was already familiar, albeit in the reverse. If we think about Moroni's visits alongside the other angelic visits and tutelage Joseph received through the years we can discern a pattern. From what we know, these visits often centered around the messenger bringing together various verses of scripture in order to teach Joseph a new reading, interpretation, or principle. Re-reading scripture as the model of divine communication already made sense to Joseph. When trying to communicate information about which he feels a similar sense of sanctity, Joseph turns, perhaps instinctively, to the very same model, i.e., the presentation and examination of a series of scriptural passages.

which our bodies, in ordinance, actually participate in the recording of the ordinance itself. This is, as Joseph asserts, "a very bold doctrine" (v. 9).

And yet, interestingly, the pen and paper (here a metaphor for whatever method of record-keeping is employed) cannot be left behind—Joseph continues to insist on the centrality of "books" and "the records which they have kept concerning their dead" (v. 8). Wherever the priesthood power has been given, "whatsoever those men did in authority, in the name of the Lord, and did it truly and faithfully, *and kept a proper and faithful record of the same,* it became a law on earth and in heaven" (v. 9; emphasis mine). The keeping of the record according to the order prescribed by God is as essential to a priesthood act as is the authority of the priesthood itself, as is acting in the name of the Lord, and as is proper form, order, intent, and faith. And the result is an addition to both earthly and heavenly law. In other words, a person authorized and acting accordingly can record law in heaven. Perhaps priesthood, writing, and ordinance are intertwined precisely because it is in this relationship that we, on earth, become like God, forming law for heaven and earth alike.

"This is a faithful saying. Who can hear it?" (v. 9).

Indeed. The doctrine of the power of the priesthood, which is the essential nature of the ordinance of baptism for the dead, is the teaching that we can become like God, authoring eternal law, effecting saving ordinances, inscribing Christ's name upon our siblings, and submitting to that inscription upon our own souls.

And then, in case we have not "heard it," Joseph starts the process of citation and interpretation again. He quotes Matthew 16:18–19 and then tells us that he is going to explain "the great and grand secret of the whole matter," which "consists in obtaining the powers of the Holy Priesthood" because with them "there is no difficulty in obtaining a knowledge of facts in relation to the salvation of the children of men" (v. 11). There is here a hint of the difficulty Joseph is facing in trying to write out his understanding: with/by the power of the priesthood, one may understand salvation completely and without difficulty, but there is no guarantee that this understanding can be shared with others. In fact, it would seem that this knowledge is of a type and intimacy that explicitly denies straightforward transmission.

There is a bit of a catch-22 here: knowledge comes with the priesthood, but the priesthood, it seems, only comes then to those without a full knowledge or understanding who have demonstrated faith and covenanted to accept the terms of salvation. For this reason, Joseph must instead return again and again to this pattern of quotation and interpretation, speaking through other texts, retranslating in an attempt to circle around this knowledge to the point that others may be brought to it through inspiration and the power of the priesthood.

Joseph gives it a good try in verse 12:

> Herein is glory and honor, and immortality and eternal life—The ordinance of baptism by water, to be immersed therein in order to answer to the likeness of the dead, that one principle might accord with the other; to be immersed in the water and come forth out of the water is in the likeness of the resurrection of the dead in coming forth out of their graves; hence, *this ordinance was instituted to form a relationship with the ordinance of baptism for the dead*, being in likeness of the dead. (Emphasis mine.)

Again, our expectations are reversed here. Baptism on earth was instituted in order to forge a link to the prior ordinance of baptism for the dead precisely because there needs to be accordance of form and record between heaven and earth (recalling, as we saw in verse 9, that to be like God is to create agreement between the heavenly and earthly spheres). Given the temporal train of our earthly experience, we expect baptism for the dead to be imitative of the earthly ordinance of baptism, but instead we find the reverse. What is the significance of this reversal?

If baptism for the dead is a foundational ordinance, then the framework within which we understand the plan of salvation is adjusted. The plan is not for everyone on earth to accept or reject the gospel. The plan is already for the majority to never receive the gospel, never receive Christ, live, be tested under those circumstances, die, and then wait. Wait for others—statistically insignificant others—to develop faith, receive the proper ordinances, continue faithfully, and then develop a desire to share what they have gained such that they begin to seek out the records of those who have died, find them, locate time to travel to a specific sacred site in which heaven and earth coincide through priesthood power and earthly record keeping, and then finally initiate the ordinance(s) through which the waiting dead are inscribed with the name of Christ.

If I may, what an odd plan!

We return again to the theme of accord between heaven and earth—the very physical qualities of submersion and the lowered baptismal font evoke the grave (interestingly, the resurrection is not mentioned here), "that which is earthly conforming to that which is heavenly" (v. 13). We are baptized, then, in part because the dead must be baptized. Our covenant at baptism is a covenant to be Christ's, to submit our bodies to the grave repeatedly on behalf of our brothers and sisters who cannot perform this work for themselves. We take Christ's name upon us not (only) for our own salvation, but to bring the powers of heaven down to earth, to work on earth so that the law may be written in heaven and those waiting may receive that which was promised to them by their Father at the foundation of the world.

Again, this accordance is tied to a parallel accordance in records. Joseph quotes 1 Corinthians 15:46–48, a somewhat complicated passage that regretfully I will not take up in its entirety here. In essence, Joseph sees the accordance between heavenly and earthly records as essential—even necessary—to salvation, and as a key of knowledge through which the kingdom is opened. Joseph interprets this passage to relate directly back to the prior discussion of record-keeping that initiated and sustains this letter: "And as are the records on the earth in relation to your dead, which are truly made out, so are the records in heaven. This, therefore, is the sealing and binding power" (v. 14). This summary seems like another repetition of what has been said before, but what exactly is the relation between our earthly records and our dead as detailed here? There are two types of earthly records implicit in this discussion: the records that allow us to discover our dead, and the records we make following the prescribed order regarding our dead and the ordinances they have received by proxy. The description"truly made out" seems to favor the second, in which case the relationship can be described in salvific terms: these records witness the ordinance of baptism for the dead, and in doing so participate in the creation of a link between heaven and earth through which one dead may receive the name of Christ. And, apparently, the records in heaven are the same because things have been executed precisely in order to align heaven and earth, bringing the two spheres into agreement regarding the salvation of a soul. Understanding this multi-sphered sealing power is, for Joseph, a key: it opens the kingdom through an opening of knowledge (see verse 14).

For that reason, I find the next sentence almost humorous in its understatement: "And now, my dearly beloved brethren and sisters, let me assure you that these are principles in relation to the dead and the living that cannot be lightly passed over, as pertaining to our salvation" (v. 15). It is almost as if Joseph is saying "I know I'm appearing to be a bit repetitive here, but I promise this is really important!" The reason, as he explains with 1 Corinthians 15:29, is that this sealing extends multi-laterally. The Saints' own salvation depends upon their understanding these principles and putting them into action. Once written over with the name of Christ on earth, one must live up to that name through the continual effort at the salvation of those already dead: "Their salvation is necessary and essential to our salvation" (v. 15). This subject—the salvation of those dead through the ordinance of baptism for the dead—is the "*most glorious* of all subjects belonging to the everlasting gospel" (v. 17; emphasis mine). In the past, I have not often paused to ponder this ordinance, but I believe Joseph is telling us that we should.

Verse 18 follows a quotation of Malachi 4:5–6 and provides a review of all the content covered so far, recontextualized by Malachi in terms of the necessity of "a welding link" between the generations. This is Joseph's final attempt to describe what is at stake in the relationship between the ordinance and the records. He does not read Malachi as saying that we will be condemned for neglecting something important. Rather, Joseph's expansion of Malachi's words relies on an understanding of an inter-generational necessity—the dead for the living equal to that of the living for the dead. "We without them cannot be made perfect; neither can they without us be made perfect" implies that the dead are necessary to our own salvation precisely because it is through them that we are ultimately and familially connected back to the original covenants and covenant makers. There is no use in integrating ourselves into a chain that stops, for the point of the chain, according to Joseph, is that "it is necessary in the ushering in of the dispensation of the fullness of times" and "that a whole and complete and perfect union, and welding together of dispensations, and keys, and powers, and glories should take place." We return back, and are welded to, Adam and Eve. The "dispensation of the fullness of times" is revelatory in nature, and one of its main revelations centers precisely around the "whole and complete and perfect union" that will "be revealed from the days of Adam even to the present time." We cannot be connected back to the beginning and to the promises of the fathers unless we have the unification and sealing found only in the power of the priesthood, in the ordinance of baptism for the dead. Our need for them, and them for us, is quite literal, embodied, and here recorded. The plan remains odd: it centers around the arising of relatively few dispensations or restorations, none of which comparatively grows to a great size, and then the subsequent linking of those dispensations through the ordinance of baptism for the dead.

The way in which Joseph frames his review of Malachi 4:5–6 in verse 18 is likewise significant. Responding to the text of Malachi, Joseph explains that he "might have rendered a plainer translation to this, but it is sufficiently plain to suit [his] purpose as it stands" (v. 18). And here Joseph subtly highlights his interpretive method: he has been responding to scriptural texts, providing interpretations that simultaneously may be read as translations of those texts. Not a word-for-word translation, but a translation through the key of knowledge provided by the power of the priesthood and its accompanying visions such that the scriptural text is transformed, recontextualized, re-read, reinterpreted, and even radicalized by the truth of the doctrine under discussion. I think it is significant that Joseph redirects our attention to his methodology at this crucial, summative point. Joseph has already let us know that he cannot necessarily speak plainly and directly regarding the things taught to him by the Spirit. His repeated attempts at elucidating the relationship between the ordinance of baptism for the dead, salvation, recording, and priesthood show this. But they also demonstrate another relationship under (silent) discussion: the relationship between scripture and voice.

Joseph has returned again and again to the scriptures, opening them with his own individual interpretive voice. He provides a pattern for the seeking and gaining of knowledge, and that pattern centers around reading and rewriting scripture. His methodological reminder at this juncture foregrounds the importance of the individual voice speaking in response to the voices of the dead.[3] Just as we are saved in conjunction with our dead, welded together against the potential cursing of the earth, we are saved together with our dead in our conversations with their words. The written scripture, Joseph reminds us, contains an imperfect impression of a once-living voice and as such, demands our own vocal response. The converted converse. They seek their dead, and they reanimate their words through their own witness received and testimony borne. And in doing so, they engage in a re-articulation that directs our attention once again to the relationship between writing and salvation.

* * *

I find it impossible at this point to go on without a brief, speculative break. In considering what Joseph presents to us here in section 128, I keep returning to the idea that the relationship among writing, ordinance,

3. This relationship between the individual voice and the multiple voices of the dead is a theme that Joseph had already encountered in a both a textual and personal way in his translation of 2 Nephi 27: "And it shall come to pass that the Lord God shall bring forth unto you the words of a book, and they shall be the words of them which have slumbered. . . . But the book shall be delivered unto a man, and he shall deliver the words of the book, which are the words of those who have slumbered in the dust" (vv. 6, 9).

priesthood, and salvation functions on multiple levels. And at one level, I find a highly symbolic, metaphoric image. We must write our name over with the name of Christ because he has already written his body over with ours: our corrupted, mortal, piercing names.

Why unite baptism for the dead with an emphasis on ordered record keeping? Why bring the grave to our remembrance, if not to recall that the grave has been overcome? The very act of recording, of writing down a name, an ordinance received and witnessed, parallels the resurrection in which we all hope. Letters—signs—are organized in an effort to re-present a living soul, and in doing so necessarily submit that soul to death. There is no way in which a word, a name, can capture the essence of a life. And yet, in the act of recording, that name is preserved against the losses of memory, time, and death. The writing of the name permits death, but it does so precisely with the hopeful knowledge that that name will be read again and enter into life. Only the written—only the dead—can be reborn through resurrection.

Christ tells us that he has written our selves upon his palms (see Isa. 49:16). His scars witness suffering and redemption; they are a physical source of hope pressing upon our souls—as are the eternal inscriptions we forge in our lives. Joseph lays out for us a plan in which we have the ability to seal the tear between heaven and earth if we so choose. In which we may write, record, inscribe, seal, bind, and weld, creating records that will witness on earth and in heaven the ordinances of salvation. We must write not only to create the record that accords with those in heaven, but to participate in a physical, embodied act that evokes death and creates the scarred, inscribed, witness. These eternal inscriptions, forged illogically in earthly circumstance, witness as do Christ's own palms the ordinances prepared from the foundation of the world. And in them we all, together, dead and living, waiting and distracted, have hope.

* * *

I would like to return to the text of section 128 and continue reading. There are some fantastic things that await, including Joseph's own witness of the returning, living voices of those once dead—the voices of the angels of the restoration—eternal, witnessing voices that intersect precisely with the earth itself and who are, in turn, the patriarchs of the dispensations to be welded together under discussion in verse 18. And I find it hard to resist Joseph's "Brethren, shall we not go on in so great a cause?" (v. 22)—in context, an invitation to participate in *the* cause under discussion: the performance and recording of ordinances for the salvation of the waiting dead and the bringing of heaven to earth as we become as God is, now, in our mortality.[4] And yet for the present purposes of this discussion, I believe it time to return to methodological considerations.

Reflections on a Mormon Scriptural Theology

What type of reading have I performed here? Mechanically, I have worked through a scriptural text fairly sequentially, closely considering various specific phrases as they arose while attempting to discern what they might be saying, at least in part. I have not examined the text line by line or word by word with exhaustive commentary on each, but rather through a sequential movement through the text, which has been countered by a vaguely fragmentary sensibility in which the textual specifics brought under consideration have been removed from their original structure and placed somewhat organically into the reading itself. I have tried to clear a space around the text. I have deliberately avoided bringing in traditional academic structures of explicit criticism and citation, although there are clearly modern critical and theoretical concerns that underlie the reading. I have tried to question what the text is saying in a faithful and responsible manner, and in so doing hopefully opened up the text to several of its multiple potential readings.

What I am left with after this exercise is a series of questions: Is this reading process useful when applied to a scriptural text? Is it productive? What do we mean when we say something is "useful" or "productive" with regard to reading scripture? Is there anything essentially "Mormon" in this reading, other than the text itself? In other words, is a Mormon scriptural theology concerned with Mormon texts or with a peculiar Mormon approach to scripture?

I have spent a considerable amount of time pondering what is meant by the phrase "Mormon scriptural theology" itself. Latter-day Saint doctrine is fairly clear on the point that the study of the scriptures will bring

4. Joseph realizes what he is asking, and knows that seeking such an end will necessitate the fire of trial and purification: "he shall sit as a refiner and purifier of silver, and he shall purify the sons of Levi, and purge them as gold and sliver, that they may offer unto the Lord an offering in righteousness. Let us, therefore, as a church and a people, and as Latter-day Saints, offer unto the Lord an offering in righteousness" (v. 24). The offering? It is, of course, "a book containing the records of our dead, which shall be worthy of all acceptation" to be presented "in his holy temple" (v. 24). For, after all we can do, what remains are our welding records to witness our Christ and his atoning, graceful gift.

one closer to God, helping one to understand his teachings and opening one to the inspiration and direction of the Holy Ghost. Thus, on its most basic level, any understanding of Mormon theology will necessarily involve an understanding of the scriptures as well. While at various times throughout its history Church leaders have advocated the study of a particular book of scripture,[5] as a whole, the leadership has tended to emphasize the importance of the act of scripture study itself, occasionally suggesting various ways in which said study might occur, but generally leaving the particulars to the individual members themselves.

There is, however, a common tendency or theme in the messages regarding the doctrinal importance of the scriptures in the lives of Church members: over and over, ecclesiastic leaders advocate a *daily* interaction with the scriptures.[6] I find the nuances underlying this particular emphasis intriguing. Members are *not* regularly asked to learn biblical languages, to study history, or to enroll in academic courses in order to study the scriptures. While these activities are not discouraged, they are explicitly not the doctrinal emphasis or impetus underlying the study of scripture for Latter-day Saints. In short, members are not asked to achieve any sort of measurable scholastic achievement or reach a specific level of mastery through their study of scripture. If this were the case (for example, if members were asked to study the New Testament writings of Paul in the original Greek), then a doctrinal emphasis on daily scripture study would not make any sense. While such discrete achievements are reached through study, this study could occur daily, weekly, or even monthly and still eventually reach the desired result. In a study of the scriptures oriented toward measurable achievement, the focus shifts away from frequency and toward finishing a

---

5. One well-known example is that of President Ezra Taft Benson whose 1986 discourse "The Book of Mormon: Keystone of Our Religion" asks members of the Church to pay greater attention to and express greater gratitude for the Book of Mormon through increased study of the book. Ezra Taft Benson, "The Book of Mormon—Keystone of Our Religion," http://www.lds.org/ensign/1986/11/the-book-of-mormon-keystone-of-our-religion?lang=eng (accessed July 6, 2012).

6. A quick perusal of the articles available on the Church website regarding scripture study confirms this assertion. For example, see Henry B. Eyring, "A Discussion on Scripture Study," http://www.lds.org/ensign/2005/07/a-discussion-on-scripture-study?lang=eng (accessed July 3, 2012); Julie B. Beck, "My Soul Delighteth in the Scriptures," http://www.lds.org/ensign/2004/05/my-soul-delighteth-in-the-scriptures?lang=eng (accessed July 3, 2012); and Dallin H. Oaks, "Scripture Reading and Revelation," http://www.lds.org/ensign/1995/01/scripture-reading-and-revelation?lang=eng (accessed July 3, 2012).

predetermined task. In such a scenario, the scriptures become merely the means to an end—in which a quantifiable goal is mastered—and thus are emptied of their spiritual potency. All this is not to say that goals such as reading Paul in the original Greek should be discouraged, but rather that, when scripture study occurs within a temporal paradigm emphasizing frequency over the measurable content of study, reaching such a goal does not in and of itself terminate one's relationship with scripture.

What I propose, then, is that the LDS doctrinal emphasis on daily scripture study serves an important purpose: that of universalizing scriptural texts. If the command from God, via his authorized representatives, is that one studies the scriptures, and if that command is consistently contextualized in terms of the frequency of that textual encounter (i.e., daily study), then it is now possible for anyone, anywhere, to perfectly keep that command.[7] In this very universality lies an essential ordinariness. To study the scriptures according to God's command is precisely something that is *not* singular, unique, or in any other way exceptional. To encounter the text of scripture via daily devotion is to repeat, day after day, the outward form of a common event. It is in this unremarkable repetition that we find the innate potential for the common and communing human experience. To be human is to participate in the shared language of the ordinary: we eat, we breathe, we defecate, we sleep, we wake, we thirst—and, in Mormon doctrine, we study the word of God.[8] We encounter God's word daily and in doing so we testify to the universality of his word and his love. In this scenario, what is essentially Mormon with regards to a scriptural theology is not the content of the texts, nor the method of study, but rather the actuality and ordinariness underlying the potential for a daily encounter with God.

Mormonism is consistently concerned with the fleshy reality of God's existence and, as such, repeatedly witnesses the overlap between the divine and the earthly. Joseph's first vision of God the Father and his son Jesus Christ inflects modern Mormonism with this witness: the divine is manifest here, now, on a corruptible and impure earth to sinners seeking truth. The final third of section 128 witnesses not the singularity of that First

7. Assuming literacy and access to the text, factors which are increasingly available in the current global community. While literacy and access to the text have historically limited access to scripture, it is important to recall that these thoughts concerning Mormon scriptural theology take place in the present sociohistorical context of the Information Age.

8. This same logic can, of course, be applied to other devotional aspects, such as prayer or church attendance.

Vision, but rather its function as a repeatable form that continues to reverberate down through our modernity. "What do we hear?" Joseph asks.

> Glad tidings from Cumorah! Moroni, an angel from heaven, declaring the fulfilment of the prophets—the book to be revealed. A voice of the Lord in the wilderness of Fayette. . . . The voice of Michael on the banks of the Susquehanna. . . . The voice of Peter, James, and John in the wilderness between Harmony . . . and Colesville. . . . And again, the voice of God in the chamber of old Father Whitmer in Fayette. . . . And the voice of Michael, the archangel; the voice of Gabriel, and of Raphael, and of divers angels, from Michael or Adam down to the present time. (D&C 128:19–20)

These multiple divine voices communicating (as Joseph is careful to point out with his specific geographical references) in the temporal plane witness the current availability (and perhaps as well the universality) of the word of God. While these encounters may seem extraordinary, the point I believe that Joseph wishes to convey is that they shouldn't be. My reading of section 128 asserts the realities of recording simultaneously on earth and in heaven. It promotes the idea that we can, now, in our current state, create records that bind together heaven and earth and seal souls to their salvation. While these acts and powers are holy, they are not, or should not be, uncommon. In order for the plan to work, in order for the baptism for the dead to be effected, these overlaps between heaven and earth should be, must be, daily, common, and in that sense, ordinary.

The records and writings of section 128 must eventually be universal—open and available to every human soul—in order for the plan to be completely fulfilled. Likewise, I believe that a Mormon scriptural theology advocates an ordinary universality underlying the encounter with the scriptural text. Why are we asked to study the scriptures daily? Not to reach some quantifiable goal. Rather, we are asked to participate in an act that assumes the real potential for a daily encounter with the divine. Daily, ordinary study clears a space for the actuality of the divine in our sinning yet striving lives. If the devotional goal of the practicing Latter-day Saint is to return to the presence of the Father and live throughout eternity within the sound of and obedient to his celestial voice, then it follows that part of that preparation lies in becoming accustomed to his words. If we fail to accept the ordinary act of his speaking into our lives—if we fail to become anxiously engaged by his recorded voice available here and now—then it seems no small stretch to imagine that we might also fail to hear him in the eternities.

NINE

Faith and the Ethics of Climate Change

George B. Handley

We can only be ethical in relation to something we can see, feel, understand, love, or otherwise have faith in.
–Aldo Leopold[1]

Developments in science and in our understanding of the world historically have posed new problems and questions for religious communities.[2] A test of the vitality of religious tradition is not only its ability to resist change that would be either unnecessary or even deleterious to human moral health but also its ability to be flexible, adaptive, and creative in response to emerging problems and concerns that demand innovative and proactive responses. In other words, scripture reading as an act of searching for deeper understanding of revealed truth neither can nor should take place in a cultural vacuum. We read from where and who we are, with the concerns of our day. And yet any reading that is merely and only motivated by ideology and a desire to extract ideas to confirm a pre-established worldview can hardly be described as an honest search for truth. I only mean to suggest that scripture reading requires a willingness to experiment with the word to see what fruit it bears in relation to our evolving understandings of the world.

This essay performs such an experiment in relation to the challenges posed by environmental degradation generally and global climate change

1. Aldo Leopold, *A Sand Country Almanac* (New York: Oxford University Press, 2001), 214.

2. A slightly different version of this paper appeared as George B. Handley, "Faith and the Ethics of Climate Change," *Dialogue: A Journal of Mormon Thought* 44, no. 2 (Summer 2011): 6–35.

more specifically. I will begin by exploring the environmental issues raised by contemporary science at some length in order to then turn to the text of the Book of Moses. I do not mean to suggest that an environmental reading provides an exhaustive account of the meaning of our restored accounts of the creation or that scripture should be subordinated to political or scientific concerns. Instead, my reading is a faithful attempt to see what fruit the restored account of the creation might bear in relation to one of the most pressing problems in the world today. I say "faithful" because it is a reading done in trust that latter-day revelations, as I hope to show, manifest their divine origins, in part, by proving their ongoing relevance to the chief concerns of our times.

Aldo Leopold expresses one of those concerns in my epigraph. The reach of environmental problems today urges us to consider more carefully how interdependent we are with one another and with the entirety of ecological processes across the globe. Environmental degradation has reached a scale that the otherwise forward-thinking conservationist Leopold had not yet imagined in 1949, making his call for a land ethic even more urgent. However, we can only see, feel, understand, love, or otherwise have faith in those things that our experiences, culture, and values have taught us are real—or at least that help stimulate our minds to imagine.

History shows that human communities often fail to think in global terms because it brings unwanted complexity, uncertainty, and responsibility. In religious communities, such attitudes end up compromising religion's universal and cosmological reach because believers forego the needed expansion of their imagined sphere of responsibility. Climate change tests our culture's capacity to imagine the remote and often unseen threads of interconnectivity that knit all human communities together and that make social and environmental concerns inseparable. This requirement, of course, means we need deep environmental awareness stimulated by direct experience as well as by a truly planetary imagination that acknowledges realities that lie beyond our lives. Moreover, climate change requires faith in our unique human capacity to live morally in the context of uncertainty that a newly expanded sense of community has created. What is needed, then, to cultivate an ethics adequate to the problems we face is a restored sense of what it means to be a human being in the broadest of biological contexts and a concomitant reinvigorated faith to consider the well-being of the entire human family and of the planet itself.

Learning to See the Unseen

As a complex phenomenon that implicates all human communities and that has begun to drive the climate globally, anthropogenic climate change is unprecedented in human history and unprecedented in the demand it makes of us to be answerable to unseen, complex, and global processes of degradation.[3] Although all religions attempt to imagine and explain the correlation between human behavior and climate conditions, earlier assumptions about the environmental manifestations of this relationship were often understood as local, not global. Moreover, climate changes that resulted from human behavior were traditionally directly attributed to God, not humankind.

And culturally speaking, human populations were not aware of the reach of the planet and its diversity of cultures and geographies until relatively recently in human history. Even today in the age of satellites, aeronautical travel, and world geography, the human mind's capacity to assimilate the diversity of the world's peoples and climates remains a major obstacle to global ethics. For example, it is not uncommon for people to gauge their reaction to climate change politics merely on the basis of their own local experience, even though this is scientifically absurd. Consider, for example, that the Intermountain West in 2010 experienced an unseasonably cool summer in the midst of the most scorching summer recorded globally since records have been kept.[4] While the bumper sticker adage adjures us to "Think globally. Act locally," our capacity to imagine the global often derives from and rarely extends beyond the conditions of local experience.

Thus, it is not surprising that climate change has been relatively easy to deny or ignore altogether as a problem. Even the kind of heightened

3. McKibben argues that climate change has transformed the very meaning of nature as something we once imagined to be outside of human history but which is now within it. Bill McKibben, *The End of Nature* (New York: Random House, 2006). For further reading about the causes, range, and impact of climate change, see Timothy Flannery, *The Weather Makers: How Man Is Changing the Climate and What It Means for Life on Earth* (New York: Grove Press, 2001).

4. According to the National Oceanic and Atmospheric Administration's (NOAA) National Climatic Data Center, 2010 tied for the hottest year on record. See "NOAA: 2010 Tied for Warmest Year on Record," http://www.noaanews.noaa.gov/stories2011/20110112_globalstats.html (accessed February 15, 2011); and "Summer 2010 Is Breaking Heat Records," http://www.grist.org/article/2010-08-17-summer-2010-is-breaking-heat-records-video/ (accessed October 15, 2010).

environmental awareness of one's home and region that Leopold hoped would stimulate a land ethic might not provide sufficient evidence or impetus to respond to the problems that climate change is causing. Modern life over the last 150 years has provided the means for a fortunate fraction of the world's population to enjoy an unprecedented level of comfort, with increased mobility, larger shelters of controlled climates, and an extraordinary diversity of foodstuffs available at the modern grocery store. These circumstances have had no small influence on the way its beneficiaries have come to see their lives compartmentally, as a distinct reality, sheltered from the ravages of nature and separated from the deprivations of the world's poor. The modern citizen of the developed world, in Leopold's terms, is able to see, feel, and touch the human-made world that is his or her home, but is perhaps less likely to have interest or faith in social, geographical, or ecological realities that lie beyond the reassuring appearance of the comforts modernity provides, especially when those realities challenge the perception that all is well.

The irony, of course, is that we are arguably more connected as a human family—affecting and being affected by communities across the globe—than at any point in human history, because the home economy has been globalized by industrialization, international trade, massification of production, and increased reliance on technology. Quality of life for any one individual, group, or nation has become inseparable from questions concerning the whole of the planet and the entirety of humanity. Moreover, because the modern way of life has compromised the atmosphere itself and thus destabilized the climate across the planet, it requires faith to believe in this complex web of interdependency that often seems invisible, intangible, or at least unreliably measurable.

Despite these narrowing tendencies in our ethics, globalization and climate change present a unique opportunity to resist the spiritually deadening effects of modernity and restore our values and faith to their original potency. If we are more capable of affecting large-scale damage to the planet, we are also called upon more than ever before to act collectively and on principle on behalf of the human family. Perhaps no Christian religion today offers a more direct scriptural account of the mandate to imagine our place in a world of unknown diversity. We read a direct condemnation of geographical chauvinism in the Book of Mormon when Christ chastises his Old World disciples for their "iniquity" in failing to understand that the "other sheep" not only included the Gentiles of the Old World but the millions of inhabitants of the New World who were at the time entirely unknown to the Old World (3 Ne. 15:15–24). If it seems unfair to describe a people's capacity to imagine the unknown as a form of "iniquity," consider what it means in our Information Age to fail to concern ourselves with the millions of the earth's poor who live in close proximity to vulnerable coastlines, in drought zones, and in other areas already dramatically affected by climate change. To imagine, even to insist, on ideological grounds that our consumption of natural resources cannot possibly be relevant to the well-being of others on the planet, ignores the very foundation of the law of consecration.[5] What kind of imagination is required to conceptualize problems of unseen complexity and to act responsibly in the face of the challenges they present? To answer this trenchant question, we must examine the roots of climate change skepticism.

Political Ideology as Obstacle to Faith

First, it is important to distinguish between principled and honest questioning and ideological and dogmatic denial. While the former is vital to the ongoing process of scientific discovery and of moral judgment and leads to dialogue, the latter is an enemy to learning and leads to self-confident mockery. Moreover, the latter position is motivated more by ideological and lifestyle preference than by deeply considered religious principles. Consider, for example, the profoundly irreligious confidence many have cultivated in progress and technology, which in turn inspires apathy or denial about the relationship between excess luxury and the plight of the poor, or between wasteful living and the often remote or delayed environmental consequences of our way of life. Inspired by philosopher Hannah Arendt, ethicist Michael Northcott has argued that environmental apathy is at its root caused by the fact that we "defer [our] capacities for moral and political deliberation to the autonomous procedures of the market" and to the promise of the next ad-

5. Of course, Doctrine and Covenants 104 makes it clear that this is indeed a form of iniquity. There is "enough and to spare," the Lord tells us, but He qualifies this promise: "It is expedient that I, the Lord, should make every man accountable, as a steward over earthly blessings, . . . [But] it must needs be done in mine own way. . . . Therefore, if any man shall take of the abundance which I have made, and impart not his portion, according to the law of my gospel, unto the poor and the needy, he shall, with the wicked, lift up his eyes in hell, being in torment" (D&C 104:17, 13, 16, 18).

vance in technology.[6] To the degree that we have ignored our responsibility to the world as a whole or have shrunk from the challenges such responsibility poses to our modern values and way of life, we have not only lost touch with the earth but also with religious principles; we have, in other words, preferred ideology to theology and the arm of flesh to the arm of God.

In a way, this attitude is understandable. The material benefits of industrialization are patently and tangibly obvious, while its environmental costs are often delayed or remote enough to deny or ignore, at least for those who enjoy its benefits. Indeed, the denial of the connection between the burning of fossil fuels and the warming of the planet has arguably been most adamant in the world's most developed nation and greatest producer of carbon in the atmosphere—the United States. Several authors have documented a devastating and long history in this country of obfuscating scientific fact in the interest of maintaining the economic status quo.[7] Addiction to the idea of unlimited growth without restraint, an idea that took firm grasp of the American mind following the devastations of the Great Depression and World War II, is nurtured today by think tanks devoted to fabricating reasonable doubt about climate change and other evidence of the consequences of growth. This doubt, however, has not taken root in the developing world where the consequences of climate change are patently obvious to populations whose sustainability is vulnerable to local shifts in climate patterns.

Just to sketch the vulnerability I'm talking about, consider that 60 percent of the world's population lives within 100 kilometers of the ocean. In Bangladesh alone, the population is 140 million, 120 million of whom live near or on waterways vulnerable to floods. The Intergovernmental Panel on Climate Change (IPCC) predicts that a mere 40 centimeter rise—likely in the next century due to global warming—will see an increase in the number of people worldwide whose lands will be annually flooded from 13 to 94 million, almost 60 million in South Asia alone. Further, 1.3 billion people live in areas affected by glacial retreat; they are likely to experience increased flooding at first and then increased water

6. Michael S. Northcott, *A Moral Climate: The Ethics of Climate Change* (Maryknoll, N.Y.: Orbis Books, 2007), 6.

7. See, for example—in addition to ibid., 18, 31, 158, 84—Naomi Oreskes and Eric Conway, *Merchants of Doubt: How a Handful of Scientists Obscured the Truth on Issues From Tobacco Smoke to Global Warming* (New York: Bloomsbury Press, 2010); and James Hoggan and Richard Littlemore, *Climate Cover-Up: The Crusade to Deny Global Warming* (Vancouver: Greystone Books, 2009).

shortages. About 50 million people will be subject to starvation with a 2.5 centigrade increase in temperature, which is a reasonable expectation by century's end if we do not make significant changes in our dependence on fossil fuels. An estimated 150,000 people are already dying every year due to climate change, not to mention the thousands who have been displaced by increased weather extremes.[8] The fact that the developed world is primarily responsible for the increase in carbon emissions, resulting in disproportionate suffering for the world's poor, has led many theologians and religious leaders to conclude that improving access to renewable and clean energy sources and reducing our carbon footprint have moral urgency.[9]

Of course, the claim to moral urgency falls apart if we can convince ourselves that climate change perhaps doesn't exist, that it's immeasurably slow and therefore harmless, that it would be too expensive to do anything about it, or at least that there is no definitively proven link between fossil fuels and climate change. Or does it?[10] If climate change at least suggests the need for more modest and conservative consumption of natural resources

---

8. For an LDS perspective on the impact of environmental degradation on the world's poor, see Gary Bryner, "Theology and Ecology: Religious Belief and Environmental Stewardship," *BYU Studies* 49, no. 3 (2010): 21–45; and James Mayfield, "Poverty, Population, and Environmental Ruin," in *New Genesis: A Mormon Reader on Land and Community*, ed. Terry Tempest Williams, William B. Smart, and Gibbs M. Smith (Layton, Utah: Gibbs Smith, 1998), 55–65.

9. This is the argument, for example, of Northcott, *A Moral Climate*. See also Lyndsay Mosely, ed., *Holy Ground: A Gathering of Voices on Caring for Creation* (San Francisco: Sierra Club Books, 2009); and, indispensably, Roger Gottlieb, *This Sacred Earth: Religion, Nature, Environment* (New York: Routledge, 1995).

10. Of course, the claim that fighting climate change is too expensive and will hurt the poor may very well be a principled and honest reason for skepticism, but if the hesitancy to move to action is based on the categorical denial of a link between consumption and the well-being of the rest of the world, such a position contradicts the fundamentals of Christian stewardship—especially as they are outlined in sections 104 and 49 of the Doctrine and Covenants. If the hesitation comes from a preference for small government, then genuine dialogue, not denial, about the best solutions should ensue. As Bryner has recently written: "Working out the details of political action requires compromise, patience, and time; environmental policies also tend to conflict with other pressing priorities. But our obligations to each other and to those who come after us cannot be discharged by our mere acceptance of worthy goals and true principles. Those obligations require that we plunge into the world of politics and work with others who may disagree with us on many issues in order to find common ground and workable solutions to the problems we face together." Bryner, "Theology and Ecology," 41.

and if it suggests the need for more creative and innovative use of all of the world's energy sources, then why the resistance to mitigation efforts?

If our addiction to fossil fuels is directly linked to what Thomas Friedman aptly calls "petrodictators" across the world and to increased political instability, why is it not a form of patriotism to embrace the opportunity to make the world safer, cleaner, and more sustainable?[11] A recent case in Kansas shows that people don't need a belief in climate change to be motivated to act in a way consistent with reducing the human carbon footprint. Instead, community leaders focused on "thrift, patriotism, spiritual conviction and economic prosperity" and thus motivated changes in behavior known to reduce contributions to greenhouse gases without saying a word about climate change.[12] In other words, much of what can be done to fight climate change is consistent with traditional Christian values of good stewardship and modest living. To the degree that we prefer to debate, yet again and ad nauseam, the comparative values of conservative and liberal approaches to governing instead of doing the hard work of living up to our environmental stewardship, we allow ideology to trump religious principle.[13]

Since the Kansas case reminds us that politically conservative values are not inconsistent with the theological principles of environmental stewardship, we might wonder what kind of theology we are using when we convince ourselves that the very possibility of something like anthropogenic climate change is absurd or of no concern. I can think of three main objections. First, some might say: "Worrying about human-caused climate change is absurd because we can always have confidence in unlimited growth and in the further development of technology as an answer to all of our environmental problems. Stop moralizing about the market or trying to move it in any particular direction." As indicated earlier, according to Michael Northcott, this is a symptom of a misplaced faith in the

---

11. Thomas Friedman, *Hot, Flat, and Crowded: Why We Need a Green Revolution and How It Can Renew America* (New York: Farrar, Straus, and Giroux, 2008), 23.

12. Leslie Kaufman, "In Kansas, Climate Skeptics Embrace Cleaner Energy," *New York Times*, October 18, 2010.

13. For an exploration of how directly political ideology is linked to attitudes about climate change, see Michael Hulme, *Why We Disagree about Climate Change: Understanding Controversy, Inaction, and Opportunity* (Cambridge, England: Cambridge University Press, 2009); and A. Leiserowitz, et al., *Global Warming's Six Americas, June 2010*, http://environment.yale.edu/climate/files/SixAmericasJune2010.pdf (accessed October 15, 2011).

superstructures of liberal democracies, which have "[given] up on deliberation over ends, or on what kinds of taking up with the world make for a good society. Technological modernization sustains the illusion that it is possible to create procedures and policies that ensure that such good ends as justice or prudence can be achieved *without the people being good*."[14]

This argument, in essence, claims that it is more important to advocate and live in unfettered freedom than to articulate and live up to responsibility. Not only do such attitudes ignore the many ways in which markets are already subject to incentives intended to maintain the status quo but they also give carte blanche to its consequences. It is hard to reconcile such confidence in an invisible mechanism of the economy with the consistent moral critique of the human economy offered by Old Testament prophets who repeatedly decry civilizations that ignore the creation or abandon the vulnerable and the poor. Indeed, if we allow the market to be free of moral restraint, we abdicate responsibilities to deliberate how or why the economy grows and what its impact on the poor and on the earth might be. We pretend that economics isn't about human choices and human consequences. In other words, we have imagined our fate and well-being as radically separate from the well-being of others, as if no conditions of interconnectivity brought us together as part of the same community.

A second, equally theologically specious kind of reasoning justifies inaction with a very different attitude. This reaction insists: "This is a problem of such complexity I can only throw up my arms and exonerate myself of any responsibility to do anything about it. God doesn't expect me to be worrying about global problems and will forgive me for ignoring something I couldn't have done much about anyway. It's not fair that driving my son to his soccer practices is somehow connected to the suffering of the world. Besides, to worry too much about it shows a lack of faith in God's plan. Who am I to doubt his purposes?" Indeed, I have heard some ask: "If the earth is going to die anyway, why should I bother taking care of it?" This apathy and insistence on inaction is akin to urging "eat, drink, and be merry for tomorrow we resurrect." It is utter nihilism offered in the name of religion.[15] Large, complex events have the feeling of inevitability about

14. Northcott, *A Moral Climate*, 115; emphasis mine.

15. I have criticized the absurdity of this kind of logic before, as have others. See Handley, "The Environmental Ethics of Mormon Belief," *BYU Studies* 40, no. 2 (Summer 2001): 187–211; and George Handley, Terry Ball, and Steven Peck, eds., *Stewardship and the Creation: LDS Perspectives on the Environment* (Provo, Utah: BYU Religious Studies Center, 2006).

them, but they do not obligate us to accept them, especially if it is apparent they harm the vulnerable. Jesus warned: “It must needs be that offences come; but woe to that man by whom the offence cometh!” (Matt. 18:7).

It takes faith to act on principle, even—and especially when—there is no tangible or immediate evidence that we are making a difference, which is to say that if we were collectively committed and proactively working to alleviate poverty and to care for the creation, our differing views of the proper role of government, or of the United Nations, Al Gore, and the IPCC, would not have the power to stop principled and faith-based action. Faith is relevant here because, if climate change proves to be false or vastly overstated as many skeptics hope, and if the current unanimous view of every major scientific organization in the world on anthropogenic climate change proves to be based on massive and widespread error, we will have at least acted on good principle. That’s a wager that seems far more religiously principled and far less reckless than the leap of faith it takes to actively dismiss every corroborating fact across the globe and across the wide spectrum of the sciences to retain dogmatic confidence that the theory of human-caused climate change is a colossal mistake.

I have also heard some say: “Why would God allow something like that to happen?” This is a bad application of a good theological question. Spontaneous abortions, sudden infant death, and birth defects happen, to name just three examples, and they are much more challenging to consider theologically, so it hardly seems rational to dismiss a *human-caused* problem on theological grounds. Some Mormons might wonder why the very technologies that allow the prophet to travel across the world or missionary work to go forward must now be considered harmful. The horse and buggy made progress possible in their own day, but now we have also seen the wisdom of no longer putting manure in our streets. The fact that fossil fuels still exist is not a theological mandate to continue to make use of them. While the abundance of cheap fossil fuels has made modern life possible, are there not also abundant supplies of geothermal energy, sunshine, and wind? Why are they also not considered God-given for our use?

What we should not be ashamed to admit—and what religion certainly can stand behind—is the idea that we need to repent of our excess consumption and our luxury uses of fossil fuels. Again, a comparison between the ideological and materialistic values that justify doing nothing and the Christian faith to live according to values of modest living, concern for the poor, and respect and care for the creation shows clearly that there is little room or need for dogmatic denial.

I have occasionally heard fellow LDS members wonder why, if climate change is such a big problem, we haven't heard more from Church leaders on the question. While the silence of the LDS Church on this question is perplexing, it would be looking beyond the mark to conclude that this means climate change is not a serious issue that should concern members. The Church made no formal announcement that we should worry about what was happening in Darfur, for example, but that was not an excuse to remain ignorant or indifferent. No statement was read over the pulpit when the Church acted on behalf of flood victims in Pakistan. What should be our inspiration is the fact that doctrines throughout the restored gospel point us to careful stewardship over natural resources and that the Church has taken revolutionary steps recently to green its architecture, putting it in the very vanguard of religious institutional action on behalf of climate change.[16] As modern revelation reminds us, "It is not meet that I [the Lord] should command in all things" (D&C 58:26).

I do not mean to suggest that it is our religious duty to believe that climate change is real and human-caused, but it *is* our duty to inform ourselves as honestly and as carefully as we can and to respect those who act out of deep concern for the issue. One of the first clues that religious-minded skeptics are allowing ideology and not religious principle to be their guide is how often they employ nouns such as "alarmist" and "extremist" to describe—and hence to dismiss, as if by definition—anyone crazy enough to believe that climate change is human-caused. If we insist that anthropogenic climate change can't be real simply because in our minds it can't be possible, we will never be in a position to assess data rationally. Moreover, if we can't make a reasonable distinction between an alarmist and a concerned citizen, then the charge of alarmism is meaningless.

It seems rational and within the realm of theologically defined responsibility to disagree about policy matters or about which end of the spectrum of possible outcomes is worth our greatest attention, but to dismiss the science outright because it conflicts with or presents complica-

---

16. Kristen Moulton, "LDS Church Shows Off its New 'Green' Prototype," *Salt Lake Tribune*, June 4, 2010, http://www.sltrib.com/sltrib/home/49478671-73/church-lds-meetinghouse-davies.html.csp (accessed June 6, 2010). An article that cites the LDS Church's advances in architecture in conjunction with the greening of Islamic architecture is Christina Koningisor, "The Ground Zero Mosque and the Greening of Faith," *The Atlantic*, August 24, 2010, http://www.theatlantic.com/national/archive/2010/08/the-ground-zero-mosque-and-the-greening-of-faith/61967/ (accessed October 15, 2010).

tions for a worldview that has largely been shaped by economic, partisan, or ideological values is neither religious nor ethical.

The Dialectic of Faith

Perhaps part of the problem in mustering faith sufficient to respond to global climate change is a fundamental misunderstanding of the nature of faith itself. Faith acquires meaning in a dialectic relationship to uncertainty. If we stipulate that climate change calls for a capacity to imagine the known world as part of a much broader whole that is not yet visible or accessible by direct experience but one that we are answerable to, then we might describe faith as a poetic capacity, one that allows us to see our place in the world humbly, as contingent upon a greater and as yet still unknown whole of interdependent relationships. Moral action similarly acquires meaning in a dialectic relationship to uncertainty and in the context of interdependence.

Moral action is, by definition, courageous because it is a genuinely free choice to take the risk of faith; it shows a willingness to act, even and especially when we don't have guarantees about the outcomes of our action, because we feel answerable to a broader, though not perfectly comprehended, set of relationships. As Leopold noted, "All ethics so far evolved rest upon a single premise: that the individual is a member of a community of interdependent parts."[17] This is one reason why religious faith is not only compatible with addressing a problem like climate change, but indispensable in doing so, since it is in the business of cultivating this kind of morality. Religious faith is no guarantee that we cannot be wrong about the world, as evidenced by Christ's chastisement of his Old World disciples, but this risk is not sufficient reason to dismiss religion's relevance or to categorize religion as the opiate of the deluded. It is not less religion that we need, but deeper and more careful consideration of our contingent understandings of the world which faith asks us to learn to live with.

To have faith is to inhabit that space between what we know and what we might know at some future point; it is not an expression of human certitude but an expression of trust in God's knowledge. It is to accept, as King Benjamin puts it simply, that "man doth not comprehend all the things which the Lord can comprehend" (Mosiah 4:9), which may be one reason why continual revelation is necessary. Similarly, novelist and

17. Leopold, *A Sand Country Almanac*, 203.

essayist Marilynne Robinson posits that religious faith cannot be reduced to a system of assertions about ultimate realities; instead it is a trust in an ultimacy that remains beyond our full cognitive grasp, but that nevertheless generates a rigorous rethinking, rereading, and reconsideration of our most basic impulses and assumptions. In an interview, she described faith as "trying to understand at a level that almost absents you from what you were trying to understand."[18] She further argues that, in its addiction to a secular and materialist confidence in progress, our civilization has lost such faith. Because of the seductions of modernity, civilization fails to value self-distrust, self-chastening, or confessions of ignorance, all of which are fundamental to religion. The result has been increasing levels of epistemological certainty about the nature of the world and of our humanity, what Stanley Fish calls "a naive and untenable positivism."[19] Religious faith can offer in the stead of radical certitude such principles and values as modesty, humility, mercy, justice, and stewardship that can guide us *meaningfully* through a complex and sometimes uncertain universe.

Jeremiads of moral certitude are, of course, not uncommon for environmental writers who see stakes so high that only a browbeating from a loin-clothed prophet will do. However, if environmentalism does not also have room for the kind of profound self-questioning that religion motivates, it closes the door on its own moral argument. Such problems

18. George Handley and Lance Larsen, "The Radiant Astonishment of Existence: Two Interviews with Marilynne Robinson, March 20, 2004, and February 9, 2007," *Literature and Belief*, 27 no. 2 (2007): 132.

19. In response to atheists who wrote in to his blog to criticize religion's intolerance for doubt and dissent, Fish wrote: "What religion are you talking about? The religions I know are about nothing but doubt and dissent, and the struggles of faith, the dark night of the soul, feelings of unworthiness, serial backsliding, the abyss of despair. Whether it is the book of Job, the Confessions of St. Augustine, Calvin's Institutes, Bunyan's 'Grace Abounding to The Chief of Sinners,' Kierkegaard's 'Fear and Trembling' and a thousand other texts, the religious life is depicted as one of aspiration within the conviction of frailty. The heart of that life . . . is not a set of propositions about the world (although there is some of that), but an orientation toward perfection by a being that is radically imperfect. . . . So to sum up, the epistemological critique of religion—it is an inferior way of knowing—is the flip side of a naive and untenable positivism. And the critique of religion's content—its cotton-candy fluff—is the product of incredible ignorance." Stanley Fish, "God Talk, Part 2," *New York Times*, May 17, 2009, http://opinionator.blogs.nytimes.com/2009/05/17/god-talk-part-2/ (accessed May 18, 2010).

as global warming or species extinction are moral issues precisely because there is a margin of uncertainty in what the science presents; they require the *risk* of judgment to determine and assess the comparative effects of our choices, which means that they also require us to rely on religious principles and values. If the picture is so clear that no judgment is required, then environmentalism is reduced to mere rhetorical battles about information and regulations and nothing more. We then encourage a perpetual circulation of the same wholly redundant information and diminish the chances for genuine learning.

When environmentalism is offered as a form of radical certainty about the world, it becomes just another form of "technology" that provides solutions to human problems through mechanized means, obviating the need for honest deliberation. This means that climate change can be rhetorically debunked with even the slightest hint of inconsistency or contradiction in the science. Such debunkings belie the fact that science is by nature a process of investigation; its findings are myriad and complex and must always be placed in a contingent context. If we demand that science provide radical certainty, there will never be enough evidence to motivate any change and we fall back on ideological preference.[20]

---

20. This was painfully evident in my home state of Utah where, in 2010, the state legislature passed an anti-climate-change bill crafted to discredit the entire scientific community as corrupted by ideology, greed, and deception. After insisting on the unreliability of science and the "inconclusive" findings of climate science, the bill's sponsor, Kirk Gibson, nevertheless disingenuously suggested that we should "let the science develop" lest we make "rash" decisions. At no point did the legislature offer a standard of scientific conclusiveness that would suffice for taking action, which is not surprising, of course, since the science is already overwhelmingly conclusive and corroborated across a diverse range of fields and upheld by every major national and international scientific society. For audio files of the floor debate and for the text of the bill, see "Climate Change Joint Resolution – Gibson, K," http://le.utah.gov/~2010/htmdoc/hbillhtm/HJR012.htm (accessed February10, 2010). For an editorial response, see Handley, "Legislators, Open Minds to Science," *Deseret News*, February 12, 2010, http://www.deseretnews.com/article/700008926/Legislators-open-minds-to-science.html (accessed February 12, 2010). For more on the visit of climate change skeptic, Christopher Monckton, to Utah and his influence on Utah climate change politics, see Barry Bickmore's blog, *Anti-Climate Change Extremism in Utah*, http://bbickmore.wordpress.com, (accessed February 10, 2011). For a full report on the saga, see Bud Ward, "BYU Earth Scientists Express Concerns Over State Legislature's Climate Efforts," http://www.yaleclimatemediaforum.

As a society, we are no longer in the habit of learning about and responding to new empirical realities, since information is increasingly mediated and disseminated by partisan factions. And if we have abdicated the responsibility to honestly investigate and deliberate about an issue by surrendering our thinking to packaged ideologies, we will be tempted to believe that we are already in possession of a complete picture, on one hand, or that we can never have enough information before we act, on the other. The inevitable result is a morass of uninformed inaction and angry certitude that compromises the health of democracy.

It is imperative to understand that ecosystems are not machines and human actions are not the equivalent of coins dropped in their slot to get our bag of chips. An inherently harmonious and knowable structure in nature was initially what ecology seemed to offer. Donald Worster has suggested that whereas ecology was "basically a study of equilibrium, harmony, and order" in its beginnings, now "it has become a study of disturbance, disharmony, and chaos." Initially, the notion of ecosystems suggested the idea of a "superorganism" and the promise of meaning and manageability if we could but learn to live in balance and cooperation with natural laws. But as we observe the operations of complexly interconnected systems, we are learning that "change is without any determinable direction and goes on forever, never reaching a point of stability." The world appears to be asking us to act in faith, without foreknowledge or the assurance of predictability. As Worster remarks, "If there is order in the universe—*and there will no longer be any science if all faith in order vanishes*—it is going to be much more difficult to locate and describe than we thought."[21]

Environmentalism and religious faith alike must avoid unwarranted certainty about an inevitable trajectory of increasing degradation for humanity. Because our knowledge is always evolving, we may never be ab-

---

org/2009/11/byu-earth-scientists-express-concerns (accessed February 15, 2011). In response to the bill, eighteen BYU scientists authored a letter to the legislature, not to argue for policy, but to criticize the legislature's willingness to craft policy on the basis of erroneous and misleading interpretations of what the science of climate change has found. See Barry Bickmore, et al, "To the Members of the Utah State Legislature," http://extras.mnginteractive.com/live/media/site297/2010/0204/20100204_024750_Legislature2.pdf (accessed February 15, 2011). Despite the letter and opposition from the public, the bill, which was largely symbolic, passed.

21. Donald Worster, "Nature and the Disorder of History," *Environmental History Review* 18 (Summer 1994): 3, 8, 15; emphasis mine.

solutely certain which actions restore the world and which actions ruin it. This caution does not mean that we should abandon the hard work of identifying the best course of action. Quite the contrary, it implies that working for a particularly desired end is, ultimately, an act of faith. Catholic ecotheologian John Haught has argued, for example, that understanding nature as "unfinished" and creation as ongoing and moving toward a promised future fulfillment and perfection with God, makes us answerable to its telos. "The cosmos itself," he writes, "is an installment of the future, and for that reason deserves neither neglect nor worship, but simply the kind of care proportionate to the treasuring of a promise."[22] Eschatology can be a form of trust in the lawful way of the world without becoming a justification for asserting that we are in full possession of such knowledge or in full control of the process. Excessive and ideologically driven confidence in destiny often inspires indifference in the face of the world's suffering. It does not require judgment or the hard work of moral risk-taking; it appeals only to the Panglossian mind that has grown tired of its own freedom and inspires acquiescence to the status quo.

Instead of offering faith as a dialectic that calls us to self-questioning and self-distrust and thus makes judgment a necessary risk, religion has sometimes seemed to offer the allure of radical certitude, even though this negates life's requirement for moral judgment. As I suggested earlier, the existence of a moral universe requires that choices matter despite outcome, and that judgment must be exercised even (or especially) if we are not in possession of complete information. The notions of salvation and of condemnation can help to motivate an ethic that pertains to here and now, but too often religion, particularly the more superficial conceptions of Christianity, can offer eschatological visions of the end of times that leave believers uninterested in the hard work of assuming responsibility for the direction of civilization.

In this way, religion has proven at times to be a major obstacle to good environmental behavior, but more hopefully, it has recently begun to provide powerful impetus for change. The sociological research on the role of religion in shaping environmental behavior remains mixed, however. Some studies suggest that there is a strong correlation between religious belief and anti-environmental sentiment. The Pew Forum on Religion and Public Life, for example, reports that 47 percent of all Americans believe global warming is real and human-caused. Fifty-eight percent of

22. John Haught, "Christianity and Ecology," in *This Sacred Earth: Religion, Nature, Environment*, ed. Roger Gottlieb (New York: Routledge, 1995), 279.

Americans who are unaffiliated with any religion, however, hold this belief. White mainline Protestants are on par with the national average, but black Protestants and white Evangelicals show a precipitous decline—a mere 39 percent and 34 percent respectively.

Despite these trends, we have seen a significant shift in rhetoric, tone, and attitude toward environmentalism within religious communities in recent years, with most religious communities showing some effort to improve institutional practice, religious leaders declaring the moral principles of sustainable living, and important and numerous publications, conferences, and forums in ecotheology.[23] While the record is still unclear about how much this official concern affects believers' practices and politics, signs seem to indicate an improvement. It is no longer the case, if it ever was, that environmentalists and believers represent two distinct groups.

It behooves us then to identify the kinds of stories, beliefs, and theologies in religious culture that can attend to the contingencies and chaos that lie at the heart of our current environmental crisis. As science has begun

23. Since the 1950s, the National Council of Churches (representing mainline Protestant and Orthodox churches in the United States) has issued 133 declarations urging action on pressing environmental issues. The World Council of Churches has urged since 1964 a "better developed theology of nature and man in relation to nature." Jewish synagogues across the country have organized more than 150 educational programs related to environmental stewardship. The Ecumenical Patriarch Bartholomew, symbolic leader of more than 250 million members of the Christian Orthodox Church, has been traveling across the world to decry environmental degradation. The Catholic Church has recently added environmental degradation as a "new sin," the Dalai Lama has called for a deeper respect for nature, the Islamic Foundation for Ecology and Environmental Sciences provides resources for mosques and Islamic education centers. In 1993, a professor of environmental studies at the University of Wisconsin founded the Evangelical Environmental Network, and more than a hundred evangelical leaders signed a declaration calling for better "Care for Creation," they have worked to protect the Endangered Species Act, and in 2006 signed a call for action on global climate change. The Environmental Protection Agency estimates that congregations serious about reducing energy consumption could save 25–30 percent. If half of all congregations in the United States did so, it would have the effect of removing a million cars from the road and would make available 13.5 billion kilowatt hours of electricity for other uses, without the construction of new power plants. All statistics cited here are reported in Charles L. Harper, "Religion and Environmentalism," in "The Legacy of Lynn White Jr.: Religion and the Environment," *The Journal of Religion and Society, Supplement 3* (2008): 5–26, http://moses.creighton.edu/JRS/2008/2008-11.html (accessed February 15, 2011).

to describe our human impact on those workings in empirical language, we have also come to expect that science can provide an equally empirical map of where to go from here. We have what Daniel Sarewitz has called an "excess of objectivity" where we have grown accustomed to eschewing policies or philosophies that "favor adaptation and resilience over control and rigidity."[24] And as Michael Northcott adds, the supreme value placed on certainty only "obviate[s] the need for reasoned debate about probabilities and particular cases in moral deliberation."[25]

If secularization means that we forsake the need to act in uncertainty, to act with a suspension of disbelief, or what in religion is simply called faith, we will not have the means to act meaningfully and ethically in response to global climate change. Strict materialist atheism and religious fundamentalism are both attitudes of superstition, not forms of knowledge, since they presume to hold fast to a form of knowledge that is without the stains of an evolving, contingent, and incomplete human history.

What is now necessary is what Michel Serres calls a "diligent religion of the world," an epistemology that refuses the specialization and balkanization of knowledge that secularism has created. The word "religion," he reminds us, means to "assemble, gather, lift up, traverse or reread," implying that if religion will prove helpful to our current environmental crisis, it must be a principle-oriented gathering of knowledge from any relevant epistemologies in the ethical interest of renewing the world.[26] Religion has to rethink its role and resist the balkanization that has become its refuge, which is one reason why a religious mind ought also to be a scientific one. Science, politics and current events, international affairs, human suffering, and environmental degradation raise an enormously wide range of questions that can bring out the very best in religious belief and practice if we are willing to treat them as religious questions.

While it might be assumed that making religion more relevant to the world requires relaxing the orthodox and universalist claims of religion to obtain a more open and secular outlook, faith is still necessary because it seeks to do the hopeful and hard work of binding together all knowledge. Faith, however, is irrelevant if it only wants the triumph of epistemological

---

24. Daniel Sarewitz, "Science and Environmental Policy," in *Earth Matters: The Earth Science, Philosophy, and the Claims of Community*, ed. Robert Frodeman (Upper Saddle River, N.J.: Prentice-Hall, 1999), 91, 93.

25. Northcott, *A Moral Climate*, 67.

26. Michel Serres, *The Natural Contract*, trans. Elizabeth MacArthur and William Paulson (Ann Arbor: University of Michigan Press, 1995), 47–48.

certainty or if it means that we can satisfy the demands of truth simply by assuming that, when doctrine and empirical reality seem to conflict, it can only mean that our interpretation of empirical reality is wrong. The same scrutiny should be brought to bear on our interpretation of doctrine, as Galileo's case famously showed. Religiosity means taking all available information seriously, as potentially of moral import and therefore deserving of reverent and careful rereading, as the word religion implies. It means allowing religious principle to guide our catholic and interdisciplinary learning.

The real religious heresy is when believers become so lazy that they feel confident that they can dismiss secular knowledge categorically and in knee-jerk fashion as mere falsehoods. While secularism has had a heyday criticizing religious fanatics as flat-earthers, for example, believers must make the *religious* case that such dogmatic attitudes are inherently irreverent, uncharitable, and irreligious. By failing to make a religious case for openness to learning, religion becomes a scaffold to uphold our desire to be right instead of a ladder to motivate our aspiration to become good; and it seems unlikely that it will ever have the power to motivate social, political, and environmental transformation. So this is a problem within religion that needs to be fixed because, as I have been insisting, the crisis of global climate change is not only a crisis of the environment but also a crisis of culture that the ambitious and cosmic claims of a religion robustly interested in learning are well suited to address. The complexity of the problem requires that the solutions we offer must meet the depth and range of the problems; they must be global, they must reach into the very marrow of how we define ourselves as human beings, into what we believe to be our place on this planet, and what, ultimately, is the meaning and nature of death, of dying, and of our biology. This is certainly too much to ask of capitalism, politics, science, and technology, but it certainly shouldn't be too much to ask of religion.

To the degree that religion remains resistant to the claims of science and other secular epistemologies, it calcifies in its claims of absolute knowledge and simultaneously turns its attention away from this world and toward another one beyond it. And to the degree that secular knowledge ignores religion or insists on a categorical differentiation between the sacred and the secular, it calcifies in its claims to absolute reliability but cannot explain why we should want to make one choice as opposed to any other or choose one end as opposed to any other. In this scenario, both religion and scientific knowledge are rendered ineffective in addressing the problems that confront us. What is needed, then, is a reading of religion that is informed by the questions that scientific findings raise about the workings of the world. In what follows, I hope to model such a reading.

The Dialectic of Human Significance in LDS Belief

In the greening of various academic and religious fields pertaining to contemporary culture that has occurred over the last four decades—including philosophy, literary criticism, history, psychology, anthropology, and theology—what has emerged is a sustained and sobering discussion of the human place in the physical world. Much of this thought has focused on the first part of Leopold's formula—seeking ways to increase human awareness of the physical and tangible presence and even the subjectivity of the more-than-human realm. The environmental argument of the past several decades has been that cultures that imagine human experience in the world as an *intersubjective* phenomenon are more likely to treat nature as a presence, not as an unfeeling object.[27] This approach has raised doubts about whether we can afford any longer to believe in the exceptionalism of humanity—that is, to see the world anthropocentrically or human-centered. Consequently, the push has been for worldviews that would teach our connection to and equality with all of creation—in a word, for a biocentric cosmology.

But in the rush to find antidotes to human hubris, our suspicion that we are unique and special within the creation has never entirely left us,

27. See, for example, David Abram, *The Spell of the Sensuous: Perception and Language in the More-Than-Human World* (New York: Vintage, 1997). Abram argues that non-Western cultures, by virtue of their polytheistic and animistic traditions, experience nature in this intersubjective way but that Western culture emerged in competition with these cultures and thereby denigrated, to its own detriment, animism's claims about inspirited nature. Similarly, White, argued that Christianity's rejection of paganism by the Middle Ages led to its claims of nature as dead matter, thus rendering the question of ethics moot. Lynn White, "The Historical Roots of Our Ecological Crisis," in *This Sacred Earth: Religion, Nature, Environment*, ed. Roger Gottlieb (New York: Routledge, 1995), 190–201. Many Christian theologians have responded to these criticisms by arguing that Christianity does indeed posit the living and spiritual presence of the physical world. These ecotheological responses resonate powerfully with Mormon doctrine. Indeed, as I argue in "Environmental Ethics of Mormon Belief" and hope to further elaborate here, few systems of belief in Christianity offer a more comprehensive and unambiguous articulation of the spiritual substructure of all physical life than Mormonism.

since even the most hardened critic of humanity's environmental failings has to acknowledge that we are at least unique in our capacity for destruction and, most importantly, in our capacity to deliberate about the morality of this fact. Since I suppose it isn't a serious proposition of most environmentalists to convert the world to a doctrine of animism, it behooves the monotheistic traditions in the world to find sufficient reasons to trust in the living presence of the vast creation to temper our anthropocentric tendencies and thereby act responsibly.

To the extent that some environmentalists reject human exceptionalism, environmentalism has become increasingly incapable of articulating the moral reasons for responsible stewardship, a fact that has sometimes alienated believers. In their attempt to reconcile the environmental aims of a biocentric philosophy with the most ancient and vital claims of religion about human exceptionalism, environmentally-minded religious thinkers have begun to articulate a dialectic of human significance that, as my reading of the Book of Moses intends to show, resonates with the LDS account of the creation. Indeed, it would seem that few, if any, religious traditions offer such a satisfactory dialectic between the experience of human nothingness that nature provides and the faith in human significance and responsibility that emerges from such experience.

The Mormon account offered in the Book of Moses and echoed in the temple makes it simultaneously clear that human beings are special, even unique, in the creation and yet are also part of a vast and endless universe of planets and almost inconceivable biodiversity that should temper any hubris that the divine origins and destiny of humanity might inspire. The LDS account of the creation, then, seems to resist the polemics of choosing between a strictly anthropocentric or strictly biocentric account of humankind; it instead points us to a theocentric universe in which humanity plays a vital role in a web of biological complexity that teaches both the reasons for our profound humility and for our special moral responsibilities. LDS theology does not privilege spirit over body, heaven over earth, eternity over this moment in time, individuality over collectivity, transcendence over immanence, but rather produces an ambiguous commingling of these categories—spirit *and* body, heaven *on* earth, eternity in an hour, the individual within the collective, and so on. We cannot designate concern for the well-being of the earth, of the body, and of animals, plants, and watersheds as irrelevant to our pursuit of salvation.

The idea of an embodied God stresses the centrality of earthly physical life. While Genesis teaches that we are created in the image of God, the

Book of Moses states more explicitly that we are created in the image of the Savior. In Moses 1:6 the Lord tells Moses, "Thou art in the similitude of mine Only Begotten," and amplifies Genesis 1:27 with: "in the image of mine only Begotten created I them" (Moses 2:27). We are created, in other words, in the image of a son of God who would take upon Him flesh to become the incarnate God. This distinction, though subtle, is important, since it points to the central idea that the human condition is a combination of the body and spirit, of the divine and the earthly, and that this combination is, indeed, the very nature and sphere of the Creator Himself, a being of flesh and bone, familiar with the intricacies of the Creation as well as with the sufferings of the earthly condition. Of course, Mormon doctrine stipulates a Father of flesh and bone in any case, but these verses seem to clarify that our model is the same God who created the earth, assumed a body here, and suffered and sanctified the life of the body, perhaps culminating in that remarkable moment when Jesus eats fish and honeycomb with his disciples in a resurrected body (Luke 24:42).

Of course, it has often been assumed that this doctrine is incompatible with the story of evolution. Without getting into this important debate, suffice it to say that to exist in the body and to be in the image of God is not, in these verses, incompatible with the concept of being kin with the rest of creation. Because Mormon doctrine consistently asserts the holiness of the physical realm and the centrality of the body and of the earth to the divine destiny of humanity, it doesn't seem necessary to dismiss the evolutionary account out of hand, especially since it teaches the inherent complexity, diversity, and kinship of all living things. That the human mandate to reproduce is later echoed in God's commands to the rest of the earth's life forms suggests that the specialness of humanity is contextualized by biology's reminder of our belonging with all creation and the inherent value of all life forms. Moses 2:22, which echoes Genesis, reads: "And I, God, blessed [every living creature that moveth]: Be fruitful and multiply, and fill the waters in the sea; and let fowl multiply in the earth." This divine command implies that biodiversity is its own good end. That the temple additionally suggests all living things' inherent right to joy in their posterity suggests an ethic of protecting biodiversity.

The diversity and immensity of creation, which by implication goes beyond even what Moses sees, is a cause for the most profound humility. Almost in the same moment that Moses learns of his divine parentage, he learns that God's creations are "without end" and that "no man can behold all my works, except he behold all my glory; and no man can behold all my glory, and afterwards remain in the flesh on the earth" (Moses 1:4–5). In other words, as long as we are in the body and on the earth, even with the aid of the revelations that God grants to his prophet here, we can never comprehend the whole of God's creations. Our understanding of the specialness of our role must be couched within this broader, imagined cosmos, an imagination which is the fruit of faith. God allows Moses to witness "the world and the ends thereof," an experience of a global consciousness about which "he greatly marveled and wondered" (Moses 1:8).

The account further provides the clearest doctrinal basis for a kind of intersubjectivity we can experience in the physical world that neither denigrates the specialness of humanity nor the strangeness and diversity of the world. The cause of Moses's wonder appears to be the extent and diversity of the creation but is also the deep intersection between the body and the spirit that runs through all creation. As Moses learns, "I, the Lord God, created all things, of which I have spoken, spiritually, before they were naturally upon the face of the earth" (Moses 3:5). Spiritual creation means that all living things—human beings, animals, and plants—are "living souls." This designation implies a kind of spiritual continuum or kinship that undergirds all life forms. Granted, it does not compromise the specialness of the human condition (created in the image of God), but it does suggest that the specialness of humanity is not categorical or all pervasive. It is an ambiguous specialness, and that ambiguity seems important to ethics. Precisely because we do not know exactly on what grounds we are equal to animal and plant life and on what grounds we are distinct, it seems we are placed in a constant state of wonder, a kind of uncanny spirituality, as if by looking into the mirror of nature, now we see ourselves, now we don't.

We learn that the creation is designed, in part, for our aesthetic response and that appreciation for the strangeness and beauty of the creation should form the basis of human culture and should temper any tendencies toward unrighteous dominion. Before the Fall, God commanded that all animals should come to Adam "to see what he would call them, and they were also living souls" (Moses 3:19). His dominion, in other words, begins with a creative act of naming and continues as a responsibility to ensure the healthy reproduction of all life.[28] We learn some of this responsibil-

---

28. This notion of dominion has received a lot of attention from critics of the Judeo-Christian tradition because it seems to provide us license to do to nature whatever we want. No one has written more powerfully and persuasively in the Mormon tradition about why Adam's dominion is a "call to service, not a license

ity from the temple, which clearly teaches the right of all living things to fulfill the measure of their creation and to have joy in their posterity. Curiously, Adam is commanded to "dress" and "keep" the garden and to avoid the tree of the knowledge of good and evil.

The implications of the spiritual continuum in creation are enormous, especially with regard to the ethical treatment of animals; and while this aspect has been given some attention in Mormon scholarship, the significance of trees, for example, also as living souls has not been fully understood or explored. We are told that "out of the ground made I, the Lord God, to grow every tree, naturally, that is pleasant to the sight of man; and man could behold it" (Moses 3:9). The aesthetic value of contemplating trees and the allure of their always idiosyncratic and unique forms and colors are here placed in highest priority, as is the joy of gaining a relationship with creation, even before the value of use. It is only later that "man saw that it was good for food" (Moses 3:9). The implication is that language itself (and all of culture by implication) derives from this wonderful encounter with the strangeness of biological forms. Nature, in other words, is always central to our spiritual and cultural self-understanding, since it instructs us first about our own nothingness, a discovery that then tempers our acceptance of our significance. To the degree that we lose that sense of wonder or diminish our capacity for aesthetic pleasure, or degrade nature's beauty beyond repair, we are compromising these vital spiritual recompenses of physical life.

There is no more profound expression of the inseparability of physical life and spiritual happiness than in the marvelous cosmic chiasm Moses describes at the very heart of our human journey: "Ye were born into the world by water, and blood, and the spirit, which I have made, and so became of dust a living soul, even so ye must be born again into the kingdom of heaven, of water, and of the Spirit, and be cleansed by blood, even the blood of mine Only Begotten" (Moses 6:59). Born of the spirit before coming to earth, we are born in the womb of blood and water. Spiritual birth is a sanctification of the biological conditions of life, an echo in reverse of the voyage from heaven through the birth canal, capped by the reception of the gift of the Holy Ghost. It is only fitting, then, that God would be of flesh and bone and that the earth itself, the very site of our sufferings, our biological evolution, our toil, and our separation from God, would become the place of return and restoration of our unity with

---

to exterminate" than Hugh Nibley, "Subduing the Earth," in *On the Timely and the Timeless*, 2nd ed. (Provo, Utah: BYU Religious Studies Center, 2004), 106.

God. So, too, is it fitting that the conditions of the Fall (working for food and survival, being subject to sexual desire, experiencing sexual union, and suffering through childbirth and parenting), through the sanctification of the spirit, are not the conditions of our alienation and separation from God, as some forms of Christianity have it, but part of what redeems us.

Indeed, if the Fall is a curse and a negative, lamentable event, Christianity would seem to see no hope embedded in physical life. Such a view is precisely why so many critics in environmentalism have taken aim at the Judeo-Christian tradition. To believe that this earth, this body, and this mortal existence are conditions merely to be suffered through in the hope of a better place and a better state is to argue implicitly against the need to concern ourselves with sustainable living. But Mormonism here presents a different view, namely, that working for the health of this mortal existence is the means of truly becoming living souls. The evolutionary story of our emergence from the cell matter of the earth that once seemed so directly opposed to the story of the Creation now seems consistent with the idea that biological process and spiritual creation are not competing but cooperative processes. Indeed, it seems fitting that our bodies that evolved from dust, and blood, and the hard-scrabble struggle for survival over millennia—as evolutionary science seems to suggest—would ultimately be an image of a sanctified and perfect being, the very Son of God. There is something spiritually immanent about all biological accident and all biological process implied here.

I offer this thought as suggestive provocation, as an incentive to consider the need for us to be inherently interested in the workings of physical life, in the diversity of life forms, and in the ways in which physical life is not transcended by the spiritual but is rather informed by and informing of the ultimate verities of the spirit. Ultimately, to be human is not merely a biological story; we are not reduced to our origin and destiny as dust, but we are also given a temporary probation, like a tree, as a "living soul."

After seeing the ends of the earth and the diversity of the creation, the exhausted Moses slowly recovers and avers in awe: "Now, for this cause I know that man is nothing, which thing I never had supposed" (Moses 1:10). If we are to recover an awareness of this kind of nothingness, we must learn to imagine a wholeness far beyond our experience, and to do this, I have been suggesting, is an act of faith. We can be reassured that this experience of nothingness is a gift of a loving Father, the Creator of the universe, and not merely an empirical experience. Indeed, Moses's recovery of awareness of his own nothingness might sound like what some environmentalists have called for: a thorough debunking of the specialness of humanity. And yet Moses's discovery of his nothingness appears to be his unique human privilege, thus proving the dichotomy as false. Moses, along with all of God's children, is uniquely situated among God's creations to discover his own nothingness in relation to the complexity and beauty of the whole. Awe and wonder are his and our human privilege, not certain knowledge or possession. My reading is intended to show that the principles that should inform our environmental attitudes and that are our moral duty to act upon are deferential reverence and care for the processes that sustain that complexity.

Of course, the story also reminds us that Satan is intensely interested in distorting this sacred relationship to the creation that is so central to our spiritual health and growth. Moses successfully resists Satan's temptation to worship him precisely because he understands his own value in the proper spiritual and biological context. He asks Satan, "Where is thy glory, that I should worship thee? . . . I could not look upon God, except his glory should come upon me, and I were transfigured before him. But I can look upon thee in the natural man" (Moses 1:13–14). In other words, Moses here understands that the unique privilege of awe that comes from understanding our small but vital human place in the vast physical universe is not a merely biological fact, nor a fact that requires merely intellectual or natural understanding. It requires a spiritual transformation of our powers of perception to see with the eyes of faith, a kind of seeing that is a unique combination of the spiritual and the physical, a vivification of the human eye through spirit and blood. Only such a transformation allows him to strike the necessary and delicate balance.

Furthermore, Moses's power to resist Satan's attempt to pervert his relationship to this vast creation comes from a determination to learn more about the mysteries of the earth and our human place on it. In other words, Moses's resistance comes from two understandings. First, he does not deny his unique human station: "Behold, I am a son of God," he says (Moses 1:13). Second, he recognizes his need for greater understanding: "I will not cease to call upon God, I have other things to inquire of him" (Moses 1:18). Consequently, Moses's recognition of his nothingness is a powerful tool of resistance to Satan's temptation to artificially elevate human significance and power. Satan's interest here suggests why a problem as serious and as global as climate change demands our heightened moral attention, lest we succumb to false ideas about our place in and responsibility to the world.

In conclusion, the LDS account of the creation teaches that we can identify spiritually valuable and ethical uses of natural resources because they are facilitated by and enhance our sense of wonder of our spiritual kinship with the whole of the earth, stimulate a desire for deeper knowledge, and respect biodiversity. Only these kinds of acts (ecological restoration comes to mind) are spiritually holy and redemptive; they enact the conditions of a Fortunate Fall. Acts that decrease wonder, teach us that nature is mere dead matter, stop our growth of understanding, or insist there is no way to act in our human self-interest *and* in the interest of the web of life, are profane, tragic, and therefore enact the unfortunate conditions of humankind's profound alienation from God.

We deny the earth's holiness when we assume that we have the promise that there is enough and to spare regardless of how we use earth's resources, or when we assume that, if the earth appears to be dying or suffering, we are supposed to let it happen. These attitudes are almost fanatical in their devotion to the instrumentality of nature; they see science merely as technology—as a certain means to use the world, not as the work of naming and building relationships to other living souls, or at least trying to imagine the earth on its own terms. They are also views that are bent on avoiding self-questioning and circumspection because they are uncomfortable with circumstances that demand judgment and action despite incomplete knowledge and high stakes. In their adherence to false certainties, these attitudes reject the need to engage our own moral agency. When religious beliefs are motivated by fear rather than love, they shield us from confronting the limitations and uncertainties that science sometimes inspires. When this happens, faith becomes unnecessary, ideology takes over, and religion does not live up to its claims of universality or morality.

As I have suggested, religion can either help or hurt in rising to the moral challenges of living on the earth, challenges that have perhaps existed from time immemorial but which global climate change has only recently spelled out that we can no longer avoid with impunity. The solution is not to declare that one knows the meaning of all things, but to remember that religion is a call to faithful and moral action on behalf of what we love, which is usually more important and far-reaching than what we can claim we know. It is our choice.

TEN

The Way toward the Garden: Moses 5:1–12

James E. Faulconer

Propaedeutic: My Hermeneutical Principles (An Always Continuing Draft)

I plan to offer a reading of Moses 5:1–12, but before I do, let me sketch the principles that I think lie behind that reading. I say "I think" because I don't trust myself. Perhaps something very different is going on when I study scripture. Perhaps these are, indeed, involved in what I do, but there are other, more important things that I have overlooked. Paraphrasing King Benjamin, I cannot tell you all the ways whereby I could be wrong about how I interpret (cf. Mosiah 4:29). I love to read and study scripture. I love to talk and write about it. I feel reasonably confident that I learn new things, good things, when I do. I feel less confident that I know how to describe well what I am doing when I do it. But, reflecting on how I study scripture and thinking about things I've read about scriptural interpretation, here are eleven principles that I believe capture reasonably well what I do:

1. Canonical texts are those that the Church, broadly and narrowly conceived, has agreed to take as the standard for its self-understanding and that of individuals within it.

   What has been canonized is not purely accidental, but the canon certainly could have been different than it is—something I take to be as true of the Book of Mormon as it is of the Bible, though perhaps it is more obviously true of the latter.

2. Presumably, the Church has canonized its texts with guidance from the Holy Spirit, but that guidance may vary in its effect, both for the original writer and for the redactors.

   For me, therefore, the phrase "as far as it is translated correctly" has as much to do with the original translation of inspiration into text as it does with the subsequent transmission of that text from the past to the present and its translation from one language to another.

3. Whatever the textual history of a particular scripture, I assume that most often the final redactor (when there was one) did not do his work blindly or unintelligently. I assume that he "knew what he was doing" in the same sense that a novelist—or the writer of readable history—knows what he or she is doing. What she does, she does intentionally, though she is perhaps not conscious of all that what she does entails. Anyone who writes carefully says more than he or she knows explicitly. (Indeed, even those who do not write carefully say more than they know.) So I begin with the received text, as written. I assume that Jesus knew something of the redaction history of the Bible, a history fraught with questions and difficulties. Yet as a friend recently pointed out, "as redacted and worked over as these texts [of the Old Testament] are, they are the texts Jesus taught from, what the early Christians knew."[1] I am leery of having a textual standard for religious purposes that strives to be higher than his.

   I don't deny that a text may need emendation, but I avoid it if possible. Also, insofar as possible, the text I'm interested in is that in the original language.[2] For study purposes, the original language of the Book of Mormon, and the books of Moses and Abraham is English. Reference to Hebrew or other languages may sometimes be instructive or provocative, but English is the language in which we received those texts.

---

1. See Cherylem's comment (number 9) of May 31, 2010, on "How a Loving God Could Command the Wholesale Extermination of Nations," http://feastuponthewordblog.org/2010/05/26/how-a-loving-god-could-command-the-wholesale-extermination-of-nations/#comment-31825 (accessed May 22, 2012).

2. This is the point where textual, linguistic, and historical scholarship overlap with interpretation. It is not always a simple matter to decide what the received text is. Nevertheless, for most readers most of the time the question is moot.

4. Because it comes to us with a much less difficult history of transmission / translation (though not without questions of translation and transmission internal to it), the Book of Mormon is what Joseph Smith called it: "the most correct book of any book." No book teaches the gospel of Jesus Christ better. In virtue of that, I take it that the Book of Mormon provides a standard for understanding the Bible.

   However, in one sense, the Book of Mormon is not a standard for understanding that is always easy to use. It may sometimes provide teachings to which we can compare what we find in, for example, the Bible, but it is not fundamentally a guide to correct beliefs. Primarily it helps us remember (remember rather than recall) the gospel that we are trying to read in all scripture, a gospel that the Book of Mormon defines as Jesus coming into the world as the Messiah to be crucified for our sins, which requires that we repent and are baptized, receive the Holy Ghost, and endure to the end (3 Ne. 27:13–16, 20).[3] That is both easier and more difficult than proclaiming correct doctrine.

5. Given their deutero-canonical status, I assume that the teachings of the latter-day prophets also serve to help us understand scripture.

   Rarely are those teachings about the exegesis or even the hermeneutic of a particular passage. Like the Book of Mormon they most often help us remember the gospel that scripture preaches. I would add that all scripture has this purpose: to call us to remember more than (not "rather than") to teach us doctrine.

6. Reading scripture is about achieving self-understanding and coming to repentance (which are ultimately indistinguishable). It is only tangentially about recovering lost meaning from ancient texts. The latter is scholarship and has its place, but it isn't scripture reading.

7. Self-understanding comes more in responding to questions than in learning new facts about some state of affairs in which one finds oneself. Questions are more important than answers, but not more important than responses.

---

3. On the distinction between memory and recall, see James E. Faulconer, "Remembrance," in *Faith, Philosophy, Scripture* (Provo, Utah: Maxwell Institute, 2010), 1–17.

8. Self-understanding is unavoidably an ongoing project. It has no final point, at least not for mortals.
9. I assume that repentance comes about when a person or a church is genuinely engaged in self-understanding. In that it continually helps us repent, scripture study is an important part of continuing revelation.
10. The questions that bring self-understanding are rarely those with which I begin because I seldom know already what I need to learn about myself. Rather, I begin with questions that come to me from the text.

    Most often, these questions arise when I focus on the details of the text rather than on the big questions that I am always tempted to ask at first. Questions about details can range from the question of genre (an oft-neglected question in LDS scripture study) to grammatical questions such as "What is the referent for this pronoun?" (another neglected question).

    Questions like "What principle is being taught in these verses?" are last, though not least, in scripture study (1) because those questions too often tempt me to revert to repeating "what everyone knows" about the passage I am studying; (2) because beginning with the principles I find in scripture moves me too quickly to the general and philosophical when what I need is things directed at me in particular; and (3) because by paying attention to the details of the text—particularly its "story line," even when it isn't narrative—I will often be asked questions that I wouldn't have thought of otherwise.

    Equally, questions about historicity are seldom relevant. It does not follow that they are irrelevant. It is important to know that Jesus lived, was crucified for our sins, was resurrected on the third day, and sits at the right hand of God so that we can be saved (D&C 20:21–25). It is important that the Book of Mormon is what it claims to be. It is perhaps less important whether Jonah existed or whether he was swallowed by a large fish.

    Most questions about historicity say little about how to understand what the New Testament, the Book of Mormon, and other scriptures teach us, what kinds of lives they call us to. Historical claims give us reason for taking those books seriously, but taking them seriously doesn't require that we continue to ask the question of their historicity.

11. The most important thing one can have when reading scripture is imagination. Perhaps the most important question one can ask in order to set imagination to work is this: "How can I read this passage otherwise than I usually would and yet remain true to the text and true to the gospel preached through the Restoration and its on-going revelation?"

Body: The Way toward the Garden: Moses 5:1–12

The beginning of Moses 5 interrupts the traditional Genesis story, inserting a text between the expulsion from the Garden of Eden and the birth of Cain: Moses 5:1–16a. Part of that text (Moses 5:1–3) and the first part of verse 16 are an introduction to the story of Cain and Abel. But the introduction is itself interrupted by a reflection on prayer, obedience, and sacrifice (vv. 4–9), a reflection on the positive consequences of Adam's and Eve's transgression (vv. 10–12), and a brief homily on the need to repent (vv. 13–15). The authority of these interruptions is underscored by the fact that they are told to us by the voice of "I, the Lord God" (v. 1) rather than by the anonymous, perhaps human narrator or redactor of Genesis. This is not a story told by a human being, not even if that human being is Moses. It is God's story, and Moses is his amanuensis.

The natural interpretation of the Genesis text is that we move from the expulsion in Genesis 3:24 to the beginning of human community in Genesis 4:1 with the beginning of the family, specifically with the birth and naming of the first person to enter into that family: Cain. In contrast, in the book of Moses, we move from the expulsion to human labor, and then to the family, with multiple sons and daughters mentioned before any of them are named. However, the Moses account presents us with an interpretive problem, for we are told in verse 2 that Adam and Eve have sons and daughters, but Cain—though traditionally the first human born—is not mentioned until verse 16. According to the book of Moses, is or is not Cain the first child born to Adam and Eve?

There are two possible ways to understand this pericope in answer to that question. We can read it as a simple chronology: Adam and Eve have children who also have children and then later, after they learn about sacrifice and come to realize the effects of their transgression in the Garden, they have Cain and Abel. Or we can understand Moses 5 to begin with a general statement about Adam and Eve and their children (vv. 1–3) that returns in verse 16 to the specifics of the story of the first family by telling of the births of the first two children, Cain and Abel (vv. 16–17), after a digression on sacrifice, obedience, and repentance (vv. 4–15). I prefer the second of these readings because it creates fewer difficulties of interpretation when we compare the Genesis and the Moses texts. Choosing one reading over the other makes little difference to our understanding of the doctrines of this pericope, but as I will try to show, it enlarges the meaning we can find in it.

The first three verses of Moses 5 give us a theme that is, at best, implicit in Genesis, namely the inseparability of labor and family. In both Moses 4 and Genesis 3 Adam is told that because he has done what Eve asked him to do, eaten of the fruit of the tree of knowledge, he must labor. Eve is told that because she has eaten of the tree, she will endure the pain consequent on childbirth. One can make a case that even in the Genesis account these two results are not as distinct as they have often been thought to be.[4] But in the Moses account, their intertwining is made explicit at the beginning of chapter 5:

> Verse 1: Adam and Eve labor together.
> Verse 2: Adam and Eve have children; their children have children.
> Verse 3: Their children labor and bear children, imitating their parents.

Verse 3 brings the themes of the first two verses together as one: to be a child of Adam and Eve is to labor and bear children. This intertwining of labor and family suggests that the two are inseparable from one another. Labor and childbirth are not separable and distinct duties, but two aspects of one thing, the fullness of human life.

However, as verse 4 shows us, intertwined labor and family are not yet enough for full life. For Adam and Eve also call on God. The book of Moses directly contests the book of Genesis at this point. For though the book of Moses suggests that Adam and Eve "called upon the name of the Lord" as part of the intertwining of labor and family, we don't see that phrase until much later in the Genesis story, in Genesis 4:26: "And to Seth, to him also there was born a son; and he called his name Enos: then began men to call upon the name of the Lord." In the Genesis story, not until the third generation is anyone explicitly said to call on the name of

4. See James E. Faulconer, "Adam and Eve—Community: Reading Genesis 2–3," *Journal of Philosophy and Scripture* 1, no. 1 (Fall 2003): 2–16.

the Lord, while in the Moses story, Adam and Eve know and call on his name from the beginning.

But what does it mean to say that they call on God? The text specifically says that they call "upon the name of the Lord." This suggests that he isn't an impersonal force or someone unknown. He may not be present, but he is not anonymous. Adam and Eve call on someone they know and, using his name, their prayers have the force that the petitions of someone we know would have on us. Their use of his name suggests a covenant relation between him and them, a relation of obligation like the obligation of children to a father.

But Adam and Eve's prayer is not simple prayer. In most Genesis texts the formula, "call on the name of the Lord," suggests prayer and sacrifice. Indeed, if we pay close attention to the use of that formula in Genesis, we see that it most often appears to imply covenant, ritual worship (see Gen. 12:8, 13:24, 21:33, and 26:25). So we see here that for Adam and Eve life in the world includes ritual worship. Human life begins in work, family, and the covenant relation with God that is instantiated in ritual.

Adam and Eve *call* on God because he is not present to them. They must call on him because they are outside the Garden of Eden. They have been "shut out from his presence" (Moses 5:4). It is significant that the human life of work and family—fullness of life—comes about not in God's presence, but in his absence. But as is obvious in the story, "shut out from his presence" and "cut off" do not mean the same thing. After the expulsion Adam and Eve continue to hear the Lord speaking "from the way toward the Garden of Eden" (v. 4). They have not been abandoned, though he keeps his distance from them.

Considering the distance between the place in the world where Adam and Eve find themselves and the Garden, notice an interesting phrase in Moses 5:4: "Adam and Eve . . . heard the voice of the Lord from the way toward the Garden of Eden." There is a way, a path, leading toward the Garden. Without multiple trips from Adam and Eve's home to that garden's entrance, trips enough to wear a path, could there be such a way? I doubt it. And what would be the point of these trips toward the gate of the Garden? Logically every path goes both to and from its end points, but the text emphasizes that this way goes toward the Garden. The way is described from the point of view of someone intending to go to the Garden or, given what we know about what happened before this story, at least to its periphery. I imagine the first couple treading their way toward the garden gate, hoping for contact with the Lord and being disappointed until they return home and hear that voice from afar (as we hear his voice from afar through the scriptures and the words of the prophets). I imagine them hoping that even if they are not to be readmitted to the Garden of Eden, then perhaps by returning to its edge they will once again be brought into at least the nimbus of God's presence. But the journey on which this way leads them—presumably many times—is a disappointment. The only presence they find there is perhaps the fearful presence of the cherubim with their flaming sword (see Moses 4:31; Gen. 3:24). Adam and Eve have made a path to the Garden looking for what they can have only at home, though what they receive at home is not quite what they went looking for at the Garden. It is a voice from afar rather than a presence. As I read verse 4, the way toward the Garden of Eden is evidence that Adam and Eve are nostalgic for that garden.

Nostalgia is a common experience. Perhaps I should be embarrassed to admit it, but the older I grow, the more often I experience nostalgia. A mission reunion makes me nostalgic for the time I spent as a missionary. A message on Facebook from a high school friend makes me nostalgic for my adolescence. The visit of a grandchild makes me nostalgic for their halcyon infancy and for the childhood of my now-grown children, as well as my own. Nostalgia is a kind of yearning, and yearning is an emotion that may be uniquely human, perhaps the most inclusive form of human desire. Adam and Eve's nostalgia for the Garden shows that they are fully human. But nostalgia never yearns for what really was.

There was much about my mission that was wonderful, but it was also difficult, sufficiently difficult that I would prefer not to do it again. High school was, in fact, awful, vexed by teenage hormones and adolescent worries, driven by a brain not yet developed enough to make well-grounded moral decisions but making moral decisions anyway. I very much prefer being older, thank you. And as much as I love my grandchildren, the times for which I am nostalgic are chosen selectively from a much wider canvas on which the pastel colors of babies and loving four-year-olds are mixed with the more dramatic colors of full-blooded, real, non-halcyonic, developing children. As nostalgia, yearning is a pleasant-feeling form of self-pity—and it is a deception.

Adam and Eve's nostalgia for the Garden of Eden takes the outward form of a hope to return to the presence of God, but that hope is implicitly also a hope to return to a state of bliss, a state free of difficulty and overflowing with plenty. Nostalgia for the Garden of Eden conflates being in the presence of God with bliss, plenty, and freedom from pain. In spite of scriptural and prophetic evidence to the contrary, our dreams of heaven are often formed from such nostalgia: we dream that in heaven there is no pain and that there is no labor. Unfortunately, in such a heaven there would probably also be neither personal relationship nor even personal identity. For the nostalgic, heaven is nothing but continual bliss and, so, probably nothing at all.

I suspect those nostalgic, Edenic dreams of the heavenly garden to come also inform our hope for the possibilities of mortality. When we think about family or communal life, we often do so in nostalgic terms, hoping not only that the earth will be "renewed and receive its paradisiacal glory" (A of F 10), but that our earthly lives will approach those of Adam and Eve in the Garden of Eden. The problem with such hope is that the promised heavenly paradise and the Garden of Eden are not the same. In the Garden of Eden, Adam and Eve were not yet fully human. Their eyes were as yet unopened; they were not only blissful, but ignorant. Indeed, perhaps there is no bliss without ignorance. Perhaps "bliss and ignorance" is a hendiadys (two words for one meaning). Nostalgic dreaming that fullness of life means bliss amounts to dreaming that we can escape our humanity rather than fulfill that humanity in the labor of family.

We cannot undo the fact that as the children of Adam and Eve we too have eaten of the fruit of the tree of knowledge of good and evil. Our eyes are open and, at least in principle, we are as the Gods (Moses 4:28). Nostalgia for something like an Eden conceals from us the truth of what it means to have that divine knowledge of good and evil. The way to the Garden of Eden gives Adam and Eve nothing that they don't already have without treading its path. They can hear the voice of the Lord speaking to them from where they are without going back. His voice comes when they call on him, and verse 4 may imply that they call only after they've trodden the way to the Garden, after whatever time it would take to make that path. Perhaps our first parents call on the Lord in prayer only after they've given up their nostalgia. In any case, like them we learn that nostalgia for bliss—in other words, nostalgia for ignorance—will give us nothing. We, too, can stand some distance outside the presence of God, but we, too, can nevertheless hear the voice of the Lord. And we hear that voice, not at the gate of the Garden of Eden, but where we are within the world of labor: labor by the sweat of our brows, the labor of families, of Adam and Eve laboring together, of Adam and Eve multiplying and replenishing the earth together. The knowledge of good and evil does its work in labor and families. We become as the Gods here in the world, where we can hear the voice of the Lord but remain distant from his presence.

From outside their world the Lord responds to Adam and Eve's call, commanding them to worship and sacrifice (Moses 5:5). The Lord's answer to Adam and Eve's longing for his presence is his continued but not absolute absence and the command to sacrifice the firstlings of their flocks. He not only rejects their nostalgia for presence, he asks them to forfeit the first part of their present plenty. Human fullness requires labor, the labor to produce what we need to live, a need that tends toward the desire for fullness and plenty and sometimes excess. But we see here that human fullness is not the same as a fullness of material needs, for it requires sacrificing those material needs, giving some of them up. Surely Adam found this answer to his prayers puzzling: he calls on the Lord, asking, as it were, "Lord be with me," and the Lord answers in sum, "Worship me and offer sacrifice." Puzzled or not, as every Latter-day Saint knows, Adam obeys (Moses 5:5), trusting that God will be with him in that ritual. As verse 6 tells us, Adam does not know why he is sacrificing from his flocks, but he understands that sacrifice is more than just giving something up. More importantly it is also sacrifying, or making sacred. I assume that we have another hendiadys in the phrase "worship and sacrifice." In worship, sacrifice brings us into God's presence, though it is not obvious to Adam at this point how or why that is so.

In the next part of the pericope, though the temporal distance is great—"many days"—the spatial distance between Adam and the Garden of Eden apparently remains the same. But he no longer needs to tread the way across that distance. Now engaged in worship and sacrifice, Adam is no longer nostalgic. He has given up his yearning for presence and plenty. He lives in the world of his humanity without seeking to leave it for an inhuman realm. Nostalgia has been replaced by obedience: "Why dost thou offer sacrifices?" an angel asks after many days. "I know not, save the Lord commanded me," answers Adam (Moses 5:6).

Sometimes when we talk about this story we say that Adam doesn't know why he offers sacrifice, but that isn't quite right. He doesn't merely say "I know not." He says, "I know not, save the Lord commanded me." In other words, "I know only one reason, that I was commanded to do so." He enacts the ritual because it instantiates the relationship he has with the Lord. The desire for presence is taken up and changed (*aufheben* if we steal a word from Hegel) into something new: presence in ritual, the enactment of relation to another. Ritual worship in response to the voice of the Lord has taken the place of nostalgia for presence. Nevertheless, Adam does not yet know why the Lord has commanded this particular ritual. We can understand the angel's question to amount to "Why does sacrifice of your firstlings enact your covenant relation to the Lord?" To that question, Adam's answer would be a simple, "I don't know." The covenant of ritual worship remains as yet implicit.

The angel makes that covenant explicit by telling Adam that ritual worship is a similitude of the sacrifice of the Only Begotten of the Father (Moses 5:7). Webster's 1828 American Dictionary of the English Language gives "likeness" and "resemblance" as definitions for similitude. What Adam does in sacrifice is a likeness of what the Only Begotten will do. Compare similitude here with likeness in the King James Bible, for example in Deuteronomy 5:8: "Thou shalt not make thee any graven image, or any likeness of any thing that is in heaven above, or that is in the earth beneath, or that is in the waters beneath the earth." "Likeness" translates the Hebrew word *temuna*, clearly meaning something like "form." Covenant, ritual worship enacts the presence of God for Adam because the elevation that comes through worship is informed by God's life and condescension.

The angel adds that the Only Begotten is "full of grace and truth" (Moses 5:7), repeating a phrase that we are familiar with from John 1:14: "And the Word was made flesh, and dwelt among us, (and we beheld his glory, the glory as of the only begotten of the Father,) full of grace and truth." At first glance we might assume that this is an anachronism imported into the Moses translation through Joseph Smith's familiarity with the New Testament text. But the Johannine phrase appears to be a repetition of the Hebrew formula *hesed we emeth*, most often translated as "mercy and truth" (in, for example, 2 Sam. 15:20), but also translated "lovingkindness and truth" (Ps. 40:10–11) or "goodness and truth" (Ex. 34:6). In the Hebrew Bible the phrase describes God's covenant mercy, which is why John uses a translation of that language to describe his experience of the Son. Presumably the book of Moses uses John's language for the same reason that John uses the language of the Hebrew Bible, though he wrote in Greek. The covenant enacted in sacrifice is a covenant of mercy, not just God's promise of mercy to those who will be his people, but a demand for their mercy to others, their imitation of his mercy.

As we saw, Adam's ritual sacrifice enacts a covenant with the Lord because it has the same form as the divine life of the Only Begotten of the

Father.[5] Fullness of human life requires sacrifice rather than mere plenty because fullness of divinity requires it. Just as God's Only Begotten will give up his life, Adam must ritually repeat that sacrifice by giving up a significant token of what sustains his life. In ritual, Adam remembers the sacrifice of the Only Begotten, and by doing that he acts out the possibility of his own divinization, of being like the Gods. In covenant, ritual worship Adam and Eve remember who they are by acting out the mercy that joins human beings to the Gods through the condescension of the Son and they remember that the imitation of that mercy makes it possible for them to be like the Gods.

In that day (Moses 5:10), rather than after many days (v. 6), Adam regains what he had sought when he and Eve wore a path to the Garden of Eden, namely the presence of God. But that presence comes on him, as if by surprise. It is not something he discovers: "The Holy Ghost fell upon Adam." This is not the presence of a form. Adam cannot see God and, so, remains at a distance from him. At the same time, however, he is in the presence of God. It is not just an angelic messenger who speaks to him. It is the Godhead in their unity. The verse is clear about that, for it specifically says that the Holy Ghost came to Adam, but when he speaks, he speaks in the name of the Son: "saying, I am the Only Begotten of the Father from the beginning." Relation with God in covenant, ritual worship makes possible the presence of God for human beings. Rather than finding that presence in a well-trodden, nostalgic return to Eden, in bliss and plenty, the presence of God in covenant falls on us when we enact divine mercy and sacrifice.

With that understanding of covenant worship, Adam's eyes are finally fully open. Rejoicing he says, "Because of my transgression my eyes are

---

5. There have been speculations among Latter-day Saints about what the term "Only Begotten" means, resulting in sometimes shocking conclusions about Jesus's genesis by the Father through human modes of reproduction. Whatever the means by which Jesus was begotten, the scriptural phrase "Only Begotten" doesn't support such speculation—though, of course, it also doesn't render it false. Hebrews 11:17 refers to Isaac as the only begotten of Abraham, and Paul could not have been ignorant of Ishmael's birth. So Paul could not have meant the phrase "only begotten" to suggest that Isaac was "the only person whom Abraham has physically begotten."

The speculations in question appear to have been based on a misunderstanding of the term "only begotten," a translation of the Greek word *monogenēs*. The point of the Greek word is that Jesus, like Isaac, is unique. He is the only one of his kind. It says nothing about the process of his genesis.

opened" (Moses 5:10). He now knows what he seems to have previously grasped only sketchily, if at all: he understands that his transgression of the bounds of the Garden of Eden has made it possible for him to be like the Gods. Divine and divinely human existence is not blissful ignorance. It is not a lack of want and freedom from pain. It cannot occur within the boundaries of Eden. This means that the desire to return to Eden is a denial of human and divine existence. That existence is covenant relation to others in mercy, which requires sacrifice, and it is existence in this world rather than someplace else: "In this life I shall have joy, and again in the flesh I shall see God" (v. 10).

Though one popular Mormon understanding of the Garden of Eden is that Eve realized the necessity of eating the fruit and made the choice to do so conscious of what that disobedience would mean, the book of Moses appears to understand what happened differently. In Moses 5:11 Eve seems only now to understand the blessing consequent on her and Adam's transgression: "Were it not for our transgression, we never should have had seed, and never should have known good and evil, and the joy of our redemption, and the eternal life which God giveth unto all the obedient." With Adam, Eve comes to know that joy is the joy of labor, family, and covenant obedience.

In our pericope Adam and Eve learn that covenant life in the presence of God requires that they be outside the Garden of Eden. The way to the garden of future Paradise is not the same as the way to the Garden of Eden. The latter is trodden in nostalgia, but the former is trodden in the faith, hope, and love of work, family, and covenant, and in the imitation of God that is wrought in sacrifice. Adam and Eve learn that to be before God (fullness of life) is to be fully in this world rather than in some other hoped-for world.

Contributors

Claudia L. Bushman and her husband Richard Lyman Bushman are the 2014–2015 Distinguished Senior Scholars in Residence at the American Antiquarian Society in Worcester, Massachusetts.

Robert Couch is Assistant Professor of Finance in the Atkinson Graduate School of Management at Willamette University. In addition to finance research, he works on questions pertaining to business, ethics, and religion.

James E. Faulconer is a professor of philosophy at Brigham Young University, associate director of the Wheatley Institution, and a former holder of the Richard L. Evans Chair for Religious Understanding.

Dr. P. Jane Hafen (Taos Pueblo) is a Professor of English at the University of Nevada, Las Vegas. She has written articles and book chapters about American Indian Literatures. She recently edited a collection of essays, *Critical Insights: Louise Erdrich*.

George Handley is Professor of Interdisciplinary Humanities and Chair of the Department of Comparative Arts and Letters at Brigham Young University where he has taught since 1998. His published research focuses on literatures of the Americas, post-colonialism, ecocriticism and ecotheology. His environmental memoir, *Home Waters*, was published in 2010.

Eric D. Huntsman is Associate Professor of Ancient Scripture and Coordinator of Ancient Near Eastern Studies at Brigham Young University. He is the author of *God So Loved the World: The Final Days of the Savior's Life* and *The Miracles of Jesus*.

Bruce W. Jorgensen earned degrees from Brigham Young University (BA, 1966) and Cornell (MA, 1969; PhD, 1978). He taught creative writing, literature, and critical writing at BYU from 1975 to 2014 and has published poems and short fiction as well as critical essays on American literature and on Mormon literature and scripture.

Adam S. Miller is a professor of philosophy at Collin College in McKinney, Texas. He is the author of seven books including *Rube Goldberg Machines, Speculative Grace*, and *Letters to a Young Mormon*. He is co-editor, with Joseph Spencer, of the book series *Groundwork: Studies in Theory and Scripture*, published by the Neal A. Maxwell Institute for Religious Scholarship and he serves as the director of the Mormon Theology Seminar.

Joseph M. Spencer is a PhD candidate in philosophy at the University of New Mexico, where he studies contemporary French thought. He currently serves as the associate director of the Mormon Theology Seminar and as an associate editor of the *Journal of Book of Mormon Studies*. He is the author of *An Other Testament* and *For Zion*. He and Karen, his wife, live with their five children in Albuquerque, New Mexico.

Jenny Webb is an independent scholar living in Huntsville, Alabama with her husband, Nick Webb, and two children. She has an MA in comparative literature from Brigham Young University and works as an editor and production manager for several academic journals. Her work has appeared in *The Comparatist, An Experiment on the Word: Reading Alma 32,* and *Reading Nephi Reading Isaiah: 2 Nephi 26–27*, which she co-edited with Joseph M. Spencer.

Index

J–L

M–O

P–S

T–Z

Also available from

GREG KOFFORD BOOKS

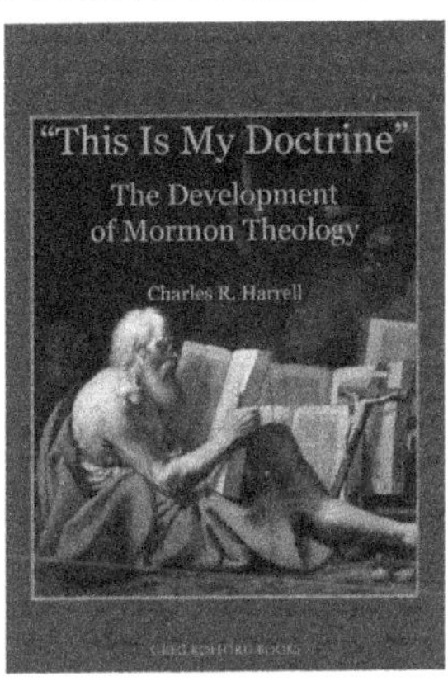

"This is My Doctrine": The Development of Mormon Theology

Charles R. Harrell

Hardcover, ISBN: 978-1-58958-103-6

The principal doctrines defining Mormonism today often bear little resemblance to those it started out with in the early 1830s. This book shows that these doctrines did not originate in a vacuum but were rather prompted and informed by the religious culture from which Mormonism arose. Early Mormons, like their early Christian and even earlier Israelite predecessors, brought with them their own varied culturally conditioned theological presuppositions (a process of convergence) and only later acquired a more distinctive theological outlook (a process of differentiation).

In this first-of-its-kind comprehensive treatment of the development of Mormon theology, Charles Harrell traces the history of Latter-day Saint doctrines from the times of the Old Testament to the present. He describes how Mormonism has carried on the tradition of the biblical authors, early Christians, and later Protestants in reinterpreting scripture to accommodate new theological ideas while attempting to uphold the integrity and authority of the scriptures. In the process, he probes three questions: How did Mormon doctrines develop? What are the scriptural underpinnings of these doctrines? And what do critical scholars make of these same scriptures? In this enlightening study, Harrell systematically peels back the doctrinal accretions of time to provide a fresh new look at Mormon theology.

"This Is My Doctrine" will provide those already versed in Mormonism's theological tradition with a new and richer perspective of Mormon theology. Those unacquainted with Mormonism will gain an appreciation for how Mormon theology fits into the larger Jewish and Christian theological traditions.

Rube Goldberg Machines: Essays in Mormon Theology

Adam S. Miller

Paperback, ISBN: 978-1-58958-193-7

"Adam Miller is the most original and provocative Latter-day Saint theologian practicing today."

—Richard Bushman, author of *Joseph Smith: Rough Stone Rolling*

"As a stylist, Miller gives Nietzsche a run for his money. As a believer, Miller is as submissive as Augustine hearing a child's voice in the garden. Miller is a theologian of the ordinary, thinking about our ordinary beliefs in very non-ordinary ways while never insisting that the ordinary become extra-ordinary."

—James Faulconer, Richard L. Evans Chair of Religious Understanding,Brigham Young University

"Miller's language is both recognizably Mormon and startlingly original. . . . The whole is an essay worthy of the name, inviting the reader to try ideas, following the philosopher pilgrim's intellectual progress through tangled brambles and into broad fields, fruitful orchards, and perhaps a sacred grove or two."

—Kristine Haglund, editor of *Dialogue: A Journal of Mormon Thought*

"Miller's Rube Goldberg theology is nothing like anything done in the Mormon tradition before."

—Blake Ostler, author of the Exploring Mormon Thought series

"The value of Miller's writings is in the modesty he both exhibits and projects onto the theological enterprise, even while showing its joyfully disruptive potential. Conventional Mormon minds may not resonate with every line of poetry and provocation—but Miller surely afflicts the comfortable, which is the theologian's highest end."

—Terryl Givens, author of *By the Hand of Mormon: The American Scripture that Launched a New World Religion*

Re-reading Job: Understanding the Ancient World's Greatest Poem

Michael Austin

Paperback, ISBN: 978-1-58958-667-3

Job is perhaps the most difficult to understand of all books in the Bible. While a cursory reading of the text seems to relay a simple story of a righteous man whose love for God was tested through life's most difficult of challenges and rewarded for his faith through those trials, a closer reading of Job presents something far more complex and challenging. The majority of the text is a work of poetry that authors and artists through the centuries have recognized as being one of--if not the--greatest poem of the ancient world.

In *Re-reading Job: Understanding the Ancient World's Greatest Poem*, author Michael Austin shows how most readers have largely misunderstood this important work of scripture and provides insights that enable us to re-read Job in a drastically new way. In doing so, he shows that the story of Job is far more than that simple story of faith, trials, and blessings that we have all come to know, but is instead a subversive and complex work of scripture meant to inspire readers to rethink all that they thought they knew about God.

Praise for *Re-reading Job*:

"In this remarkable book, Michael Austin employs his considerable skills as a commentator to shed light on the most challenging text in the entire Hebrew Bible. Without question, readers will gain a deeper appreciation for this extraordinary ancient work through Austin's learned analysis. Rereading Job signifies that Latter-day Saints are entering a new age of mature biblical scholarship. It is an exciting time, and a thrilling work." — David Bokovoy, author, *Authoring the Old Testament*

Exploring Mormon Thought Series

Blake T. Ostler

In volume one, *The Attributes of God,* Blake T. Ostler explores Christian and Mormon notions about God. ISBN: 978-1-58958-003-9

In volume two, *The Problems of Theism and the Love of God,* Blake Ostler explores issues related to soteriology, or the theory of salvation. ISBN: 978-1-58958-095-4

In volume three, *Of God and Gods,* Ostler analyzes and responds to the arguments of contemporary international theologians, reconstructs and interprets Joseph Smith's important King Follett Discourse and Sermon in the Grove, and argues persuasively for the Mormon doctrine of "robust deification." ISBN: 978-1-58958-107-4

Praise for the *Exploring Mormon Thought* series:

"These books are the most important works on Mormon theology ever written. There is nothing currently available that is even close to the rigor and sophistication of these volumes. B. H. Roberts and John A. Widtsoe may have had interesting insights in the early part of the twentieth century, but they had neither the temperament nor the training to give a rigorous defense of their views in dialogue with a wider stream of Christian theology. Sterling McMurrin and Truman Madsen had the capacity to engage Mormon theology at this level, but neither one did."

—Neal A. Maxwell Institute, Brigham Young University

Discourses in Mormon Theology: Philosophical and Theological Possibilities

Edited by
James M. McLachlan and Loyd Ericson

Hardcover, ISBN: 978-1-58958-103-6

A mere two hundred years old, Mormonism is still in its infancy compared to other theological disciplines (Judaism, Catholicism, Buddhism, etc.). This volume will introduce its reader to the rich blend of theological viewpoints that exist within Mormonism. The essays break new ground in Mormon studies by exploring the vast expanse of philosophical territory left largely untouched by traditional approaches to Mormon theology. It presents philosophical and theological essays by many of the finest minds associated with Mormonism in an organized and easy-to-understand manner and provides the reader with a window into the fascinating diversity amongst Mormon philosophers. Open-minded students of pure religion will appreciate this volume's thoughtful inquiries.

These essays were delivered at the first conference of the Society for Mormon Philosophy and Theology. Authors include Grant Underwood, Blake T. Ostler, Dennis Potter, Margaret Merrill Toscano, James E. Faulconer, and Robert L. Millet

Praise for *Discourses in Mormon Theology*:

"In short, *Discourses in Mormon Theology* is an excellent compilation of essays that are sure to feed both the mind and soul. It reminds all of us that beyond the white shirts and ties there exists a universe of theological and moral sensitivity that cries out for study and acclamation."

-Jeff Needle, Association for Mormon Letters

Authoring the Old Testament: Genesis–Deuteronomy

David Bokovoy

Paperback, ISBN: 978-1-58958-588-1

For the last two centuries, biblical scholars have made discoveries and insights about the Old Testament that have greatly changed the way in which the authorship of these ancient scriptures has been understood. In the first of three volumes spanning the entire Hebrew Bible, David Bokovoy dives into the Pentateuch, showing how and why textual criticism has led biblical scholars today to understand the first five books of the Bible as an amalgamation of multiple texts into a single, though often complicated narrative; and he discusses what implications those have for Latter-day Saint understandings of the Bible and modern scripture.

Praise for *Authoring the Old Testament*:

"*Authoring the Old Testament* is a welcome introduction, from a faithful Latter-day Saint perspective, to the academic world of Higher Criticism of the Hebrew Bible. . . . [R]eaders will be positively served and firmly impressed by the many strengths of this book, coupled with Bokovoy's genuine dedication to learning by study and also by faith." — John W. Welch, editor, *BYU Studies Quarterly*

"Bokovoy provides a lucid, insightful lens through which disciple-students can study intelligently LDS scripture. This is first rate scholarship made accessible to a broad audience—nourishing to the heart and mind alike." — Fiona Givens, co-author, *The God Who Weeps: How Mormonism Makes Sense of Life*

"I repeat: this is one of the most important books on Mormon scripture to be published recently. . . . [*Authoring the Old Testament*] has the potential to radically expand understanding and appreciation for not only the Old Testament, but scripture in general. It's really that good. Read it. Share it with your friends. Discuss it." — David Tayman, The Improvement Era: A Mormon Blog

For Zion: A Mormon Theology of Hope

Joseph M. Spencer

Paperback, ISBN: 978-1-58958-568-3

What is hope? What is Zion? And what does it mean to hope for Zion? In this insightful book, Joseph Spencer explores these questions through the scriptures of two continents separated by nearly two millennia. In the first half, Spencer engages in a rich study of Paul's letter to the Roman to better understand how the apostle understood hope and what it means to have it. In the second half of the book, Spencer jumps to the early years of the Restoration and the various revelations on consecration to understand how Latter-day Saints are expected to strive for Zion. Between these halves is an interlude examining the hoped-for Zion that both thrived in the Book of Mormon and was hoped to be established again.

Praise for *For Zion*:

"Joseph Spencer is one of the most astute readers of sacred texts working in Mormon Studies. Blending theological savvy, historical grounding, and sensitive readings of scripture, he has produced an original and compelling case for consecration and the life of discipleship." — Terryl Givens, author, *Wrestling the Angel: The Foundations of Mormon Thought*

"*For Zion: A Mormon Theology of Hope* is more than a theological reflection. It also consists of able textual exegesis, historical contextualization, and philosophic exploration. Spencer's careful readings of Paul's focus on hope in Romans and on Joseph Smith's development of consecration in his early revelations, linking them as he does with the Book of Mormon, have provided an intriguing, intertextual avenue for understanding what true stewardship should be for us—now and in the future. As such he has set a new benchmark for solid, innovative Latter-day Saint scholarship that is at once provocative and challenging." — Eric D. Huntsman, author, *The Miracles of Jesus*

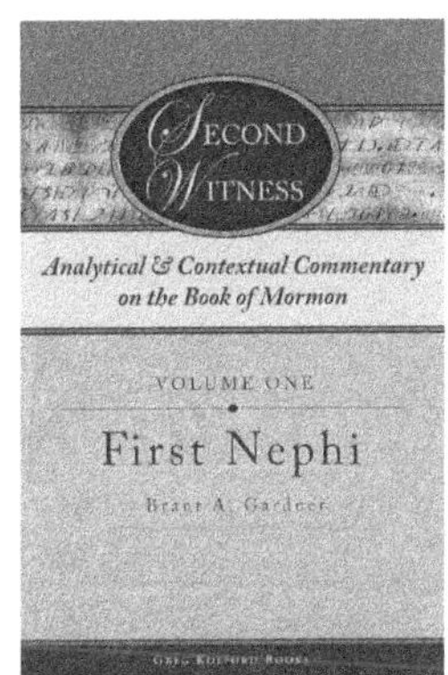

Second Witness: Analytical and Contextual Commentary on the Book of Mormon

Brant A. Gardner

Second Witness, a new six-volume series from Greg Kofford Books, takes a detailed, verse-by-verse look at the Book of Mormon. It marshals the best of modern scholarship and new insights into a consistent picture of the Book of Mormon as a historical document. Taking a faithful but scholarly approach to the text and reading it through the insights of linguistics, anthropology, and ethnohistory, the commentary approaches the text from a variety of perspectives: how it was created, how it relates to history and culture, and what religious insights it provides.

The commentary accepts the best modern scholarship, which focuses on a particular region of Mesoamerica as the most plausible location for the Book of Mormon's setting. For the first time, that location—its peoples, cultures, and historical trends—are used as the backdrop for reading the text. The historical background is not presented as proof, but rather as an explanatory context.

The commentary does not forget Mormon's purpose in writing. It discusses the doctrinal and theological aspects of the text and highlights the way in which Mormon created it to meet his goal of "convincing . . . the Jew and Gentile that Jesus is the Christ, the Eternal God."

Praise for the *Second Witness* series:

"Gardner not only provides a unique tool for understanding the Book of Mormon as an ancient document written by real, living prophets, but he sets a standard for Latter-day Saint thinking and writing about scripture, providing a model for all who follow. . . . No other reference source will prove as thorough and valuable for serious readers of the Book of Mormon."

-Neal A. Maxwell Institute, Brigham Young University

1. 1st Nephi: 978-1-58958-041-1
2. 2nd Nephi–Jacob: 978-1-58958-042-8
3. Enos–Mosiah: 978-1-58958-043-5
4. Alma: 978-1-58958-044-2
5. Helaman–3rd Nephi: 978-1-58958-045-9
6. 4th Nephi–Moroni: 978-1-58958-046-6

Parallels and Convergences: Mormon Thought and Engineering Vision

Edited by A. Scott Howe and Richard L. Bushman

Paperback, ISBN: 978-1-58958-187-6

If there is "no such thing as immaterial matter," and "all spirit is matter," then what are the implications for such standard theological principles as creation, human progression, free will, transfiguration, resurrection, and immortality? In eleven stimulating essays, Mormon engineers probe gospel possibilities and future vistas dealing with human nature, divine progression, and the earth's future. Richard Bushman poses a vision-expanding proposal: "The end point of engineering knowledge may be divine knowledge. Mormon theology permits us to think of God and humans as collaborators in bringing to pass the immortality and eternal life of man. Engineers may be preparing the way for humans to act more like gods in managing the world."

From the foreword by Richard L. Bushman:

Mormon theology leads us to see eternal implications in engineering. Engineers enable us to make the world more comfortable and to perform incredible feats of movement and communication. But their work may go beyond the amelioration of the human condition. The end point of engineering knowledge may be divine knowledge. Mormon theology permits us to think of God and humans as collaborators in bringing to pass the immortality and eternal life of man. Engineers may be preparing the way for humans to act more like gods in managing the world.

Kindliness, wise parenting, righteousness, and service are probably more fundamental in leading humans toward eternal life. But improving our physical world fits serves divine purposes, too. In constructing better worlds, engineers may be learning godly skills. From a Latter-day Saint perspective, they may be incipient creators.

The papers in this volume capture the thought of a group of LDS engineers exploring the interactions of their work and their belief at the beginning of the twenty-first century. Ideally these essays will launch a discussion that will continue for many years to come.

Fire on the Horizon: A Meditation on the Endowment and Love of Atonement

Blake T. Ostler

Paperback, ISBN: 978-1-58958-553-9

Blake Ostler, author of the groundbreaking Exploring Mormon Thought series, explores two of the most important and central aspects of Mormon theology and practice: the Atonement and the temple endowment. Utilizing observations from Søren Kierkegaard, Martin Buber, and others, Ostler offers further insights on what it means to become alienated from God and to once again have at-one-ment with Him.

Praise for *Fire on the Horizon*:

"*Fire on the Horizon* distills decades of reading, argument, and reflection into one potent dose. Urgent, sharp, and intimate, it's Ostler at his best." — Adam S. Miller, author of *Rube Goldberg Machines: Essays in Mormon Theology*

"Blake Ostler has been one of the most stimulating, deep, and original thinkers in the Latter-day Saint community. This book continues and consolidates that status. His work demonstrates that Mormonism can, and indeed does, offer profound nourishment for reflective minds and soul-satisfying insights for thoughtful believers." — Daniel C. Peterson, editor of *Interpreter: A Journal of Mormon Scripture*

Dead Wood and Rushing Water: Essays on Mormon Faith, Culture, and Family

Boyd Jay Petersen

Paperback, ISBN: 978-1-58958-658-1

For over a decade, Boyd Petersen has been an active voice in Mormon studies and thought. In essays that steer a course between apologetics and criticism, striving for the balance of what Eugene England once called the "radical middle," he explores various aspects of Mormon life and culture—from the Dream Mine near Salem, Utah, to the challenges that Latter-day Saints of the millennial generation face today.

Praise for *Dead Wood and Rushing Water*:

"*Dead Wood and Rushing Water* gives us a reflective, striving, wise soul ruminating on his world. In the tradition of Eugene England, Petersen examines everything in his Mormon life from the gold plates to missions to dream mines to doubt and on to Glenn Beck, Hugh Nibley, and gender. It is a book I had trouble putting down." — Richard L. Bushman, author of *Joseph Smith: Rough Stone Rolling*

"Boyd Petersen is correct when he says that Mormons have a deep hunger for personal stories—at least when they are as thoughtful and well-crafted as the ones he shares in this collection." — Jana Riess, author of *The Twible* and *Flunking Sainthood*

"Boyd Petersen invites us all to ponder anew the verities we hold, sharing in his humility, tentativeness, and cheerful confidence that our paths will converge in the end." — Terryl. L. Givens, author of *People of Paradox: A History of Mormon Culture*

CPSIA information can be obtained
at www.ICGtesting.com
Printed in the USA
LVHW09s1943270818
588287LV00007B/37/P

9 781589 587120